P9-CMF-890

Laura
Laura

20000 5/d

Visits in Other Lands

By

WALLACE W. ATWOOD

and

HELEN GOSS THOMAS

GINN
AND
COMPANY

Boston · New York · Chicago · Atlanta · Dallas
Columbus · San Francisco · Toronto · London

COPYRIGHT, 1947
COPYRIGHT, 1943, BY GINN AND COMPANY
ALL RIGHTS RESERVED
446.3

THE PICTURES IN THIS BOOK ARE BY

Marjorie Quennell

AND THE COLORED MAPS ARE BY

Eugene Kingman

The Athenæum Press
GINN AND COMPANY · PRO-
PRIETORS · BOSTON · U.S.A.

Foreword to the Teacher

This is a book of imaginary visits with children in widely scattered parts of the world; children whose geographic environments, cultural backgrounds, and ways of living differ markedly from one another and from those familiar to American children. Its purpose may be summarized briefly as follows:

To give American beginners in geography some idea of the widely varying types of physical environment with which the earth as a whole challenges its peoples.

To demonstrate the fact that adaptation to conditions of physical environment imposed by nature underlies the life of all peoples, from those of the most primitive cultures to those of the most advanced.

To create a feeling of friendly fellowship with peoples who live otherwise than we do, and thus to counteract the tendency, natural to all children, to consider such peoples queer, strange, or inferior.

To lay in a background of knowledge of such geographic facts and terms as are necessary in preparation for the more formal study of subsequent years.

To give simple, progressive training in the ability to read and interpret maps and map symbols.

It is to the accomplishment of these ends that the carefully integrated text, pictures, and maps of the book are dedicated. To insure freedom from reading difficulties, the text is written simply and informally, and the vocabulary conforms to the Buckingham-Dolch Graded Word Book.

Illustration requirements for a book of this type are exacting and cannot be met satisfactorily from the ordinary run of photographs available from either commercial or private sources. To the publishers the authors are deeply indebted for their willingness to go to the expense of having the book illustrated to order by a highly qualified artist whose field of specialization is the historical development of modes of living, past and present.

Published at a time when the world is torn asunder by war, the book nevertheless adheres to the normal peacetime life of the peoples whom it depicts, — the life which they can and do live under the conditions of freedom within the law which our side in the global conflict is fighting to perpetuate where they have been previously enjoyed, and to establish wherever they have been previously denied. Since the book seeks to point out basic adaptations to physical environment as they develop when people are free to apply their abilities in a normal way to the problems of living, it would be folly to base it on the abnormal and tragic conditions of war which have thrown the world into chaotic confusion. To do so would be, merely, to defeat its end.

Many teachers, no doubt, will wish to employ the book as an opportunity for pointing out the tragedy of the war in its effect on innocent peoples, and the supreme righteousness of the cause of the United Nations. The life of Erik and Inger in Norway has been turned into a bitter, hand-to-mouth struggle for survival under the cruel, ruthless heel of the Nazi invaders. Likewise the life of Sumai and Lota in China, around whose once peaceful village rage the tides of war set in motion by the Japanese. Suvan and Nara, in the steppes of Asiatic Russia, have no doubt seen the young men of their clan ride off to do battle with the would-be despoilers of their country.

For Abdul and Zakia in Egypt, for Roshik and Moti in Bengal, for Simba and Panya in the Congo, the quiet, unoffending life to which they were born is imminently threatened; no one can say how soon they too may feel the scourge and the privations of war. Even Bunga, hidden away in the forested depths of Malaya, may very likely have caught sight of Japanese soldiers creeping through the jungle, or heard the ominous drone of Japanese planes overhead.

Living as we are in a world of stark reality, it is right and proper that even children as young as those who will study this book should know of the evil forces which threaten us and of the choice which confronts us: either to destroy those forces, or to be destroyed by them. Every experienced teacher knows that in the vivid imagination of nine- and ten-year-olds other children, clearly pictured and described, "come alive." Therefore, in view of the future in which American children of today must live and work, and perhaps fight, for a better world, certain of the imaginary friends in this book have a special significance. Through the initiative of the teacher they may be used toward an understanding of the intolerable abuses against which we are fighting and of the wrongs which must ultimately be righted. Were they actual flesh-and-blood friends, they could render no greater service to their American contemporaries.

WALLACE W. ATWOOD
HELEN GOSS THOMAS

iv

Contents

v

Colored Illustrations

Bunga—
A Jungle
Boy

LITTLE PEOPLE OF THE FOREST

A Negrito Boy

Bunga is a boy who is older than you would think from his size. He was ten his last birthday, but he is only about as tall as you were at seven or eight. The reason he is so small is that he is a Negrito boy, and all the Negritos are small. If Bunga measures five feet when he grows up, he will be taller than most of the Negrito men.

The Negritos are among the peoples of the world who are called *pygmies*. Pygmies are little people, smaller than the rest of us. They all have dark skin, and they live in far-away lands. Bunga's people are one group of the Negrito pygmies.

Although Bunga's people are small, their muscles are strong from plenty of exercise. Their skin is chocolate-brown color, and their hair is black and very curly.

Bunga's Forest Home

The far-away land where Bunga lives is never cold. It is never even cool enough for Bunga to need any clothes. The weather is hot the year round, and there is a great deal of rain. Almost every afternoon a heavy shower soaks the ground and leaves the air feeling steamy. Often there is thunder and lightning during the showers. At all times of year the weather in Bunga's land is what we call "muggy," — warm and very damp.

Hidden away in a thick forest in this warm, moist land is the tiny village where we shall find Bunga. It isn't really a village, but just a camping place where Bunga's people spend part of their time.

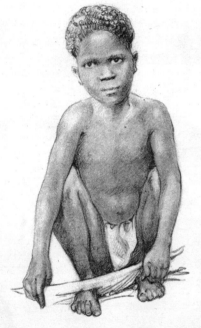

Bunga.

The forest is the kind which you will find only in the parts of the world that are hot the year round and very rainy. It is the kind which we call a *jungle*. Some people call it a "three-story" forest because of the way in which the trees grow.

First, there are the giant trees with tall, straight trunks. They are about 150 feet high, and their branches are at the very top. They are rather like huge posts holding up a roof of branches and leaves. In some places the high, leafy roof is so thick that only narrow streaks of sunlight can get through it.

Next, there is a lower story of trees that grow in the shade of the giant ones. Among them are palm trees and bamboos. Their tops are from 20 to 50 feet above the ground. Then, finally, there is a ground story of low bushes, plants with large leaves, and mosses and ferns. The forest is always green, for there is no time of year when the branches of the trees are bare.

Climbing some of the giant tree trunks from the ground to the leafy roof are plants with stems like ropes, and in places the ropy stems are strung in great loops from tree to tree. The three-story forest is damp and shady and is very still.

The forest is the home of many wild animals, some of them large and dangerous. There are elephants in the forest, and tigers, panthers, and leopards. There are monkeys and wild pigs, and many small animals such as squirrels, bats, and rats. High in the treetops bright-colored birds flit about.

1

The place where Bunga's people are camping is just a little open space in the jungle. Here they have built tiny huts of sticks and leaves. Let us pretend that we are in this little camping spot, watching what is going on.

It is early evening, and the stars are out, high above the treetops. There is a smell of wood smoke in the air, for a small fire is burning in front of each hut. Supper is over, and the people are resting and talking before going to bed.

Story-Telling Time

The children have gathered round an old man. They call him Tak, which means Grandfather, and he really is the grandfather of several of them. They are begging him to tell them a story.

The story the children are asking for is an old, old one which tells how the Negritos got their curly hair. Try to imagine that you are listening as Tak begins:

"Once upon a time, long, long ago, our people lived in a forest with the Gray Monkeys and the Black Monkeys. One day the king of the Gray Monkeys and the king of the Black Monkeys quarreled and started a war.

"The Gray Monkeys fought for their king, and the Black Monkeys fought for theirs. It was a terrible war, and it frightened our people away.

"Our people ran and ran. They ran away from the forest. They hid in a plain that was covered with tall grass.

"The Gray Monkeys beat the Black Monkeys in the war, and the Black Monkeys ran away from the forest. They ran away and hid in the very plain where our people were hiding. The Gray Monkeys chased them and set the tall grass afire.

"Then the Black Monkeys ran away again, and the Gray Monkeys ran after them. But the fire was left behind. It raced through the tall grass. It hissed and snapped. It came nearer and nearer to the place where our people were hiding.

"Our people were terribly frightened. They thought the fire would surely burn them up. They ran to some porcupine holes. They hid in the holes, hoping the fire would not find them.

"But the fire did find them. It went right over the porcupine holes where our people were hiding. But it went by so fast that it only scorched their hair.

"After the fire had gone, our people crept out of the holes and ran back to the forest. Not one of them was hurt, but their hair was

Tak is telling the children an old Negrito story.

Monkeys like these live in the forests of Malaya.

scorched to a crisp. From that day to this all our people have had curly hair."

The story we have heard is one of Bunga's favorites. He wishes Tak would tell another, but it is time to go to bed.

Bunga goes to his little hut and lies down on his bed. It must be a very hard bed, for it is nothing but a low platform built of sticks, but Bunga is used to it. Hardly has he closed his eyes before he is fast asleep.

Finding Bunga's Land

Would you like to know where you would be if you were really with Bunga in his forest home? You would be in a land called the Malay Peninsula, thousands of miles from your own home. To find out where the Malay Peninsula is, look at the picture of the globe on page 5.

If you have a globe in your schoolroom, you know that it is a very small model of the big round earth on which we live. On most globes the oceans and seas are blue, and the lands are shown in other colors.

Perhaps *peninsula* is a new word to you. It means "almost an island." Maybe you know that an island is a piece of land with water all round it. Below is a drawing that shows the difference between a peninsula and an island.

There are a great many peninsulas in the world, each with a name of its own. A shorter name for the Malay Peninsula is Malaya. Look at the globe again and prove that Malaya is really a peninsula.

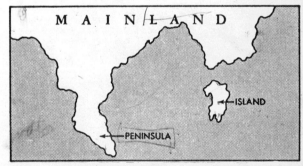

How a peninsula is different from an island: a peninsula has water almost, but not all, round it.

Something about Continents

The picture of the globe on page 9 shows that Malaya is a small part of a very large body of land called Eurasia. Long before people knew that Eurasia was all one huge stretch of land, the western part had been named Europe, and the eastern part Asia. When the truth was known, a name for the whole of it was made up in this way:

$$Europe - ope = Eur$$
$$Eur + Asia = Eurasia$$

You will want to remember about Europe, Asia, and Eurasia, for you will hear people using all three names.

The very large divisions of the lands of the earth are called *continents*. Although Europe and Asia are joined together, they count as two of the continents. Of which one of them is Malaya a part?

There are seven continents in all. Asia is the largest of them, and Europe is next to the smallest.

While you are studying the pictures of the globe, you will like to find the continent where we live. Its name is North America. When you have found North America, you will see that it is separated from Asia by the broad Pacific Ocean. To reach Bunga's land you would cross this great ocean in a ship or an airplane.

A picture of the globe like the one on page 9. The broken black lines show the division between the two continents of Europe and Asia. Europe and Asia make up the great stretch of land called Eurasia.

Can You Do This?

Each of these sentences has three endings. One ending is right and the other two are wrong. Can you find the right ending for each sentence?

1. Bunga's people are

    Indians.   Negritos.   Americans.

2. The Negritos are

    pygmies.   giants.   monkeys.

3. Bunga lives in a land that is always

    cold.   warm.   dry.

4. That is why he doesn't need

    food.   a house.   clothes.

5. Bunga's land is very

    dry.   rainy.   snowy.

6. That is why it is covered with thick

    forest.   grass.   ice.

7. This kind of forest is called a

    woodland.   park.   jungle.

8. The name of Bunga's land is

    Malaya.   America.   Europe.

9. Malaya is

    an island.   an ocean.   a peninsula.

10. Malaya is a small part of the continent of

    Europe.   North America.   Asia.

Some Questions to Think Out

Here are some questions for you to talk over in class and think out the answers.

1. How is the weather in Bunga's land different from the weather where we live?

2. Do you think there could be a forest in a land where there was no rain? Why, or why not?

3. Could we travel all the way to Malaya by train or automobile? Why, or why not?

4

NORTH

WEST

ASIA

INDIA   Yangtze   R.

BENGAL   CHINA

PACIFIC

MALAY
PENINSULA

OCEAN

EAST

INDIAN

OCEAN

AUSTRALIA

SOUTH

A DAY WITH BUNGA

Bunga Has His Breakfast

It is six o'clock in the morning now, and the people in the little camp in the jungle are up and about. There are less than thirty of them in all, for the Negritos live in small groups of a few families each.

The sun has just risen, but the air is misty, and the camping place still lies in the shade of the tall trees. Not much sunshine will reach it until noon, when the sun will have climbed high enough in the sky to be directly over Bunga's head. The early morning air is warm, and by noon it will be hot.

Bunga is sitting on the ground in front of his hut. He is eating a mangosteen. A mangosteen is a fruit about the size and shape of an orange, but its skin is reddish brown. It is juicy and sweet, and Bunga is very fond of it. At the time of year when the mangosteens are ripe, he can have as many as he likes.

Bunga will not have any cereal with milk or cream for breakfast. He will not have any buttered toast or eggs. His people have no cows to give milk, no hens to lay eggs, and no grain for making cereals or bread. When Bunga has eaten a mangosteen or two, and perhaps a few berries or nuts, he will have finished his breakfast.

No matter what time of year you visit Bunga, you will find him eating fruits, berries, seeds, and nuts from the trees and plants that grow wild in the forest. The different kinds ripen at different seasons, and so there is always a supply of one kind or another. Bunga's people eat the tender young shoots of bamboo trees and palm trees, too, and the roots or other underground parts of certain wild plants. They have no gardens or orchards as people in so many lands do, and they carry on no farming of any kind. Bunga's food would seem strange to you, but yours would seem just as strange to him.

6

Bunga is eating his breakfast of mangosteens in front of his little hut.

Spearing fish in the rivers is one of the Negrito ways of getting food.

Bunga Goes Fishing

While Bunga is eating his breakfast, his father and the other men are standing in a group, talking. Some of them have spears in their hands. The spears are made of palm wood, and they are twice as long as the men are tall. Each spear has an iron point, and Bunga's father is trying his to see if the point is fastened on firmly.

Bunga knows what this means. The men are going fishing. He swallows a last mouthful of berries and runs over to his father, for when the men go fishing the boys may go, too.

Walking single file, the men and boys follow a narrow path through the forest. The trees are so thick that the path is in deep shade. There are fallen trunks to climb over, and branches that must be pushed aside.

Soon they come to a river. The water is not very deep, and Bunga can see some good-sized fish swimming about. Now the men and boys spread out in small groups at some distance

from one another along the river. Bunga stays with his father and uncle. The fun will soon begin.

Bunga's father hides behind a fallen tree that lies in the shallow water, stretching out from the river bank. Bunga wades in, too, and hides behind the tree with his father. Meanwhile his uncle has waded into the water farther downstream.

Bunga's uncle begins driving the fish upstream. He frightens them by splashing the water. The fish dart away. Bunga knows that some of them are almost sure to swim toward the fallen tree.

Yes, here comes a fish now! Bunga's father lifts his spear and strikes swiftly. The spear goes through the fish. Bunga's father lifts it out of the water and swings it over his shoulder. A second later the fish is flopping on the bank.

Bunga's father almost never misses his aim. He is very clever at spearing fish and getting them out of the water before they can break away.

7

NORTH

WEST

EAST

SOUTH

NORTH
AMERICA
UNITED STATES
MEXICO

BAFFIN

ATLANTIC

OCEAN

PACIFIC

Isthmus of
Panama

OCEAN

MOUNTAINS

SOUTH
BRAZIL
AMERICA

Altiplano

ANDES

ARGENTINA
Pampa

Bunga's mother weaves a basket to wear on her back.

Sometimes Bunga and the other boys are allowed to try their luck at spearing fish. They use shorter spears of wood sharpened at one end. Bunga's aim is pretty good, but he has trouble landing his fish. Often the fish slips off the spear and drops back into the water with a splash. But Bunga keeps on practicing. Some day he will be as good a fisherman as his father.

The men are having good luck this morning, and that means a meal of fish for everyone when they get home. The fish will be baked over the wood fires.

Bunga Helps His Mother

While the men and boys are off fishing, the girls and their mothers are weaving baskets. They weave them of strips of split bamboo. There are plenty of bamboo trees in the Malayan jungle, and they are useful to the Negritos in many ways. Bunga's mother is finishing a basket which she can wear on her back like a knapsack.

It is afternoon now, and Bunga's mother has strapped on another kind of back-basket. She is going into the forest to dig yams. In her hand she carries a digging-stick with a point that has been hardened in fire. Bunga is going along to help her.

Perhaps you know that a yam tastes rather like a sweet potato. It grows underground, but it is not a root. It is an underground growth known as a *tuber*. The tubers that we eat most often are white potatoes. They are cultivated tubers; that is, they come from plants grown on farms. Bunga eats yams and other tubers and roots that come from wild plants.

Bunga knows the yam plant by its leaves. When he and his mother find one among the different plants on the forest floor, they start digging. Bunga's mother loosens the earth with the stick, and together they scoop out the dirt with their hands. The yams are two or three feet underground, and getting them out in this way is hard work. Bunga's people have no iron forks or spades.

Bunga's mother carries the yams home in her basket and cuts them in pieces. Then she takes

Bunga helps his mother to gather yams in the forest.

them to the river and puts them in the water for a good soaking. This is because yams of this kind have a poisonous juice in them. Soaking takes away the poison and makes them safe to eat.

Later Bunga's mother will grate the pieces of yam much as your mother grates cheese. For a grater she will use a piece of bark with sharp thorns on it. Then she will squeeze the gratings and dry them. When they are dry, they will be ready to be cooked.

There are other kinds of yams and other tubers which are not poisonous and do not have to be soaked. These can be roasted just as they come from the ground. Bunga likes them as much as many of us like baked potatoes.

Bunga Has His Supper

For supper tonight Bunga will have a sort of pudding made of yam gratings that his mother dried yesterday. His mother mixes the gratings with a little water and steams them. For a cooking dish she uses a hollow piece of a freshly cut bamboo trunk. This makes a tube about two feet long, open at one end and closed at the other. The bamboo wood is so green that it does not burn when put into the fire.

When the pudding is done, Bunga's mother divides it into three shares and puts each one on a fresh green leaf. Bunga takes his share and sits down on the ground. He holds the leaf in one hand and eats the pudding with the fingers of the other hand. His father and mother eat their pudding in the same way. Bunga has never seen a knife and fork or a spoon.

If Bunga is still hungry when he has finished his yam pudding, he can have a mangosteen. Or, if there are berries or nuts on hand, he can have some of those. Perhaps he will roast a few nuts in the fire before he eats them.

Now and then Bunga has a meal of rice cooked in a bamboo tube. His father gets the rice from people who live on the edge of the

Bunga's yam pudding is being cooked in a bamboo tube.

forest and who carry on farming. In exchange Bunga's father gives the farmers such things as fruits or bamboo that he gets in the forest.

While Bunga and his family are having supper, the other families are having theirs. When they have finished, perhaps Tak will tell a story as he did last night. Or perhaps there will be music.

Bunga's people love music, and some of the men and older boys play homemade flutes of bamboo. They like to sing together, and when they sing, some of them beat time with bamboo tubes. They spend many an evening singing in the stillness of the forest.

Making Sure of New Words

In the story of Bunga's fishing trip you found the words "upstream" and "downstream." *Downstream* means the direction *toward* which the water in a stream is flowing, or running. *Upstream* means the direction *from* which the water is flowing. Here are two questions to help you to make sure of the meaning of these new words.

1. When you stand on a river bank, which way must you face to have the water flowing away from you — upstream or downstream?

2. Which way must you face to have the water flowing toward you?

11

A Menu to Make

You know what a menu is — a list of things to eat. On the blackboard write as a heading *Bunga's Menu*. Then write under the heading a list of things that Bunga eats. Don't erase the list, for you will soon have some other things to add to the menu.

A Missing-Word Game

Now try this missing-word game. From the list of missing words choose the right one to fill the blank space in the first sentence. Then go on, choosing the right words for the blank spaces in the rest of the sentences. You must not write in this book, but if you wish you may write the sentences, with the blanks filled, in your notebook.

List of Missing Words

digs   fish   gardens   spear
farms   forest   mangosteens   yams

1. Bunga eats many things that come from plants and trees that grow wild in the _____.

2. Among the fruits that Bunga likes best are _____.

3. Among the tubers that Bunga eats are wild _____. They grow underground, and Bunga's mother_____ them with a stick.

4. The rice that Bunga sometimes eats comes from _____ outside the forest. Bunga's people have no farms or _____.

5. Bunga eats ____ from the rivers. His father uses a _____ in catching them.

HOW THE NEGRITOS HUNT

A Strange Weapon

You have found that Bunga's people gather much of their food from trees and plants in the forest, and that when they are near a stream they fish. They never have much extra food on hand. They get what they need from day to day.

There is still another way in which the Negritos get food in the forest. This, as you might guess, is by hunting.

People who get food by hunting must have weapons for killing the animals. In most parts of the world hunters use guns. Among people who have no guns the weapons most often used are spears and bows and arrows. Some of the Negritos hunt with bows and arrows, but most of those who live in Malaya use a weapon which perhaps you have never heard of. It is called a blowgun.

Here is a picture of Bunga's father holding his blowgun to his mouth. The blowgun is a long, hollow tube of bamboo with a mouthpiece at one end. Into this end Bunga's father pushes a pointed dart. The dart is less than a foot long. It is made of the stiff middle rib of a palm leaf smoothed and scraped down until it is no bigger round than a fine knitting needle.

Behind the dart in the blowgun Bunga's father puts a wad of palm fluff. This is feathery stuff, a little like the fluff that comes off woolen

Bunga's father holds his blowgun ready to shoot.

blankets. He lifts the gun to his mouth and takes aim. With a quick, hard puff he blows the dart from the gun, and it flies straight to the target.

The Negritos shoot so well with their blowguns that they almost never miss their aim. They kill birds, small animals, and even monkeys with this strange weapon.

Perhaps you wonder how a little dart from a blowgun can hit an animal hard enough to kill it. It can't. The darts kill because they are poisoned. The Negritos get the poison from the sap of certain trees and smear the points of the darts with it.

The dart has a cut behind the point so that when an animal is hit the poisoned point sticks in its flesh and the rest of the dart breaks off. In this way the poison gets into the flesh and the animal soon dies.

More about Hunting

It may seem to you that hunting with poisoned darts is cruel, and that no one should do such a thing. But there are three things you must remember about the Negritos: (1) they need food like everyone else, and hunting is one of the few ways they can get it; (2) they have no guns; and (3) their darts cannot be shot hard enough to kill. You see, then, why these pygmies of the forest use poison.

Bunga's people do not hunt the large animals of the forest, such as elephants or tigers, because their weapons are not good enough. They seldom kill anything larger than a monkey, and Bunga will tell you that monkeys are getting rather scarce. Now and then his people kill a wild pig, but most of the meat they eat comes from small animals and from birds.

Bunga's people often find the hunting poor, and of course they can fish only when they are near a stream. For this reason most of their food is what they can gather from the trees and plants in the forest.

He slashes a tree for sap to poison his little darts.

There is a special name for people who get their food by hunting and fishing or from wild plants and trees. They are called *food-gatherers*. Bunga's people are food-gatherers in a warm, rainy land where there are plants and trees of many kinds.

Some Things to Do

1. Add to Bunga's menu on the blackboard another kind of food that he eats.

2. Write a sentence telling how Bunga's father gets this kind of food for his family.

3. Draw a picture of Bunga's father hunting with his blowgun.

Some Questions for the Class to Talk Over

1. How are food-gatherers different from farmers?

2. Why can we have many more kinds of food than Bunga can have?

13

MOVING TO A NEW CAMP

A Journey through the Forest

In a few days Bunga's people will leave the camp where we have seen them. They have gathered about all the food to be found just now in this neighborhood, and so they must move on. Moving is easy, for they have little to carry. They have no housekeeping things to take with them, and no clothing except the little they are wearing.

When moving day comes, Bunga's mother and the other women strap on their baskets, for they will gather whatever food they find on the way. Each man carries a blowgun over his shoulder, a knife stuck in his belt, and a quiver fastened by a grass string round his waist. The quivers are bamboo tubes for holding darts. They are decorated with patterns cut in the wood with a knife.

Tak leads the way into the forest, and the rest of the people follow. They walk single file along a narrow footpath among the trees. Soon one of the men starts singing, and everyone joins in. Bunga's people like to start their journeys with a song.

The little band of pygmies moves slowly, for there is no need to hurry. The women stop here and there to pick berries or nuts, which they put in their baskets. The children sometimes scamper ahead and sometimes lag behind. They never leave the path, though, for if they did they might get lost. Now and then they stop to swing on a hanging vine.

The men keep a sharp lookout for things to shoot, for by evening everyone will be hungry. A meal of roast meat, if they can get it, will taste good. If they see a squirrel or any other little animal within shooting distance, one of the men lifts his blowgun. Puff! and a dart flies through the air. If it hits the mark, — and it usually does, — another bit of food goes into one of the women's baskets.

During the day Bunga's people will walk five or six miles through the quiet, shady jungle.

Which things in this picture belong to Bunga's father, and which to his mother?

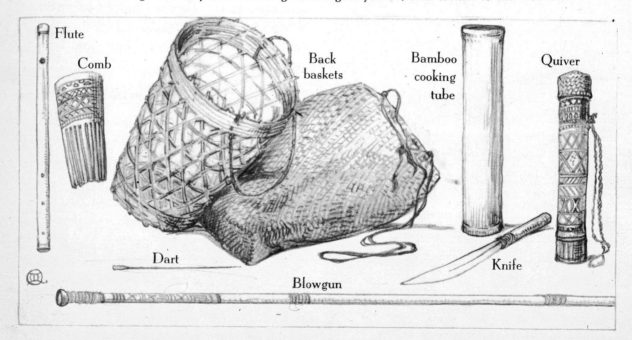

Flute

Comb

Back baskets

Bamboo cooking tube

Quiver

Dart

Knife

Blowgun

The old huts of sticks and leaves have blown down, and so the Negrito mothers build new ones.

In the afternoon they will be caught in a heavy shower of rain, but they are used to getting wet and no one will mind.

Our Negrito friends are on their way to another of their camping places. Bunga has been looking forward to this trip for a long time because there is something at the new camping place that he likes very much. You will soon find out what it is.

Building New Houses

As the sun drops lower in the sky in the afternoon, the light in the forest fades. The shadows grow deeper and deeper. By sunset the forest floor is dark.

But before sunset our friends have reached the new camp. Like the old one, it is just a patch of open ground with the forest all round it. Since Bunga's people were last here, their huts have blown down, and so they set about building new ones. The women do this work, and the older children help them.

You can see from the picture that the huts are nothing but rough shelters from wind and rain. Each one is made of sticks tied together with vines. The covering, or thatch, is of large leaves. This makes a sloping roof, which sheds the rain easily.

While the women build the huts, the men make the sleeping platforms. With their knives they cut down small bamboo trees and split the trunks into sticks. For each platform a number of sticks are tied side by side on a wooden frame a foot or so above the ground. The platforms are beds as well as bedsteads, for there are no coverings of any kind. They are the only furniture in the Negrito huts.

Soon fires are kindled and Bunga's people have supper. They eat whatever they have collected on the day's journey through the forest. As soon as they have finished supper they go to bed, for they are all tired and sleepy. Curled up on his bed of sticks, Bunga feels safe and happy. He goes to sleep thinking about the fun he is going to have tomorrow.

15

Gathering the Durians

What Bunga has been looking forward to in this camping place are the durians. They are the fruit of a certain kind of tree that grows in the Malayan jungle. Round this camp there are a good many of these trees. The durians are ripening now, and Bunga's people have come here to gather them.

Another day has begun, and the men and older boys are climbing the durian trees. The picture shows what good climbers they are. They pick the durians and drop them on the ground. Each fruit is almost round, and from six to eight inches through the middle. It has a hard, thorny shell.

The children help their mothers to pick up the durians and put them in the back-baskets. Bunga will tell you that when you split the shell

Durians and mangosteens. The real fruits are five or six times their size in this picture.

of a durian open you find a cream-colored pulp that is oh, so good to eat! And then there are the big seeds that taste so good after they have been roasted in the fire.

You yourself might not care for durians, but Bunga likes them as much as you like ice cream. Do you blame him for looking forward to durian time?

Bunga's people will stay in this camp for some time, and they will feast on the durians. Of course they will eat other things from the forest too, but they will have durians and roasted durian seeds every day.

Gathering durians is fun for everybody.

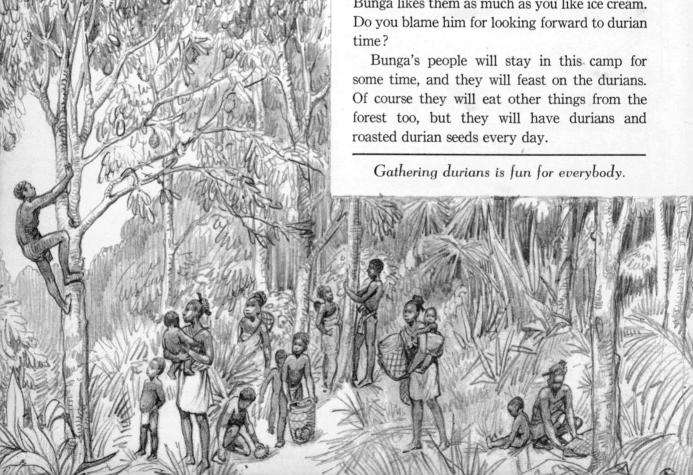

Bunga's people celebrate the durian harvest with music and dancing.

A Celebration

Perhaps you know that the gathering of any food crop, wild or cultivated, is called a harvest. You may have heard people speak of the "wheat harvest" or the "apple harvest."

For some reason the durian harvest is the happiest event of the year for our pygmy friends in Malaya. Perhaps it is because of all the fruits of the forest they seem to like the durians best.

So, during the harvest, Bunga's people have a celebration. They all dress up for it. The women and girls put on necklaces of seeds or monkeys' teeth, and each one wears a prettily decorated bamboo comb in her hair. The men and boys make wreaths of vines and flowers to wear on their heads.

On the evening of the celebration Bunga's people have a wonderful time. They sing and dance and listen to the flute-players. They dance to the beat of bamboo tubes thumped on a fallen tree trunk, and as they dance they sing. They have a special song for the durian harvest, a song so old that no one knows who made it up.

Some Things to Do

1. Add another kind of food to Bunga's menu on the blackboard.

2. Draw a picture of Bunga's house.

3. Tell why Bunga looks forward to durian time.

Some Questions about Houses

1. Here are five reasons why people need houses. Which ones are reasons why you need a house?

    (1) Shelter from rain
    (2) Shade from hot sunshine
    (3) Protection from cold
    (4) Shelter from snow
    (5) Protection from wind

2. Which one is the principal reason why Bunga needs a house?

3. How are the Negrito houses built to give the people the kind of shelter they need most?

4. Why do Bunga's people often have to build new houses in old camping places?

5. Where do they get the materials for building their houses?

6. Why is it, do you think, that the Negritos do not build houses that will last as ours do?

17

NOMADS OF THE FOREST

A Wandering People

Bunga would be surprised to know that you have only one place and one house that you call home. His people never stay in any one place very long at a time. They have a good many camping spots, and they keep moving from one to another.

All their camps are in a part of the forest which they think of as their own. The land doesn't really belong to them, but they use it as if it did, and no one minds.

There are many other small bands of Negritos in the Malayan forests, and they all live much as Bunga's people do. Each one has its own part of the jungle and its own camping places, but it is not unusual for one band to hunt or gather food on another's land. The Negritos are good-natured little people, willing to share what they have with others.

What the people of each little band care most about are the durian trees on their land. These they count their very own, and no one from another band may take any of the fruit. They all understand this rule so well and they are so honest that there is almost never any stealing.

If you should ask Bunga why his people move so often, this is what he would say:

"We move about to get our food. We get it mostly from plants and trees in the forest. Even with a little hunting and fishing to help out, we can't get enough food in any one place to live there long at a time."

Bunga's people know where the different foods grow in the greatest plenty. They know, too, just when each kind will be ready to be gathered. They plan their moves from camp to camp so as to be in the right place at the right time.

People who live wandering lives as our pygmy friends do are called *nomads*. You will want to remember the meaning of this word because later on you will meet some other nomads in other kinds of lands. Bunga's people are nomads of the warm, moist forests of Malaya.

Trading with Other People

You have learned that now and then the Negritos trade fruit or bamboo for rice. They do this trading with people who live outside the forest. They like the rice to eat, and so they are glad to make the exchange.

There are a few other things that the Negritos get by trading with other people. Among these things are the pieces of cloth that they wear round their waists, and the knives that they use. Salt, too, comes from outside, and now and then a brass kettle for cooking. The things they trade for are things that they cannot make or get for themselves.

But, as you have seen, our pygmy friends depend mostly on what the forest gives them for the taking. They spend most of their time getting food. This is not very hard work, but they must keep at it day after day. If they didn't, they would soon starve.

Years ago the Negritos lived without carrying on any trade with other people. They made clothing material of pounded bark, and they used sharp stones for knives. They got all their food from the forest. Even today they could get along without any trading if they had to.

Good-by to Bunga

Durian time is over now, and Bunga's people are starting for another of their camps. Bunga feels much as you do when summer vacation is over. In a way he is sorry, but he knows that plenty of interesting things will happen before durian time comes round again next year.

Tak has already started down the shady forest path, and the others are following.

Bunga and his father are the last to leave the little camping place. Bunga is carrying a blow-gun. His father has made it for him and will teach him how to use it. Bunga feels very proud, for before long he too will be a hunter.

There he goes, down the forest path with his father. He is singing now, but the song is growing fainter. In a few hours Bunga will be sleeping in another camping place in the forested land that he calls home.

When you slip into your own bed tonight, perhaps you will think of Bunga in far-away Malaya, and of how different his home is from yours. Would you like to change places with him?

Some Things to Explain

1. Explain why Bunga's people are called (1) pygmies; (2) food-gatherers; (3) nomads.

2. Explain just why it is that they keep moving about in the forest instead of living in one place all the time.

3. Explain why Bunga's people carry on a little trading with people outside the forest.

Something to Do

Here is a list of the things that Bunga's people need most. Tell how they get each one.

Food
Knives
Blowguns
Back-baskets
Digging-sticks
Materials for building huts

A Matching Game

Below are the beginnings and the endings of five sentences. Find the correct ending for sentence 1. Then match the other beginnings and endings correctly.

BEGINNINGS

1. Bunga doesn't need clothes because
2. Bunga needs a house because
3. Most of Bunga's food comes from
4. Bunga has meat to eat because
5. Bunga's people move often because

ENDINGS

his father is a hunter.
they cannot get food for very long in one place.
he lives in a land where the weather is always warm.
trees and plants in the forest.
he lives where it rains very often.

A Bamboo Contest

You have found that the bamboo tree is very useful to Bunga's people. Each pupil in the class may write down from memory the different ways in which Bunga's people use bamboo. Then compare the lists to see whose memory is best. The pupil who has the longest list will be the winner of the contest.

A Model to Make

See if you and your classmates can make a little model of a Negrito camp in the forest. If you make a good one, perhaps your teacher will let you invite the children from some other room to come and see it.

19

The shady path through the forest leads to another camping place.

Netsook and Klaya in the Far North

From the Greenland ice cap great glaciers like this one move slowly down to the sea.

LANDS OF ICE AND SNOW

Where Icebergs Are Born

"Br-r-r-r, it's as cold as Greenland!" Haven't you heard people say this when the weather was terribly cold? Haven't you wondered what Greenland is, and why people often seem to shiver when they speak of it?

Greenland is the largest island in the world, and it is far away in the north. Its northern coast borders the frozen Arctic Ocean and is within 500 miles of the north pole. Perhaps you know that the north pole is the point farthest north on the earth.

It is strange that this great island of the Far North should be called Greenland. Whiteland would be a better name, for most of it is buried under a thick cap of ice and snow that never melts away. The only places that ever look green are along the shores, and those are green only in the short, cool summers.

For such a large island, Greenland has very few people. Most of them are Eskimos. They live in scattered groups along the coast, where the land meets the sea. The Eskimos are brown-skinned people with straight black hair. Few white people care to make their homes in this cold, frozen land.

From the Greenland ice cap huge tongues of thick ice, crumpled and broken, creep slowly down to the shores. For miles and miles they wind their way down to the sea. People sometimes call them "rivers of ice," but they move so very, very slowly that they seem to be standing still. The correct name for these creeping tongues of ice is *glaciers*.

At the shores the glaciers push out into the water. Here, in the summer, giant blocks of ice break away from the ends of the glaciers with a noise like thunder. Then they float off to the south.

NORTH

NORTH
POLE

ARCTIC OCEAN

GREENLAND

BAFFIN

EUROPE

NORTH
AMERICA

WEST

A T L A N T I C

EAST

AFRICA

O C E A N

SOUTH

AMERICA

SOUTH

What you can see of this drifting iceberg is only a small part of the giant block of ice.

Ships crossing the northern part of the Atlantic Ocean in summer often come in sight of these giant blocks of floating ice from Greenland. "Icebergs!" the passengers say to one another, and they get out their field glasses for a better view.

Drifting icebergs are a wonderful sight, especially on a sunny day. Near the water-line they look bluish-green, and above they are snow-white against the blue of the sky. Waves, dashing against them, break into showers of sparkling spray.

Ships, though, keep well away from icebergs. If you ask a ship's captain why, he will explain that you cannot see much of an iceberg. Huge as they look, the part below the water is seven or eight times as large as the part above water. If a ship gets too near an iceberg, it may run into the under-water part, and such accidents are very dangerous.

As the icebergs drift southward they come into warmer waters and meet warmer air. Little by little they melt and disappear.

Baffin Island

The picture of the globe on page 21 shows that Greenland is not very far from the northern part of North America. Nearer still to North America is Baffin Island. This is another cold land where nearly all the people are Eskimos.

During the long, cold winter Baffin Island is much like Greenland. The whole island is blanketed with snow, and the waters round about it are covered with thick ice. In winter it is hard to tell where the land ends and the water begins.

In summer Baffin Island looks quite different, for in only a few places are there ice caps that do not melt away. As the snow disappears, it uncovers bare rock and big stretches of grass, flowering plants, and low bushes. The ice on the water breaks up, and much of it melts. But even in summer you will see pieces of ice drifting about in the water.

Children Who Dress in Furs

Baffin Island is the Far Northern land where we shall find Netsook and Klaya. They are Eskimo children. Klaya is a little girl, and Netsook is her younger brother. Here are their pictures.

Klaya's picture was taken in the wintertime. Her fur suit, as you can see, is prettily made. The coat is of sealskin, and the hood is lined with soft fox fur. The trousers are sealskin, too, and they reach to Klaya's ankles. They are tucked into sealskin boots that come up to her knees. Fur mittens keep her hands warm.

Under this suit Klaya wears another made from skins of wild reindeer. She wears it with the fur inside, next to her body. Dressed in these two suits, Klaya plays outdoors in the coldest winter weather.

Netsook is the boy at the left in the next picture. This picture was taken in the summertime. Because it is warmer now, Netsook is not wearing his deerskin undersuit. His hooded jacket is of sealskin, and his white bearskin trousers are tucked into knee boots like Klaya's.

Klaya and one of her father's sledge dogs.

Next to Netsook in the picture is his mother, and beyond her are his aunt and two little cousins. You can see that the baby cousin rides in his mother's hood. All Eskimo babies are carried about in this way.

Stop and Think

It is time now to stop and think what you have discovered about the weather in the Far North, where Netsook and Klaya live. Here are some questions to answer.

1. How is the weather in the Far North different from the weather in Malaya, where Bunga lives?

2. Why are winter storms in the Far North always snowstorms, never rainstorms?

3. How can you tell from the picture of Netsook that summer in the Far North is much cooler than summer where you live?

Netsook's mother and aunt make all the fur clothes that keep the children warm.

The trading post on Baffin Island where Netsook's people are camping in their tents.

IN CAMP WITH NETSOOK AND KLAYA

A Baffin Island Trading Post

Try to imagine that it is early in July, and that we are with Netsook and Klaya in the Far North. A ship from the south has brought us to a trading post on the coast of Baffin Island. The trading posts in the Far North are places where white men from warmer lands trade for furs with the Eskimos. This one is on the shore of Baffin Bay. Perhaps you know that a *bay* is a part of an ocean or a sea that reaches into the land.

It is a bright, sunny day, but a chilly wind is blowing. Netsook and Klaya think it a very warm day, but it doesn't seem so to us. It is much cooler than any summer's day we ever remember at home.

Netsook's people are living in tents near the buildings of the trading company. The tents are their summer houses. The small sailing boats in which the Eskimos have come to the trading post are drawn up on the beach.

How different everything is from the camp where we first met Bunga! There we saw trees wherever we looked. Here there is not a tree in sight. But we do see patches of grass and bright-colored flowers. Netsook says that over the hills, farther back from the shore, there are low bushes with berries that will soon be ripe, and big patches of moss and heather. The heather is a low-growing plant with pink blossoms.

Why do you suppose there are no trees in Baffin Island? It is because the weather is too cold for trees to grow. It is also too cold for any of the plants or farm animals which are raised for food in warmer lands. For that reason there are no farms in Baffin Island.

The trading post is a lively place this summer day. Everyone is moving about, talking and laughing. Eskimo dogs are sniffing round the tents, hoping to find something to eat. There are a great many of them, for every Eskimo family needs a team of dogs for traveling in the wintertime. The dogs draw the big sleds that are called sledges. Netsook's father has a team of ten dogs to draw his sledge over the snow.

The children are running about the camp, having a fine time. Some of them are playing with the puppies, and some are playing tag and other games. Netsook and another boy are playing at seal-hunting. A skin bag stuffed with grass is their seal, and they are throwing toy spears at it. This is good practice, for all Eskimo boys must be first-class hunters when they grow up. It is good fun too.

Eskimo Tupiks

Some of the tents in the Eskimo camp are made of sealskins sewed together and stretched over a framework of poles. Others are made of canvas, which is a heavy kind of cloth. Netsook's family has a canvas tent, and Netsook is very proud of it. His father got it last year from the traders, — the men who run the trading post, — and he gave some furs in exchange for it. Netsook and Klaya call it a *tupik*, for that is the Eskimo word for tent.

Years ago all the Eskimos made their own tupiks of sealskin, and many still do so. Netsook says that his father and mother like the new canvas tupik better because it is easier to carry when they move.

If Netsook invites you into his tupik, you will see that at the back there is a bed for the family. The bed is made by spreading the ground with heather and covering the heather with deerskins. The deerskins are soft, and the heather makes a good mattress. There are other deerskins for blankets, for even in summer the nights are too cool for sleeping without covers.

You will not find any furniture in Netsook's tupik, but you will see some things that he calls *kudliks*. They are made of stone and they look like shallow dishes with rims. But they are much more important than dishes. They are lamps.

In these strange lamps the Eskimos burn oil from blubber which has been pounded or melted. Blubber is the fat that lies between the

26

skin and the flesh of sea animals such as seals and walruses. It is very oily, and the oil burns with a bright, hot flame.

The kudliks are all that the Eskimos have in their houses, winter or summer, for heat and light. You can see, then, how important they are. Without the kudliks the Eskimos would freeze to death in the wintertime.

Some Animals That Netsook Knows

You have found that Netsook's people use sealskins for clothing and tupiks and that they burn seal oil in their kudliks. If you were to spend a year with your Eskimo friends, you would find that they eat more seal meat than anything else.

Netsook has never seen a cow or a sheep or a pig, but he knows all about the wild animals that are pictured on page 27. Here are some things that he would like to tell you about seals.

"Seals," Netsook says, "are animals that live in the water. They swim under water like fish, but they cannot breathe there. Every little while they have to lift their heads out of water for a breath of air.

"When your father takes you seal-hunting, you must wait very quietly at the water's edge until you see a seal's nose. Sometimes you have to wait a long while without moving the least little bit. If you move, you may scare a seal away, and your father will send you home.

"The minute your father sees a seal, he throws his harpoon at it. The point of the harpoon goes deep into the seal's neck. The harpoon has a rope tied to it. Your father pulls the seal out of the water by the rope. Then you help your father to drag the seal home, and you have seal meat for supper."

Netsook's father is harpooning a seal.

Arctic hare

Caribou

Walrus

Arctic fox

Polar bear

Seal

Narwhal

White whale

Some animals of the Far North that Netsook knows. Which ones are sea animals?

Netsook has told us of one way in which the Eskimos hunt seals. The harpoon which he speaks of is a special kind of spear. The Eskimos also hunt seals with guns, especially in the spring. At that time of year seals like to crawl out of the water and sun themselves on the ice along the shore.

All through the year, in the coldest weather as well as the warmest, Netsook's people must hunt seals. They need the meat for food. They need the skins for clothing and the blubber for their kudliks. If it were not for the seals of the Far North, the Eskimos would go hungry and cold much of the time.

Other sea animals that the Eskimos hunt are walruses, white whales, and narwhals. They are not so plentiful as seals, and they are harder to kill, because they are fierce fighters. Walruses and narwhals fight with their sharp tusks, and whales strike out with their strong tails. But the Eskimos have plenty of courage, and

they never miss a chance of hunting these big sea animals. They are always glad to get one, for it supplies much meat and blubber, and its tough hide, or skin, makes good leather.

The big white polar bears are rather scarce and very dangerous. They spend most of their time on the sea ice or swimming in the water. Netsook's people do not make a habit of hunting polar bears, but when they see one they always try to kill it. They like the meat, and the fur-covered skin can be used for clothing or sold to the traders.

On land there are caribou, which are wild reindeer. From these animals the Eskimos get the deerskins which they use for winter clothing and for bedding. There are hares too, and wolves and white foxes. The hares are good to eat, and their fur makes soft linings for hoods. The foxes are animals that the Eskimos catch in traps mostly for trading. The traders will always take all the foxskins the Eskimos can get.

The Eskimos are paying with furs for the things they buy from the trader.

Netsook's People Do Some Trading

Netsook's people are one of many small groups of Eskimos in Baffin Island. Each group is made up of a number of families, and all the groups live in much the same way.

In summer all the little bands of Eskimos live wandering lives. They move about, camping in their tupiks wherever they please. At least once during the summer each band visits a trading post to exchange furs for supplies needed for the winter.

Netsook's people have been camping for several days at the trading post where we have found them. Suppose we go down to the trading house and see what the men are getting in exchange for foxskins and other furs.

Last year, you know, Netsook's father bought a canvas tupik. This year he needs a new gun. Netsook's uncle is buying a new sail for his boat. All the men are getting supplies of

bullets and matches, and some are picking out big hunting knives.

Netsook's mother has asked his father to get her some large needles and some strong thread. You can easily guess why. It is because she is the family tailor. She makes all the clothing, even the boots. She sews beautifully with homemade needles of bone and with animal sinews for thread, but she likes steel needles and real thread better.

First the Eskimos buy the things they really need. Then, if they have enough furs to buy more, they choose such things as tea, tobacco, molasses, and hard crackers. Netsook and Klaya are hoping very much that their father will get some molasses. They love sweet things, but there is no way of getting them except from the traders.

Giving Reasons

Here are five facts which you have learned about Netsook's people. For each fact there is a good reason which you will be able to give if you think carefully.

1. Netsook's people do not have any farms or gardens because _ _ _

2. They do not keep any cows or raise any pigs or sheep because _ _ _

3. They never have wood fires because _ _ _

4. They need plenty of fur-covered skins because _ _ _

5. They need a great deal of blubber because _ _ _

Something to Do

Draw pictures of some of the wild animals that Netsook knows. Under each picture print a few words telling why this animal is hunted by the Eskimos.

Let's Pretend

If you like games of make-believe, you can have fun pretending that the schoolroom is a trading house, and that you and the other children are Eskimos and traders. It will be like playing store, with the Eskimos paying in furs for the different things they buy.

AN AFTERNOON WITH THE ESKIMOS

How the Afternoon Begins

It is afternoon now, and Netsook's father and the other men are going seal-hunting out on the bay. They are getting into their *kayaks* with their guns and harpoons.

A kayak is a one-man boat. It is long, narrow, and very light. The frame is made of pieces of wood, and over this is stretched a covering of sealskins sewed together very carefully so that the seams will not leak. In the middle is a round opening just big enough for a man to slip into.

Now the men are off. Each one is paddling hard and fast. The kayaks fairly skim over the water. Soon they are out of sight beyond a rocky point of land. If the hunters have good luck, each one will come home towing a seal behind his kayak.

Netsook's mother and the other women are sitting on the ground near the tupiks, sewing and talking. They are mending old clothes and making new ones for their families.

Netsook's mother is making a new sealskin coat for Klaya. Watch her as she cuts out the pieces with a sharp knife. She has no pattern, but she knows exactly how to cut the skin in

Klaya is having a lesson in tailoring.

pieces of the right size and shape without wasting any of it. As she sews the pieces together, her stitches are as even as any dressmaker's.

Klaya and the other little girls are sewing, too. They are making fur clothes for the dolls which their fathers have carved from walrus tusks. They are having fun doing it, and they

Netsook's father is hunting seals in his kayak.

are learning to be good tailors when they grow up.

The boys are kicking a ball about, playing a game a little like football. When they tire of that, they will run races, and some of the big boys will practice wrestling. Eskimo boys like sports and games just as much as other boys do.

How the Afternoon Ends

Several hours have passed, and now the children are watching for their fathers. Is that a kayak coming round the point? Yes, and there's another, and another! Are they towing any seals? They must be, because they are coming over the water rather slowly. The hunting has been good this afternoon.

The children and their mothers run down to the water's edge. They help to pull the kayaks and the seals ashore. The children are laughing and shouting. They are thinking about the seal meat they will have for supper.

The hunters are back, luck has been good, and there is seal meat for supper.

Now the men are cutting up the seals with big knives. First they take off the skin and then the thick layer of blubber beneath it. Then they slice off big chunks of meat and hand them to the women. In every tupik, seal meat is soon cooking in a kettle of boiling water hung over a lighted kudlik.

Netsook and Klaya can hardly wait for the meat to be done. They don't have to wait long, for their mother doesn't cook it very much. She brings the kettle outside, and as soon as the water cools a bit, the children and their parents dip into it with their fingers. They cut off mouthfuls of the meat with their knives, but they have no forks.

Netsook and Klaya will invite you to have some seal meat, but they will not be surprised if you don't like it. They know that people from warmer lands have to get used to seal meat before they enjoy it. If you would rather get some canned food at the trading house for supper, they will not think you rude.

Nights without Darkness

After supper the camp quiets down. First the children go to bed in the tupiks, and later the grown-ups go. But the sun is still shining. Midnight comes. The sun is in the north now, but it is still above the horizon. The horizon is the line where the earth seems to meet the sky.

After midnight the sun moves on toward the east, rising a little higher in the sky as the hours go by. Another day has come, but there has been no sunset and no darkness. What a strange way for the sun to act!

Strange to us, but not to Netsook and Klaya. They will tell you that there has been no sunset since the last of May. What has happened is this: we have come to Baffin Island at the time of year that is called the "summer day." In this part of the Far North the summer day lasts for nearly two months. During all that time the sun stays above the horizon night and day, and there is no darkness.

If you should spend a whole year in the Far North, you would find that there is a time in the winter when the sun never once rises. The days come and go, but the sun is hidden below the horizon. This time of darkness in the Far North is called the "winter night."

At the north pole the winter night lasts six months, or half the year, and so does the summer day. Southward from the pole the winter night and the summer day both become shorter. In the part of Baffin Island where Netsook and Klaya live the winter night begins late in November and lasts until the middle of January.

30

Look at the picture at the bottom of the page. It was copied from a photograph taken late in June at a place about as far from the north pole as Netsook's home. The interesting thing about the picture is that it was taken at twelve o'clock at night. It is a picture of the midnight sun, something that we never see in the part of the world where we live.

How good seal meat tastes!

Which Is Right?

Which ending for each of these sentences is right — *a, b,* or *c?*

1. Netsook's people are hunters because

a. they like hunting better than any other sport.

b. they must hunt in order to get food and clothing.

c. they must protect themselves from wild animals.

2. They wear fur clothes because

a. they do not like the feeling of cloth.

b. they think they look well in furs.

c. fur is the warmest clothing material.

3. Netsook's people eat more seal meat than anything else because

a. they do not like beef, lamb, or pork.

b. there are more seals than any other kind of sea animals in the Far North.

c. seals are easy to raise on Eskimo farms.

4. The Eskimos keep many dogs because

a. they need dogs for drawing their sledges.

b. they are very fond of pets.

c. the dogs scare away wild animals.

5. The Eskimos live in tents in summer because

a. tents are cooler than houses.

b. they are fond of camping out.

c. they move about in the summertime.

Volunteer Teamwork

Volunteers are people who offer to do things. Each pupil in your class may volunteer to do one of the things suggested below. All who volunteer for the same thing must work together as a team. Here are the rules for teamwork:

(1) Plan the work together.

(2) Decide just what part of the work each member of the team is to do.

(3) Do your best on your part.

(4) When the work of your team is finished, ask the rest of the class to say whether or not they think you have done well, and why.

Here are the three suggestions:

1. Draw on the blackboard a set of pictures which will tell the story of a summer afternoon with the Eskimos at the trading post.

2. Make a model of the trading post as it looks on a summer's day.

3. Hunt at home in old magazines for pictures of Eskimo life in the Far North. Arrange the pictures for a schoolroom show.

31

Midnight, and the sun is still shining.

Into the boats go all the things that the Eskimos carry on their summer travels.

SUMMER WANDERINGS

Nomads of the North

When you were reading about Bunga, you learned that his people are called nomads because of their wandering life. You found that they move about because they cannot get all their food in any one place in the forest.

The Eskimos are often called "nomads of the North." They lead a wandering life in the warmer part of the year. They move about in the summertime because the only way they can make a living in the Far North is by hunting.

People who live by hunting cannot settle down somewhere and wait for wild animals to come to them. The very word "hunting" means going in search of something. The Eskimos must go in search of animals to kill for food and other needs. They cannot live in one place all the year round.

In the Far North hunting is much easier in summer than in winter. There are more wild animals to be found in the warmer part of the year, and the Eskimos can get about more easily. The winter cold and darkness make hunting harder and more dangerous.

Do you see now why Netsook's people hunt all they can while the warmer weather lasts, and why they are nomads in the summer? It is because they must lay in supplies of meat, blubber, and skins for the winter. If they were lazy in the summertime, they would run the chance of starving or freezing to death in the wintertime.

Although summer is a time of work for Netsook's people, they enjoy it as much as if it were a long vacation. They love to travel, and they always have a good time at the trading post. Then, too, summer is the time when they most often meet other bands of Eskimos. Nothing pleases them more than to meet some of their friends and have a day or two of hunting and visiting with them.

Travels Along the Coast

Netsook's people have finished their trading for this year, and now they are ready to leave the trading post. There is a great deal going on in the camp this morning. The women are taking down the tupiks and tying all the family belongings in bundles. The men are busy loading the traveling boats.

Into the boats go the tents and the tent poles. In go bundles of meat, blubber, and skins. In go supplies bought from the traders and everything else that the Eskimos carry when they are traveling. The kayaks are tied on the decks. The dogs jump in and curl up among the bundles. Then the families climb aboard.

The men raise the sails, and the boats are off. Soon they are out of sight of the trading post, sailing along the coast. One man in each boat does the steering. The others keep a sharp lookout for seals or walruses, their guns and harpoons ready for use the minute they see one. The women sew as they sail along. If the wind dies down, they lay aside their sewing, get out the oars, and row.

Netsook and Klaya are watching for seals.

It takes "a long pull, a strong pull, and a pull all together" to get a walrus ashore.

The children love the long, sunny days on the water. They play with their toys, take naps when they are sleepy, and eat when they are hungry. They spend a good deal of time watching for seals. They are always hoping they will see one before the grown-ups do.

At the end of the day Netsook's people go ashore for a night's rest. The women put up the tupiks and make the beds. Soon the kudliks are lighted and seal meat is boiling for supper.

Sometimes Netsook's people stay but one night in a camping place. But wherever they find good hunting, they stay longer. Every day the men go out hunting on the water, either in the traveling boats or in their kayaks. Day by day they add to their supplies of meat, blubber, and skins for the winter.

The extra supplies of meat and blubber are left at the camping places. They are stored away among the rocks where the sun cannot reach them. This keeps them cold, so that they do not spoil. Later Netsook's people will be coming back this way, and they will stop and get the meat and blubber.

33

Eskimo children may gather birds' eggs, because the eggs are needed for food.

the place where it ends is its *mouth*. River mouths along a coast are where the rivers empty into the sea.

In the rivers of Baffin Island there are trout and other kinds of fish, and so the Eskimos often do some fishing during their summer travels. They like eating fish as a change from meat.

Netsook and Klaya like fish, but they like berries even better. They always look forward to the days in late July and early August when the berries ripen. Often they go berrying with their mothers while their fathers are off fishing.

Berries, fish, birds, and eggs are foods which Netsook's people enjoy during the short period when they can get them. But meat is what really counts with the Eskimos. Meat is the only food they can get enough of to keep them from starving.

Other Kinds of Food-Gathering

Every spring thousands of sea birds come flying north to Baffin Island from warmer lands where they have spent the winter. They nest on the rocky cliffs along the shores. Here they lay their eggs and raise their families.

When the Eskimos first start their summer wanderings, they often stop at the nesting places along the coast to gather eggs and to catch some of the birds in long-handled nets. What feasts they have, and how good the birds and the eggs taste! Remember that the Eskimos never have any chicken or turkey to eat, or any hens' eggs either.

Sometimes the women catch hundreds of little birds called auks. They kill each one so quickly that it does not suffer. They put the birds in a hollow under a pile of stones. This is like putting them in a refrigerator. In the winter, if Netsook's people are short of other meat, they can come with a dog sledge and get the frozen birds.

Now and then Netsook's people camp at the mouth of a river that flows down from the hills. The place where a river begins is its *source*, and

Caribou-Hunting

Netsook's people have now reached a place on the coast where they will stop for the men to go caribou-hunting. Caribou, you will remember, are wild reindeer. Before the cold weather comes, Netsook's people must get deerskins for winter clothes and blankets.

There are caribou in many parts of the Far North. They wander about in large herds, feeding mostly on a kind of moss which is named for them: reindeer moss. In winter they scratch away the snow with their sharp hoofs to get at the moss beneath.

Leaving their families in camp on the shore, the men start off for the hills where the caribou are feeding. They take their guns and knives and some of the dogs.

How Netsook wishes he were old enough to go caribou-hunting! His father has told him how carefully the hunters must creep up on a herd of caribou so as not to frighten them away. When they get near enough, each hunter takes careful aim, and it isn't often that anyone misses. Usually every man in the hunting party brings down a caribou.

Then comes the work of skinning the caribou. The skins are tied in bundles — large bundles for the hunters to carry and small ones to be strapped on the backs of the dogs. Sometimes the hunters get all the deerskins they need in a week or so, but at other times it takes longer.

The End of Summer

The caribou hunt is over, and Netsook's people are starting for the place where they spend the winter. It is early in September, and the days are growing very short and the nights very long. The weather is getting cooler, and winter is just around the corner. Autumn in the Far North is so short that winter seems to come on the very heels of summer.

Our Eskimo friends sail back along the coast, hunting as they go. They camp out each night, and they pick up the meat and blubber that were left behind earlier in the summer. But there are no long stops now. Netsook's people must hurry to reach their winter home before the sea freezes over.

Soon they reach the end of their journey. Here, on the shore of a sheltered bay, is the place that Netsook and Klaya call home. The summer wanderings are over, and there will be no more boat trips until spring comes round again.

35

Some Questions to Answer

1. Why are Netsook's people called nomads?
2. Why are they called nomads of the North?
3. Why do they wander about in the summer?
4. How do they travel on their summer wanderings?
5. What kind of houses do they live in, and why?
6. Why do they hunt sea animals such as seals and walruses?
7. Why must the men go caribou-hunting?
8. What other kinds of food besides meat do the Eskimos get in the summer?
9. Why do they enjoy their summer travels?
10. Why can't they live this wandering life the year round?

A River Test

In taking this test remember that water always flows downhill, never uphill.

Below are the beginnings and the endings of four sentences. Find the correct ending for sentence 1. Then match the other beginnings and endings correctly.

BEGINNINGS

1. The source of a river is
2. The mouth of a river is
3. Upstream is toward
4. Downstream is toward

ENDINGS

the mouth of the river.
where the river begins.
where the river ends.
the source of the river.

The dogs help to carry home the caribou skins.

WHEN WINTER COMES

Building Winter Houses

Netsook's people live in their tupiks until enough snow has fallen so that they can build their *igloos*. The igloos are their winter houses. In some parts of the Far North the Eskimo igloos are built of rocks and earth. But in Baffin Island and its neighborhood they are built of snow.

The work begins as soon as the snow is solid enough to be cut in big blocks. The picture shows Netsook's father building his igloo. The pictures on page 37 show how the igloo looks when it is finished. Doesn't it remind you of two big white bowls turned upside down?

The larger bowl is the main igloo. The smaller one is the vestibule, or entranceway. The vestibule helps to keep the cold air out of the main igloo, and it makes a good storage room. Notice that the doorway is so low that the grown-ups must stoop to get through it. Igloo doorways are always small. Can you think why?

Igloo-building is work in which the children can help, for all the cracks between the blocks must be packed tight with soft snow. The snow freezes in the cracks and keeps out the wind. Netsook and Klaya have great fun climbing the igloo and filling the cracks.

The inside of the igloo must have a lining, so that when it is warmed by the kudliks the snow will not melt and drip. For a lining Netsook's father uses an old sealskin tupik covering.

Opposite the doorway in the main igloo Netsook's father builds a broad platform of snow blocks for the family bed. Then he builds two side platforms for use as benches. The platforms take up so much room in the igloo that there is not much floor space.

After the men have built the igloos, the women furnish them. Netsook's mother spreads the platforms with heather and throws deerskin blankets over them. Then she arranges her kudliks and cooking dishes where she wants them.

The igloos are built and furnished so quickly that in a few hours Netsook's winter home looks like a different place. The little group of tupiks has disappeared, and a tiny village of snow houses has taken its place.

36

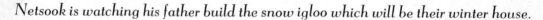

Netsook is watching his father build the snow igloo which will be their winter house.

Packing the cracks is fun for the children.

The kudliks are lighted, and soon the igloos begin to warm up. Netsook and Klaya think their igloo very comfortable. It protects them from the wind, the cold, and the storms of winter. Don't imagine, though, that a snow igloo is ever as warm as your house is in the wintertime. If it were, it would melt from the inside out and fall to pieces.

Any house is a good house if it gives people the kind of shelter from the weather that they need. So, when you think of Netsook and Klaya, remember that while their igloo would often seem chilly to you, it is warm enough for them. Remember, too, that Netsook and Klaya wear fur clothing and sleep between fur blankets.

Winter Life in the Snow Village

Can you picture Baffin Island in the wintertime? It is a cold, frozen picture, with snow on the land and ice on the sea. It is a rather dark picture too, for the winter days are very short and the nights are very long. You may think it a lonely picture, for there are no towns, cities, or roads. The only signs of life are in the tiny snow villages scattered far apart along the coast.

But each little village is as busy as a beehive. The Eskimos are not afraid of the cold, and they do not lead a shut-in life in the winter. The children play outdoors, and the men go hunting with their dogs and sledges. The women are busy with their housework, but they always have time to visit back and forth in the different igloos.

Sometimes there are terrible storms — the kind called blizzards. The wind sweeps down from the hills and brings with it clouds of stinging snow. Then everyone has to stay indoors, even the men. But usually there is more clear weather than stormy weather, and Netsook's people are not often shut in for very long at a time.

When the men cannot go hunting, there is plenty to do at home. Netsook's father must keep his gun cleaned and oiled and his harpoons in good shape. The sealskin dog-harness gets hard wear, and often needs mending. The sledge, too, must be kept in good repair. It is a big sledge, made of pieces of wood with runners of steel. If it gets smashed on a trip over the ice, Netsook's father has a big repair job to do.

The finished igloo with its vestibule looks like two big white bowls turned upside down.

Netsook's mother is just as busy as his father. She cooks the meals, prepares seal oil for the kudliks, and takes care of the clothes for the whole family. Wet clothes must be dried and torn clothes must be mended. New clothes and boots must be made when the old ones wear out.

The older girls help their mothers, and the older boys often go hunting with their fathers. The younger children spend most of their time at play. In good weather they play out of doors. If you could see the fun they have coasting, snowballing, and building toy igloos, you might almost wish you were an Eskimo yourself.

Netsook and Klaya like the evenings in the igloo almost as well as the days of outdoor play. After supper their father tells them stories, or plays on the mouth organ that he bought years ago from the traders. Often another family drops in for a call, and the men talk of the exciting adventures they have had in hunting. Netsook likes the hunting stories best of all.

The "Winter Night"

As time goes on, the days grow shorter and shorter, and the nights longer and longer. The sun rises later each morning and sets earlier each afternoon. Late in November comes the first day when there is no sunrise. This is the beginning of the "winter night." It will be nearly two months before Netsook's people will see the sun again.

Think of it — a night that lasts nearly two months! Not one glimpse of the sun in all that time! It sounds dreadful, doesn't it? But there is one thing that helps out, and that is the moon.

Twice during the two months of winter night the moon is above the horizon for eight days and nights without once setting. When the sky is clear, the snow-covered land is silvery in the moonlight. Of course there are times when clouds hide the moon's face, but Netsook's people usually have a good many hours of moonlight to help to make up for losing the sun.

On winter evenings in the igloo the children's father often tells them stories.

The children's father comes back to the little snow village from a hunting trip.

Hunting and Trapping

The supplies of meat and blubber which the Eskimos get in the summer are never enough to last through the long winter. So, in spite of the cold, the men must keep on hunting. They must keep on getting meat and blubber or their families will be hungry and cold before the winter ends. The dogs, too, must have meat, and they have big appetites.

Although the sea is covered with ice, the Eskimos can still go seal-hunting. Seals, you will remember, cannot breathe under water. So, when the water begins to freeze over in the fall, they scratch breathing holes in the ice. All winter they come to these holes for fresh air. They come often enough so that the holes never freeze over too solidly to be broken open by the push of a seal's nose.

Perhaps you can guess how seals are hunted in the winter. First a breathing hole must be found. Then the hunter waits very quietly until he sees a seal through the thin ice. Just as the seal cracks the ice, the hunter spears it with his harpoon. Often the hunter has to wait hours in the cold before a seal comes along.

Nearly every day, except in bad weather, Netsook's father and the other men go off with their dog sledges to hunt seals. If they have good luck, they come back with the sledges well loaded and the dogs pulling hard. But luck isn't always good, and often the sledges come home nearly empty. There are times when the supplies of meat and blubber nearly give out in the snow village.

Winter is also the time when Netsook's people catch white foxes in traps. You remember that foxskins are among the furs that the Eskimos take to the trading post. They use them as money for buying supplies that they cannot get in any other way. Trapping foxes is important work, but hunting the animals that supply meat, oil, and clothing materials is much more important. Getting enough to eat and keeping warm mean more than anything else to our friends in the Far North.

Harpooning a seal at a breathing hole.

39

A winter sledging trip is a happy holiday for Eskimo children and their parents.

Sledging Trips

During the winter night the darkness makes it hard for Netsook's people to do much hunting. So, if they have a good supply of meat and blubber on hand, they often go off on sledge trips to visit friends in other villages.

Netsook and Klaya always look forward to these trips. Their father harnesses the dogs to the sledge and ties on some bundles of meat, blubber, and deerskins. Their mother tucks in a pair of kudliks and a cooking pot. When all is ready, the children and their mother seat themselves on the sledge and wrap up in deerskin blankets.

Netsook's father cracks his long whip, shouts to the dogs, and off they go. What fun it is to skim over the snow behind the racing dogs! Netsook's father runs beside the sledge. He keeps cracking his whip and shouting to tell the dogs which way to go. When the going is smooth, he jumps on the sledge and rides for a while.

Netsook's family usually make these trips during the time of moonlight. Whenever they are tired, they stop to rest. They build a small snow igloo, have a meal of meat, and then roll up in deerskins for a good sleep. Sometimes they are away from home for a week or more. Netsook and Klaya have a wonderful time. They love sledging, and they have fun playing with the children in the village where they visit.

The End of Winter

One day, after the middle of January, the sun rises again. It doesn't stay above the horizon very long, but its return means the end of the winter night. You mustn't think, though, that the end of the winter night means the end of winter. Each day the sun will stay above the horizon longer than it did the day before, but many weeks will pass before the days are longer than the nights. The weather will still be cold, and spring will be late in coming.

At last, toward the end of March, the days are as long as the nights, and with more sunshine, the weather is a little warmer. After this come longer and longer days and shorter and shorter nights. The snow starts to melt, and the ice on the water begins to break up.

When the birds begin to come back from the south and the igloos begin to melt, Netsook and Klaya know that spring has really come. The people of the little village move out of their melting igloos and into their tupiks. The men go off for days at a time hunting seals and walruses out on the floating ice. When they are at home they are busy repairing the kayaks and the traveling boats.

Soon after the middle of June the day comes to take down the tupiks and pack everything in the boats. Once more Netsook's people are starting off for a summer of wandering, hunting, and trading. The happiest time of year has come again.

Now that you have been round the year with Netsook and Klaya, you can see that life is much harder for the Eskimos than it is for the Negritos in the warm forests of Malaya. The Eskimos spend most of their lives fighting off two enemies: hunger and cold. Yet they are among the most cheerful people in the world. They take good luck and bad luck as it comes, and keep smiling through it all.

Some Things to Do

1. Write or tell a short story explaining how Netsook's people manage to keep from freezing in the wintertime. Use these words in the story:

igloos	snow	cracks	doorways
kudliks	oil	blubber	deerskins
clothes	fur	hoods	mittens

2. Write or tell another story explaining why the Eskimos need sledges and dogs. Draw pictures to go with your story.

3. Plan a little play in four acts about seal-hunting in the wintertime. Here are suggestions for the four acts:

Act 1. Why we must go seal-hunting.
Act 2. Starting off on the hunt.
Act 3. At the breathing holes.
Act 4. Bringing home the seals.

Something to Prove

Here is a chance for you to prove that you remember what you have learned about the winter night and the summer day in the Far North. Give the words that are missing in the sentences.

1. During the winter night the sun never once ------. It stays below the ------- day and night.

2. During the summer day the sun never once ----. It stays above the ------- day and night.

3. At the north pole the winter night and the summer day each last six ------.

4. Where Netsook and Klaya live the winter night and the summer day each lasts nearly --- months.

If You Were Netsook or Klaya

Put yourself in Netsook's place or Klaya's. Answer the questions as you think they would.

1. Would you want your father to be a good hunter? Why?

2. Would you care whether or not he went caribou-hunting in the summer? Why?

3. Would you want him to trap as many foxes as he could in the winter? Why?

4. Would you want your mother to be a good tailor? Why?

5. Which would you rather have — an automobile or a sledge and a team of dogs? Why?

Something to Talk Over

Talk over what you know about the food, clothes, and houses of Netsook's people and of Bunga's people. Are they different because the Eskimos and Negritos are such different people or because they live in such different lands?

41

Once more Netsook's people are off for a summer of wandering, hunting, and trading.

DO YOU KNOW YOUR DIRECTIONS?

How to Find the North

You have learned that Netsook and Klaya live in the Far North. *North*, you know, is a direction. Can you point toward the north?

If you do not know which direction is north, here is a way in which you can find out for yourself:

Go outdoors any clear day *at noon* and stand in the sunshine. Your shadow will point toward the north. Stand so that your shadow points straight ahead of you, and you will be facing north. Remember this: *In the part of the world where we live noonday shadows always point north.*

How to Find the Other Directions

Besides north, there are three other main directions: *south*, *east*, and *west*. Wherever you are, if you know one of the directions, you can easily find the others. Here are some drawings that show how.

As you can see from the drawings, there are four rules to remember:

1. North and south are opposite each other.

2. East and west are opposite each other.

3. When I face north, east is on my right and west is on my left.

4. When I face south, east is on my left and west is on my right.

You will need to learn these rules. Then work out for yourself two others:

5. When I face east, north is on my ____, and south is on my _____.

6. When I face west, north is on my _____, and south is on my ____.

Some boys and girls are never sure of their directions unless they are facing north. Facing any other way, they often make mistakes. If you want to be a winner in direction-finding, practice it facing first one way and then another. Keep at it until you get so used to the directions that you just can't make a mistake. It is fun to know you can do something so well that no one can beat you.

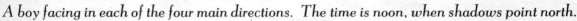

A boy facing in each of the four main directions. The time is noon, when shadows point north.

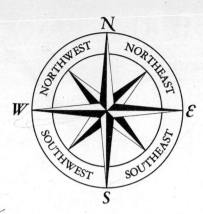

Main directions and in-between directions.

The In-Between Directions

North, south, east, and west are the four main directions, and they are the ones whose names we use the most. But we often need to name a direction between two of the main ones. As you can see from the drawing, there are four of these in-between directions, and their names are easy to remember from their places:

Northeast is between north and east.
Northwest is between north and west.
Southeast is between south and east.
Southwest is between south and west.

When you are sure you know the names of the in-between directions and their places, make a direction drawing of your own. Mark the names of all the directions on it from memory.

Schoolroom Directions

Find out which direction is north in your schoolroom, and practice finding the other directions.

When you have had enough practice, see if you can answer the questions below.

1. On which side of the schoolroom is the door by which you come in?

2. On which side, or sides, of the room are the windows?

3. How do you face as you sit at your desk?

4. On which side of the room is your teacher's desk?

5. In which direction does your teacher face as she sits at her desk?

Finding Directions at Night

On a clear night you can see the group of stars called the Big Dipper. The two Pointer Stars in the Dipper point toward the North Star. When you face in the direction of the North Star, you can tell where the other directions are. Try it tonight if the sky is clear.

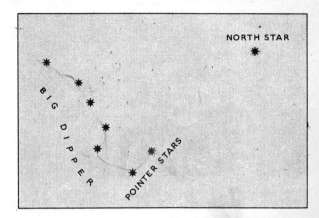

The two Pointer Stars in the Big Dipper point toward the North Star.

A Direction Match

A direction match is partly like a spelling match and partly like a drill. The whole class will stand, facing north. Your teacher will give the name of a direction, and every pupil must at once point in the direction named. Those who make mistakes and point in a wrong direction are out of the match and must sit down.

Then your teacher will name another direction, and again those who fail to point correctly must sit down. The match will go on in this way until only one pupil is left standing. That pupil will be the winner.

Some Things to Do

1. Use your schoolroom globe to show where the north pole is located. If you haven't a globe, use the picture of the globe on page 21.

2. Copy these sentences, filling in the blanks with the right words.

The north pole is the point farthest _____ on the earth. It is in the midst of the frozen _____ Ocean.

43

Suvan
of the Steppe

A KAZAK CAMP

A Boy Whose Father Is Rich

Suvan is another boy who lives part of each year in a tent. The tent is the kind which is called a *yurt*. It has a light openwork frame of wood, and the covering is a kind of cloth called felt. The whole thing can be put up or taken down in half an hour. Should you ever guess that Suvan's father is rich?

Suvan's father hasn't any money in the bank. He doesn't own any land. He has another house besides his tent, but it is nothing but a hut. Yet Suvan's father is rich and powerful. He is the headman, or chief, of his clan. The clan is one group of the people who are called Kazaks. There are many other clans of Kazaks, each with its own headman.

Suvan's father is counted a rich man because he owns so many animals. He has big flocks of sheep and goats, and many horses. He keeps cattle too, and some camels. Among the Kazaks the men who own the most animals are the richest.

The Kazaks are strong, healthy outdoor people. Their skin is a light yellowish brown, and their hair is coarse, straight, and very dark. Perhaps you have already guessed that they are nomads. They are not food-gatherers like the Negritos, nor are they hunters like the Eskimos. They live wandering lives for another reason. Soon you will learn what it is.

Where Suvan Lives

It is a hot summer day, and we have come to make a call on Suvan and his family. We have ridden miles and miles on horseback across a plain that seems to have no end. A *plain* is a stretch of land which is nearly level. This plain has no trees except a few along the streams. It is covered with short grass which has dried and turned brown in the sun. It is the kind of grassy plain which we call a *steppe*.

We are back now in Eurasia, where Bunga lives, but we are in a part which is quite different from Malaya. There, you know, the weather is

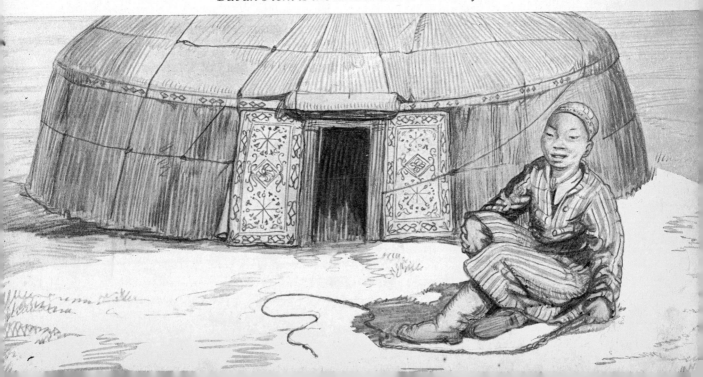

Suvan's tent is the kind which is called a yurt.

Suvan's father invites us into the yurt.

hot and rainy the year round. Here there is never very much rain, and while the summer is hot, the winter is cold.

Can you think why there are no forests here, as there are in Malaya? It is because forests can grow only in lands where there is a good deal of rain. In Suvan's land there is too little rain for forests, but there is enough for the growth of grass.

Turn to the picture of the globe on page 9 and you will see just where Suvan's land is. It is called the Kirghiz Steppe. The Kirghiz Steppe is part of Kazakstan, or the land of the Kazaks.

The globe shows that the Kirghiz Steppe is far away from Malaya. It is much farther west and much farther north in Eurasia. The globe shows also that the steppe is far inland; that is, far away from the ocean. These are the reasons why the weather is so different from the weather in Malaya.

Suvan and Nara Entertain Us

We must ride round to the back of Suvan's yurt and wait for his father to come and greet us. In Kazakstan it is very rude to ride up to a yurt and knock. If we should do that, Suvan would think we hadn't been taught good manners.

Here comes Suvan's father now. He is wearing a long coat belted in at the waist and a close-fitting cap stitched in bright colors. He was not expecting us and he has no idea who we are, but he smiles and motions us to get off our horses. He calls a boy to take the horses away and see that they are fed and watered. A Kazak always sees that his guests and their horses are well cared for.

Suvan's father leads us to the door of the yurt and invites us in. There are a number of people inside. The boy about your age is Suvan, and he is dressed like his father. The little girl is his sister, Nara. Their mother is there, and two older sisters. The girls and their mother are dressed much alike, and each one has her head bound up in a cloth that hangs down over her shoulders.

We must bow politely to our new friends and accept their invitation to sit on the floor near the doorway. There are no chairs in the yurt.

Soon Suvan's mother brings us each a wooden bowl of steaming tea and another of something that looks like milk. Suvan calls it kumiss, and says that it is made of mare's milk. Mares are mother horses. The kumiss may taste a little queer to you at first, but the more you drink of it, the better you will like it.

Right in the middle of the yurt, in a shallow hole in the ground, a small fire is burning. Over the fire hangs a copper pot of boiling water. Suvan's mother has put some pieces of mutton in the pot. Mutton, you know, is the meat of sheep. Suvan's mother is cooking it as a special treat because we are guests.

After the mutton has boiled for some time, Suvan's mother takes it from the pot and puts it on two big wooden platters. She sets the platters on a low, round table. Then Suvan's father cuts the meat into small pieces.

The next thing that happens will surprise you. Suvan will take a piece of meat in his fingers and put it in your mouth. He will give each of his guests a piece in the same way. This

46

is his way of saying "You are welcome in our house."

The boys will gather round the table with Suvan and his father and will eat from one of the platters with their fingers. Nara will set the other platter on a rug on the floor. She will invite the girls to eat with her mother and sisters and herself.

All this may seem strange to you, but it is Suvan's and Nara's way of showing you the greatest politeness. If they should visit you in your house, they would think many of your ways strange.

Suvan's Yurt

Suvan's yurt is larger than Netsook's igloo, and it has more furnishings. The ground, which makes the floor, is covered with felt. Scattered over this carpeting are felt rugs with patterns stitched in bright colors. Felt is a thick cloth made of matted wool. The Kazaks make their own felt from the wool of their sheep.

The wall of the yurt makes a circle. It is about four feet high and is built of crisscrossed rods of willow wood. From the top of the wall other willow rods slant upward like the ribs of a big umbrella, making the roof. Look up and you will see that the ribs are fastened to a small wooden ring, and through the ring you can see the sky. This is the hole that lets the smoke from the fire out.

Except for the smoke-hole, the wall and the roof are covered on the outside with layers of felt. In summer, when the weather is hot, only one or two layers of felt are used. In colder weather more layers are tied on, and at night, after the fire has died down, the smoke-hole is covered over.

47

Mealtime in the yurt, with the pot boiling over the fire in the middle.

Suvan and Nara hope you will like kumiss as much as they do.

Inside the yurt, at the back, is a big platform of boards covered with layers and layers of felt that make a mattress nearly a foot thick. This is the family bed. On the floor close by are rolls of felt bedding, sheepskin covers, and pillows stuffed with sheep's wool.

Along the wall is a row of chests, or boxes, some made of wood and some of leather. The wooden ones are carved and painted in bright colors. In these chests Suvan's mother keeps clothing and dry foods such as tea and sugar. Hanging from the wall are big leather bags made of goatskin and sheepskin, and in these Suvan's mother keeps cheese and butter. Her dishes are scattered here and there: copper pots and wooden plates, platters, and bowls.

For a tent the yurt seems well furnished, doesn't it? But don't forget that this is the home of a rich family. The yurts of the poorer Kazaks are smaller and not so well furnished.

In all there are five yurts in the little camp. Suvan's father's is the largest. Next in size are two belonging to Suvan's grown-up brothers. The brothers are married and have families of their own. They have their own flocks and herds of animals too.

The other two yurts are smaller, for they belong to some poorer cousins who own fewer animals. The cousins live and wander with their richer relatives, helping them in all their work.

Suvan calls this family group his *aul.* He will tell you that the clan of which his father is chief is made up of many auls. If you ask where the other family groups are, he will explain that in summer the clan breaks up and the people of each aul wander over the steppe by themselves.

Do You Remember What You Read?

If you do, these questions will be easy.

1. What kind of land do we call a plain?

2. What grows on the plain where Suvan lives?

3. What is such a plain called?

4. What kind of weather does Suvan's land have in summer? in winter?

5. How is the weather different from the weather in Malaya? in Baffin Island?

6. What are the tents of the Kazaks called?

7. Why are tents good houses for people who live as the Kazaks do?

8. What kinds of animals do the Kazaks keep?

9. What reason have you to think that sheep are very useful to the Kazaks?

10. What, instead of money, makes a Kazak family rich?

How Suvan's yurt is built: (1) the wall of crisscrossed willow rods; (2) the wall with the framework of the roof fastened on; (3) the finished yurt, with its covering of felt.

1
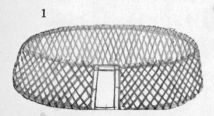

2

3

HERDSMEN OF THE STEPPE

A Horseback Ride

People whose chief work is caring for animals such as cattle and sheep are called herdsmen. Suvan's people are wandering herdsmen of the steppe.

Suvan and Nara want to take you out to see the flocks and herds. They are on their horses now, and you are on yours. Off you go, galloping over the grassy plain. Your horses are kicking up a cloud of dust.

You will have to ride well to keep up with Suvan and Nara, for they learned to ride almost as soon as they learned to walk. They are as much at home on horseback as you are on a bicycle.

Suvan's father keeps a herd of about fifty horses. A few, ready for riding at any time, are near the yurts. The rest are grazing, or feeding, at a place on the steppe where the grass is richest and best.

The horses prick up their ears as you ride up to them. One of them snorts and paws the ground. This one is the leader of the herd, and he guards it well. If a pack of wolves tries to attack the horses, they crowd together in a bunch, all but the leader. He rushes out and drives the wolves away.

You must ride farther from the camp to see the sheep and goats. There are several hundred goats and even more sheep, and they are grazing where the grass is thin and poor. Sheep and goats can get along with much poorer grass than horses can.

You will see some big boys who are riding oxen. They are the shepherds who watch over the flocks. They see that the sheep and goats do not wander away, and that they are not harmed by wild animals. The shepherds carry long sticks, slings for shooting stones, and ropes which they crack like whips. These are their weapons for scaring away the wild animals. Suvan says that in a few years he will be old enough to be a shepherd.

49

Suvan and Nara are as much at home on horseback as you are on a bicycle.

Riding back toward the camp, you will see the cattle. There are not so many cattle because they do not stand the cold winter weather so well as sheep and goats do. Then, too, cattle need richer grass than sheep and goats, and much of the grass on the steppe is poor.

Last of all, you will see a herd of about thirty camels grazing by themselves. What strange-looking beasts they are, with their long necks and the humps on their backs! Suvan says the camels are very useful because they can walk fifteen to twenty miles a day with heavy loads of goods strapped on their backs.

There are two very interesting things about camels. The humps on their backs are of fat. When the camels are getting plenty to eat, the humps grow big. When grass is scarce, the fat takes the place of food for the camels, and they can get along for some time with very little to eat. But of course the humps grow smaller as the fat is used up. The time comes when the camels must eat or starve to death.

The other interesting thing is that a camel can drink a great deal of water at one time, and then can go without drinking for three or four days. For this reason camels are the animals which can be kept most easily in lands where water is scarce.

The driest lands of the earth are called *deserts*. In the deserts so little rain falls that even grass is very scarce. The only way of getting water is from pools or wells which are far, far apart. In such lands sheep and other animals that need water every day often die of thirst. But camels can usually hold out long enough to get to some place where there is a little water.

Suvan will tell you that some of the Kazaks live farther south where the land is almost desert. They keep more camels and fewer animals of other kinds than the Kazaks of the steppe do. The steppe is a rather dry land, but it gets more rain than the desert, and so it has more grass and more water.

Perhaps you know that grazing lands where animals feed on grass and other plants are called *pastures*. Desert pastures are very poor because they are so very dry. Steppe pastures are better because they have more water and more grass. But the best pastures of all are in lands that are rainy enough so that the grass grows thick and juicy and there is plenty of water for the animals to drink.

50

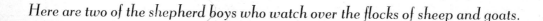

Here are two of the shepherd boys who watch over the flocks of sheep and goats.

Camels are very useful animals in lands where water and grass are not plentiful.

Milking Time

If you stay over night at the camp in the steppe, you will be there for the evening milking. Before sunset the flocks and herds are driven in from the pastures. The men milk the mares, but the women and girls milk the sheep and the goats, the cows, and the camels. Even the little girls like Nara help by milking some of the goats.

As you watch the milking, remember that there are many other Kazak camps scattered far and wide over the steppe, and that in every one of them the same work is going on. What do you suppose the Kazaks do with all the milk from their animals?

Of course they drink some of it, but they use most of it in other ways. From mare's milk, you know, they make kumiss. Kumiss is their favorite drink, and it is also a good food, but only the richer families who own many horses can have a great deal of it.

From the milk of the sheep, goats, cows, and camels the Kazak women make cheese and butter. In summer, when the animals give the most milk, the women make soft cheese for the daily meals and a great many little round dry cheeses which will keep a long time. They store away the dry cheeses in leather bags and keep them for the winter, when the animals give much less milk.

For safety at night the animals are kept near the yurts. In the morning they are milked again and then taken out to graze in the pastures during the day. They get the water they need from shallow streams that flow through the steppe, or, in some places, water is drawn for them from wells. A Kazak camp is always made near a stream or a good well.

Supper Time

After the flocks and herds have been milked and made safe for the night, Suvan's people go to their yurts for supper. If you take supper in Suvan's yurt, you will have kumiss and cheese, and perhaps some dough fried in butter or mutton fat. There will be plenty of each, but nothing else to eat.

You might think that the Kazaks would be great meat-eaters, but they are not. They never eat beef because they do not like it. They cannot afford to kill many sheep or goats for meat because they need the milk and the wool. They keep horses for riding and camels for carrying goods.

The rich Kazaks are the only ones who eat mutton fairly often, and even they live mostly on milk and cheese. The poorer families — and

Nara helps by milking some of the goats.

there are many more poor than rich — seldom kill a sheep for meat except for some special celebration.

The only time of year when much meat is eaten is in the autumn. At that time of year some of the older sheep and goats have to be killed because there is never enough grass for all the animals during the cold winter. The Kazaks enjoy the meat, but they wouldn't kill the animals if they didn't have to.

If you have ever read the story of the goose that laid the golden egg, you will understand why the Kazaks do not kill many of their sheep and goats. A dead animal cannot go on supplying milk or wool.

Evening in the Yurt

Supper is over now, and Suvan's family have settled down for a quiet evening in the yurt. The fire is blazing brightly, and even though this is a summer night, the yurt is not too warm. After sunset the dry air of the steppe cools off quickly, and the nights are rather chilly.

By the light of the fire Suvan's mother is stitching a pattern in colored wools on a small felt rug. His father is braiding a rope of hair from a horse's tail. He makes many of his ropes and whips of horsehair.

Suvan and Nara will show you some games that they like. One is a game like checkers. Another is knucklebones, which perhaps you have played at home. Both children can teach you some finger tricks with string like the finger trick you call cat's cradle. For string they use threads of twisted wool.

Nara will want to show you her dolls. You mustn't seem surprised when you see that they are just sticks tied up in felt and decorated with bits of bright-colored wool.

The felt curtain that hangs over the doorway is pushed aside, and Suvan's grown-up brothers come into the yurt. They have come to make plans with their father for moving.

The flocks and herds have eaten most of the grass round this camp, and there is not much left. In a day or two our Kazak friends must pack up and start off in search of fresh pastures for their animals.

What Do You Think?

Say "Yes" or "No" to each question and give a good reason for your answer.

1. Would it be right to call Malaya a steppe?

2. Would it be right to call Baffin Island a plain?

3. Would it be right to call the Kirghiz Steppe a pasture land?

4. Would it be right to call Netsook's people herdsmen?

5. Would it be right to call Suvan's people nomads?

Some Animal Questions

Name the five kinds of animals that Suvan's people keep. Then answer these questions:

1. Which one of these animals do we see only in zoos? Why is it a useful kind of animal for the Kazaks to keep?

2. In our country some horses are used for riding, but many more are used for farm work. For which of these uses do the Kazaks keep horses? Why don't they use them in the other way?

3. In our country cattle are raised for both meat and milk. Is it the same in Kazakstan? Why, or why not?

4. In our country we drink mostly cows' milk. What kinds of milk do Suvan and Nara drink? Why do they drink more milk and eat more cheese than you do?

5. Why don't the Kazaks kill more of their sheep and goats for meat?

Volunteer Teamwork

Make a model of a Kazak camp in the steppe. Show the grassy plain, the yurts, and the animals grazing in the pastures.

ON THE MARCH

Why the Kazaks Are Nomads

You haven't been with Suvan long, but you have had time enough to find out that his people get their living from their animals. The animals supply them with food and drink, and with the two materials that they need most: wool and leather.

All the Kazaks use wool for yurt coverings, rugs, and beds and bedding. The poorer people weave coarse cloth of sheep's wool and camel's hair for clothing, and they line their winter coats with wool for more warmth. The richer people buy cloth of different kinds, but they too need wool linings in their winter coats.

Leather, made from the hides and skins of animals that die or have to be killed, is also important for clothing and other uses. All the Kazaks — children as well as grown-ups — wear knee boots of leather, and all the men and boys need heavy leather riding breeches. Leather is needed for saddles and harness too, and for things such as bags, bottles, and chests which can be carried on the back of an ox or a camel without danger of breaking.

The Kazaks also need animals in order to get about. They have no automobiles, trailers, or trucks. When they move, they need animals for riding and for carrying their belongings.

You can see, then, that to the Kazaks their animals mean everything: food, clothing, shelter, and a way of getting about. But why is it, do you suppose, that these herdsmen of the steppe do not stay in one place with their flocks and herds? The answer to this question is grass. There is no one place in the steppe where a clan of herdsmen can find enough grass to feed their flocks and herds the year round. This is because there is so little rain.

There is not enough rain in the steppe for the growing of crops, and so the Kazaks cannot be farmers. As you will soon learn, they grow a little extra feed for their horses to eat in winter, but to do this they must water small fields from streams.

There is not even enough rain for a covering of tall grass on the steppe. The grass is short, and after it has been nibbled off by the animals, it takes it a long time to grow again.

Now you can understand why the Kazaks are nomads. Since they depend on their flocks and herds for most of their needs, they must wander in search of the grass that keeps the animals alive. The need of water is just as great as the need of grass, and streams are rather scarce in this land of little rain. There are many pastures that cannot be used at all because they are too far from any stream.

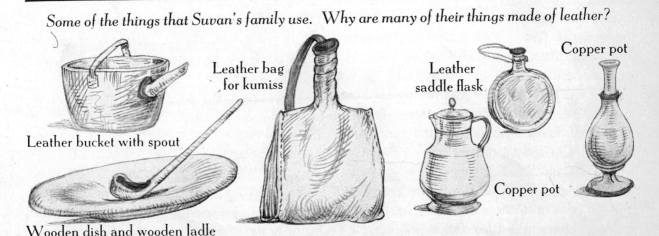

Some of the things that Suvan's family use. Why are many of their things made of leather?

Leather bag for kumiss

Leather saddle flask

Copper pot

Leather bucket with spout

Copper pot

Wooden dish and wooden ladle

The day has come to take down the yurts, pack up, and set off for fresh pastures.

Moving-Day

When the day to move comes, everyone is busy breaking camp. All the yurt coverings, rugs, and bedding are rolled up and tied in bundles. All the chests, bags, and other furnishings are brought out of the yurts. Then off come the roofs of the yurts, to be folded up rather like umbrellas. Finally the walls are taken down. They are in several parts and, like the roofs, they fold up neatly.

The oxen and the camels are waiting patiently for their loads. One by one they are loaded with all they can carry. When the work is finished, everything that Suvan's people own is tied on the backs of these strong, willing pack animals.

Now the women and the little children are getting on the backs of the riding oxen. The babies are strapped in wooden cradles, and the cradles are tied to the fronts of the mothers' saddles. The men, the boys, and the older girls jump on their horses, and Suvan's father gives the word to start.

What a long line of animals and people it is! The men and boys on horseback take the lead, and are soon far ahead. They will ride a good many miles to find the best place to stop for the night. The main line is made up of the cattle, sheep, and goats, driven by the shepherds. At the end are the women and girls on their oxen and horses, and all the pack animals that are carrying the baggage.

All day long this procession, or line, of animals and people moves slowly across the dusty, treeless plain. The camels and oxen cannot go very fast with their heavy loads. The sheep, goats, and cows want to stop to nibble the grass as they go along, and the shepherds have to keep them moving.

Fresh Pastures

Before sunset the procession stops and the pack animals are unloaded. All the things they have been carrying are dumped on the ground. The next thing to be done is the milking, and then the animals must be driven to a stream for a drink.

If Suvan's people have reached a place where there are fresh pastures, they will unpack, put up their yurts, and settle down for a few days. If not, they will set up just the roofs of the yurts on the ground and tie on some pieces of felt to keep out the chilly night wind. They will unpack only the few things they need for supper and a night's sleep. Tomorrow they will move on again.

All summer long, and until the middle of October, Suvan's people wander over the steppe in search of fresh pastures. Even where they find the most grass, there is never enough to feed all the animals for more than a few days. You might suppose that Suvan's people would get tired of so much packing and unpacking and of so many long days of travel in the heat and dust.

Suvan would be surprised if he knew you were thinking any such thing. He loves his wandering life, and he would rather be riding his horse than doing anything else in the world. All his people feel the same way. They wouldn't settle down to living in one place if they could, and they feel sorry for people who have to.

Summer, though, is hard on the animals. The grass is never very rich, and in some years it is poorer than usual. By fall the animals are thin, and many are growing weak and ailing. If a great many are in bad shape, Suvan's people have cause to worry.

The loss of a large number of animals is the worst thing that can happen to a Kazak family. It leaves them with less food and less material for clothing, yurts, and bedding than they need. The skins of the dead animals are useful, but they do not make up for too little food. Until the flocks and herds can be built up again, the family will be poorly fed and poorly clothed.

55

Ready to start. The baby is safe and happy, strapped in his wooden cradle.

A Milk-and-Weather Story

You have found that Suvan's people do not have many different kinds of food. They live mostly on milk and cheese, and the cheese is made from milk. Do you know what the weather in the steppe has to do with the supply of milk? Here is a way to find out.

1. On the blackboard draw pictures to go with this story. It is like the story of "The House That Jack Built." Or, if you would rather, ask your teacher if you and your classmates may act out the story as a little play.

This is the MILK that Suvan's people need for food.

These are the ANIMALS that give the milk that Suvan's people need for food.

This is the GRASS that feeds the animals that give the milk that Suvan's people need for food.

This is the RAIN that waters the grass that feeds the animals that give the milk that Suvan's people need for food.

2. You have pictured the story from milk to rain. Now tell it backward, from rain to milk. Give the right words to fill the blanks in the sentences.

The ____ that falls in the steppe makes the _____ grow. The _____ feeds the animals that Suvan's people keep. The animals are _____, _____, _____, _____, and _____. They all give ____ which Suvan's people need for food.

3. In some years the steppe has more rain than usual, and in other years it has less. Here are five pairs of words. If you arrange them in the right order, they will tell the story of what happens when there is less rain than usual. See if you can do it. Start with "Less rain."

Less rain   Fewer animals   Less food
         Less grass   Less milk

Some Things to Do

1. On the blackboard make as long a list as you can of the other things besides food which Suvan's people get from their animals.

2. Explain just why it is that the Kazak herdsmen are nomads.

IN WINTER QUARTERS

The Gathering of the Clan

By the middle of October the weather is getting cold and the ground is beginning to freeze. The yurts need more coverings of felt now, and wooden doors take the place of curtains at the doorways. The nights are so cold that Suvan and Nara are glad to toast themselves by the fire and then hop into bed under warm sheepskin covers.

Soon it will be too cold for the animals to graze on the open steppe, and so Suvan's people are on the way to their winter quarters. This means the place where they spend their winters. From far and wide over the plain the other auls of the clan are moving toward the same place. By November they will all be gathered at the winter quarters, and they will stay there until the middle of April.

The winter quarters of the clan are in the *valley* of a river. The valley is a strip of low-lying land through which the river flows. It is lower than the bordering land, and so it is somewhat protected from the icy winds that sweep over the steppe. Groups of willows and other trees scattered along the banks of the river give a little protection, too.

Strung out along this valley are the winter homes of the people of the clan. Each family has a piece of ground with a high wall around it. The wall is built of sticks and sods. Sods are pieces of turf (earth and grass) cut from the ground. Inside the wall are the buildings and some rough sheds for the animals.

Winter Shelter

If you should visit Suvan and Nara in the winter, you would not find them living in their yurt. Their winter house is an oblong-shaped hut built of sods. It is only about eight feet high, but the walls are three feet thick.

The roof is flat and is made of willow branches with a thick covering of sod. This kind of roof wouldn't do if there were heavy snowstorms in Suvan's land. The snow might crush it in. Even if that didn't happen, water from the melting snow would soak through.

But Suvan's people do not have to worry much about snow. There are snowstorms now and then, but not many, and they seldom leave more than a light blanket of snow on the ground. Shelter from the cold and the freezing winds is what Suvan's people need in winter. In such weather thick walls and a low, thick roof are the best protection.

Suvan's hut is like all the others except that it is a little larger. It has a tiny window at one side and another at the back. These are holes in the walls covered with a material which looks much like thin skin. This material lets in a little light, but you cannot see through it.

The hut is furnished like the yurt, and the walls are hung with pieces of felt. With a fire burning in the center the hut keeps the family warm, but it is rather dark and often smoky. The yurt is a more pleasant house, but in the part of the steppe where Suvan lives it cannot be kept warm enough in the winter.

Near Suvan's hut are a number of little sod storehouses and the sheds for the animals. The sheds are nothing but sloping roofs of willow branches built out from the sides of the wall. At night the animals lie close together for warmth in the shelter of the sheds.

Can you picture these little walled-in family homes scattered along the river valley? In other valleys, far apart in the lonely steppe, other clans have settled down in their winter quarters. In the south, where the winter weather is not so cold, the families live in their yurts instead of in sod houses in the winter. They set up the yurts within the walls of the family home and cover them with layers and layers of felt for warmth.

In the winter Suvan's family live in a little flat-roofed hut built of sods.

One of the groups of little walled-in winter homes in the river valley.

Winter Clothes

As the weather grows colder, Suvan's people put on more and more clothes. They wear woolen underclothing and felt stockings, and they put on extra coats as they need them.

Suvan's winter clothes are like those of all the other boys and their fathers. When he goes outdoors on the coldest days, he wears two thickly lined coats over his indoor coat. His woolen trousers are tucked into knee boots. On his hands are heavy leather gloves, and on his head a sheepskin cap with earlaps. Even so, he is none too warm.

Nara's mother is teaching her to embroider.

Hard Times for the Flocks and Herds

The first thing that Suvan's people do when they reach the winter quarters is to gather the hay. This is just grass which has grown in the valley since they left in the spring. There isn't a great deal of it, but it helps out in feeding the animals through the winter.

There is also a little grain for the horses. This was grown during the summer in small fields close to the river. Because there was so little rain, water from the river was let into the fields through ditches. The poorest people of the clan were left behind to do this bit of farming while the rest were off on the summer wanderings.

Before the worst of the winter sets in, some of the sheep and goats must be killed, for there will not be enough winter feed for all of them. For a while there will be meat to eat, and many skins to be cleaned and used in making leather.

As the winter goes on, the animals have a hard time. Each day they are turned out in the open to graze, but with the ground frozen and often powdered with snow, they cannot find much to eat. They often suffer from the cold, and some of them are sure to die before the winter is over. Usually, though, Suvan's people get through the winter without losing too many animals, and in the spring many baby animals are born.

58

Suvan and his friends playing knucklebones.

Winter Work and Play

Our Kazak friends find plenty to do in the winter. For the women there is the daily milking and the making of cheese. The animals give much less milk now than in the warmer months, and as time goes on the families have to dip into the supplies of cheese that were made in the summer.

The women do a good deal of sewing and embroidering, too. Their embroidering is the stitching of patterns in bright-colored wools on felt. They make and mend clothes and embroider trimmings for them. They also embroider pretty designs on the pieces of felt that are used for rugs and wall hangings in the huts and yurts.

The men spend much time making things of leather and wood. They get wood by cutting down small trees here and there along the river. Suvan's father and brothers mend the frames of their yurts or make new ones each winter. They make wooden dishes, and new traveling chests of wood and leather. They mend their saddles and make new whips and ropes.

The children have plenty of time to play. There is no school for them to go to, but they learn useful things at home. The mothers teach the girls to sew and embroider. The fathers teach the boys how to work in wood and leather, and how to make strong rope of horsehair.

All the children, big and little, help to gather fuel for the fires that must be kept burning in the huts. They gather twigs from under the trees, and dried dung, or animal manure. Fuel is a great need in this land of very cold winters.

Sometimes, for fun and exercise, the men and boys have horse races. Suvan loves the races. When he wins among the boys of his age, he can't help feeling proud of his horse and himself, but he tries not to show it. Every Kazak boy wants to be the best rider in his clan when he grows up.

Now and then Suvan's father and the other men go hunting on horseback. They hunt with guns, not for food as Netsook's father does, but for sport. They hunt foxes and wolves, and if they get a wolf, they are especially glad. Wolves are the worst enemies of the flocks and herds.

Suvan is learning to braid rope of horsehair.

Here comes the peddler with his goods.

When the Peddlers Come

What Suvan and Nara enjoy most in the winter are the visits of the peddlers. They come from towns far away in the steppe, and they visit the winter quarters of the different clans. They come on horseback with a string of pack horses, carrying bundles of goods which they hope the nomads will buy.

When a peddler comes, he calls first at Suvan's hut. He knows that the headman of the clan is likely to buy more than anyone else.

What fun it is to see what the peddler has brought!

There are rolls of cloth — cotton, woolen, and silk — that the richer Kazaks like to buy for making clothes. There are metal goods: copper pots, bowls, and teakettles, and bits and other metal parts of harness. There are bags of tea, flour, and sugar. There are needles and thread, colored yarn, and strings of beads. There are bracelets, necklaces, and earrings.

Will Suvan's father buy very much, or only a little? That depends on what he can pay. He pays not in money, but in wool and sheepskins. If he has plenty of both, he will buy many things from the peddler. If he is having a bad year and losing many of his animals, he will buy much less. Later on he may need the wool and skins much more than he needs the things the peddler wishes to sell.

Each family will buy what it can. The poor, who have but few animals, will buy little or nothing. They cannot afford things from the towns, and they must get along with what they can make or get for themselves. The well-to-do people will buy cloth and food and perhaps some new copper things. Only the rich will buy jewelry and other things that they don't really need.

Suvan's family trade wool and sheepskins for the things they want from the peddler.

From the three endings for each sentence choose the one which is right.

1. In November Suvan's people go to their winter quarters because

a. they are tired of wandering about.
b. the children must go to school.
c. the winter is too cold for wandering about.

2. Their winter houses are sod huts because

a. yurts cannot be kept warm enough.
b. they like huts better than yurts.
c. yurts are more likely to catch fire.

3. Suvan's people need heavy winter clothes because

a. they stay outdoors most of the time.
b. they have no heat in their houses.
c. the weather is so very cold.

4. Their clothes are made of wool and leather because

a. they like these clothing materials best.
b. they can get these materials from their animals.
c. they can buy these materials from peddlers.

5. Suvan's people kill some of their animals early in the winter because

a. they want meat to eat.
b. there is not enough grass at the winter quarters for all the animals.
c. they do not need milk in the winter.

6. There is plenty of work for Suvan's people in winter because

a. they make most of the things they use.
b. there are jobs for them in the towns.
c. they make things to sell to peddlers.

SPRING COMES TO THE STEPPE

Shearing Time

The first sign of spring is the thawing of the ground. The weather is still cool, but it is warm enough for shearing the sheep. During the winter their coats of wool have grown very thick, and the time has come to clip them off. The men do the shearing, or clipping, and they do it fast. The whole fleece, or coat of wool, comes off each sheep in one big piece.

After the shearing, comes the making of felt. This work takes many hands, and the boys and girls help the grown-ups. First the fleeces are pulled apart and the wool is spread in layers on a large straw mat. Then it is sprinkled with water, and when it is well dampened another mat is laid over it. The two mats, with the wool between them, are tightly rolled and tied. This is only the beginning of the work which will change the loose wool into felt.

4

Spring has come and Suvan's father is busy shearing his sheep.

The idea is to mat the wool. To do this the men, women, and children sit down in two rows opposite each other. With their feet they push the roll back and forth between them. Each time it rolls to and fro, the wool gets a little more pressing.

At last the roll is undone, but the felt is not yet finished. For two or three hours the women will beat it with the palms of their hands. Then it will be tightly matted and as firm as they want it. Each family needs many pieces of new felt, and much wool will be used in making it.

The Spring Rains

Now everyone is waiting anxiously for the thing that matters most to the herdsmen of the steppe: the spring rains. Spring and early summer are the only time of year when much rain falls, and it is rain that makes the grass grow.

About the middle of April the clan breaks up. One by one the auls, or family groups, leave the winter quarters with their flocks and herds and all their belongings. They go in different directions. The people of each aul are on their way to some part of the steppe where they hope to find good pastures. In a few days the winter quarters are empty except for the few poor families left behind to grow a little grain.

Once more Suvan and his family are out on the open steppe, living in their yurts. April is almost over, and the rains have begun. What a change they make in the steppe! New green grass springs up almost over night — fresh, juicy grass that grows fast and is good for the older animals and their young.

This is the best time of year for our Kazak friends. The animals have plenty to eat, and they grow strong and fat. It rains every few days, and there is enough grass in the pastures so that the herdsmen do not have to move very often. They can stay in each camp for several weeks.

In June it rains less often, and by the end of the month the summer drought begins. A drought is a long period of dry weather. The grass stops growing, dries, and turns brown in the hot sun. The steppe will not look green again until another spring comes round.

62

The felt is being unrolled and the women will finish it by beating it with their hands.

Another summer, and Suvan's people are again wandering with their flocks and herds.

Another Summer

The dry grass, if there is enough of it, will keep the animals alive through the summer. But will there be enough? This depends on how much rain has fallen in the spring. Suvan's father can tell you of years when there was so little rain in the spring that not much new grass came up.

Suvan's father doesn't smile when he talks of those years. He remembers all too well how many of the animals died of hunger and thirst, and how little food his people had the next winter. He knows that no one can tell when another bad year may come. But this is a good year, and the flocks and herds are getting through the hot, dry summer pretty well.

Pretend for a moment that you are flying far and wide over the great steppe. What do you see as you look down?

The little nomad camps, scattered far apart. Streams that look like crooked threads, precious because of the water they supply. Trails of dust where processions of people and animals are moving slowly toward new pastures. Somewhere, in one of those camps or one of those processions, are your Kazak friends, Suvan and Nara.

Just Suppose

1. Suppose that there should be very little rain next spring in the Kirghiz Steppe. What would happen to Suvan's people?

2. Suppose that there should be more rain than usual next summer. Would Suvan's people be glad or sorry? Why?

3. Suppose that Suvan's people wanted to stay in their winter quarters the year round. Could they do so? Why, or why not?

4. Suppose that Suvan's people wanted to keep wandering over the steppe the year round. Could they do that? Why, or why not?

The Kazak Year—A Play

Now that you have been round the year with Suvan and Nara, you know how their people live and work at different seasons, and why. Perhaps you can give a play about the Kazak year in three acts:

    I. From late spring until early fall.
    II. From early fall through the winter.
    III. Early spring.

Divide the class into three groups of actors and draw lots for the acts. Each group of actors must stick to the season it has drawn by lot. Plan your act to show what the Kazaks do at that time of year and why they do it. Ask your teacher to decide which act is given best.

63

Who Is Speaking?

Let us pretend that Bunga, Netsook, and Suvan have met somewhere and are talking. This is the way the talk begins:

Bunga: My people are nomads.
Netsook: So are mine.
Suvan: And so are mine.

You will find the rest of the talk below, with numbers used instead of the names of the boys. Tell who is speaking in sentence 1, sentence 2, and so on.

1. We are nomads because we are herdsmen.

2. We are nomads because we are hunters.

3. We are nomads because we are food-gatherers.

4. We live in a jungle.

5. We live in a steppe.

6. We live in the Far North.

7. We wear fur clothes.

8. We wear woolen clothes.

9. We don't need any clothes.

10. We eat lots of tubers and fruits.

11. We eat lots of seal meat.

12. We eat lots of cheese and milk.

13. We have tents of felt.

14. We have huts built of sticks and leaves.

15. We have tents of canvas or sealskin.

16. In winter we live in snow igloos.

17. In winter we live in sod huts.

18. We live in the same kind of huts the year round.

Learning a New Word

The word is *transportation*, and it may be new to you. Transportation is a means, or way, of getting about and carrying things. Everybody has one means of transportation: a pair of legs and a pair of arms. You can walk and you can carry things. Horses, carts and wagons, trains, boats, and automobiles are all means of transportation. You can think of others yourself.

1. What means of transportation do the Negritos use? Why don't they need any other way of getting about and carrying things?

2. What means of transportation have the Eskimos? Why do they get about in different ways at different times of year?

3. What means of transportation have the Kazaks? Why don't they need different ways of getting about at different times of year?

4. Why do the Eskimos and the Kazaks need better means of transportation than the Negritos do?

5. What means of transportation do you and your family use?

Proving That You Know

You have found that in one way Bunga's people, Netsook's people, and Suvan's people are alike. They are all nomads. Except for this, they live very differently. Here is a chance for you to prove that you know why.

1. *Food.* The Negritos, the Eskimos, and the Kazaks eat different kinds of food. Each group eats what it can get most easily. Why do the Negritos eat mostly foods from plants and trees? Why do the Eskimos eat mostly meat? Why do the Kazaks eat mostly cheese and milk?

2. *Clothes.* The clothes which the people of each group wear are what they need. They are made of the materials which the people can get most easily. How and why are their needs for clothes different? What kind of clothes does each group wear? How do they get the materials for them?

3. *Houses.* The houses are what each group needs for shelter, and they are built of the materials which the people can get most easily. Why are their needs for shelter different? What materials for houses does each group use, and why?

4. *Fuel.* Fuel, you know, is material for fire. Why do the Negritos need fire? Why have the Eskimos and the Kazaks greater need of fire than the Negritos have? How do the people of each group get the fuel they burn?

About Plans and Maps

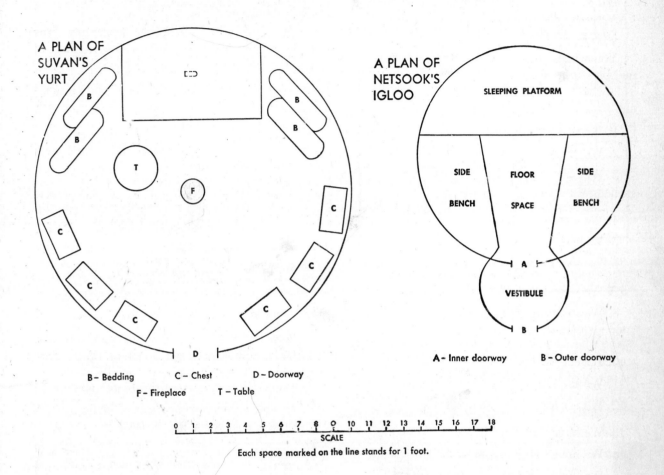

A PLAN OF SUVAN'S YURT

B — Bedding   C — Chest   D — Doorway
F — Fireplace   T — Table

A PLAN OF NETSOOK'S IGLOO

SLEEPING PLATFORM

SIDE BENCH   FLOOR SPACE   SIDE BENCH

VESTIBULE

A — Inner doorway   B — Outer doorway

SCALE

Each space marked on the line stands for 1 foot.

Suvan's Yurt and Netsook's Igloo

You have learned that Suvan's yurt is round like the main part of Netsook's igloo, but that it is larger. Here is a way for you to find out how much larger it is.

Each drawing is the kind that we call a *plan*. Under the plans is a line marked off into equal spaces. This is called the *scale*, and it gives you a way of measuring the igloo and the yurt. Be sure to read what is printed under the scale.

Lay the edge of a strip of paper along the line marking the front of the sleeping platform in the igloo. Put two pencil marks on the paper, one at either end of the platform. Now lay the strip of paper along the scale with the left pencil mark at 0. Count the number of feet that the space between your two pencil marks stands for. About how many feet across is Netsook's igloo?

Now measure the yurt. Lay the edge of a strip of paper so that it goes through the middle of the fireplace, and put a mark at the wall on either side. Use the scale as you did before, to find out how many feet the space between your two pencil marks stands for. How many feet across is Suvan's yurt? How much larger is the yurt than the igloo?

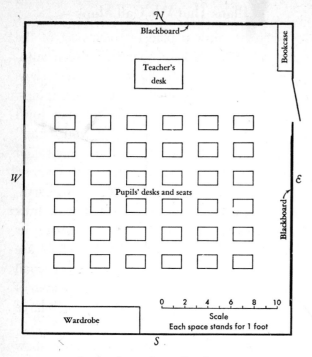

1. *A plan of a schoolroom.*

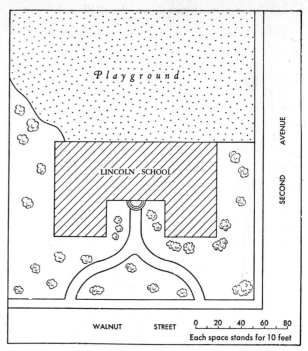

2. *A plan showing a school in its grounds.*

Three Plans to Study

On Plans 1 and 2 on this page notice that you are told the scale; that is, what each $\frac{1}{8}$ inch stands for in real distance. The letters outside the margin of Plan 1 stand for the four main directions. The directions on Plans 2 and 3 are the same as on Plan 1.

Answer these questions about Plan 1:

1. How long and how wide is the schoolroom?
2. On which sides of the room are the blackboards? Answer with the names of directions.
3. On which side of the room is the door?
4. In which corner of the room is the bookcase?
5. In which corner is the wardrobe?

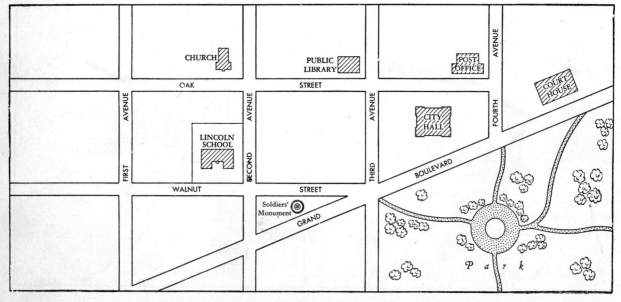

3. *A plan showing the same school in its neighborhood.*

Answer these questions about Plan 2:

1. How many feet long is the north side of the school building?

2. How long is the playground on the Second Avenue side?

3. The school faces Walnut Street. In what direction does it face?

Answer these questions about Plan 3:

1. In which direction is the Lincoln School from the City Hall, — east or west?

2. In which direction is it from the church?

3. If you were walking along Grand Boulevard from the Soldiers' Monument to the Court House, in what direction would you be walking?

A Plan to Draw

Now that you have learned about plans and scales, try drawing a plan of your schoolroom on the blackboard. First you must measure the length and width of the room in feet. Use one inch on the blackboard to show each foot in the room itself. If you measure and draw carefully, your drawing will be a plan from which anyone can tell the size and shape of the room. Perhaps you will want to add to your plan the doors and the windows.

Plans That We Call Maps

When we draw a plan of some part of the earth, we call it a *map*. You have seen automobile maps, and you know that they show roads, cities, towns, and often other things. Very likely you have seen a map of your town or city or county, or a map of your state. There is hardly a day when you cannot find maps of one kind or another in the newspapers.

A map may show any part of the earth, large or small. For example, you might draw a map showing the part of your town, city, or county where your house and your school are located. That would be a map of a very small part of the earth. Or you might draw a map of North America. That would be a map of a large part of the earth.

The maps at the bottom of the page show the Malay Peninsula, where Bunga lives, and Baffin Island, where Netsook and Klaya live. Both maps are drawn on the same scale. This means that an inch stands for the same number of miles on both maps. Which is the larger piece of land, Baffin Island or the Malay Peninsula?

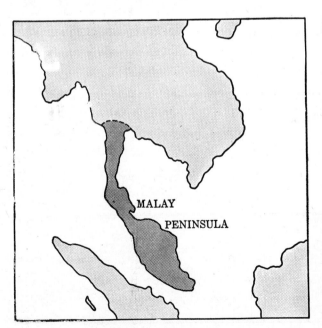
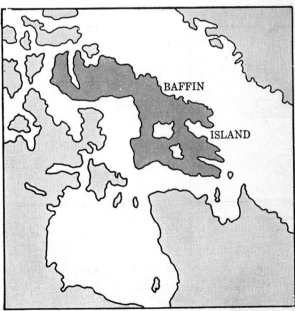

Maps of the Malay Peninsula and Baffin Island on the same scale.

67

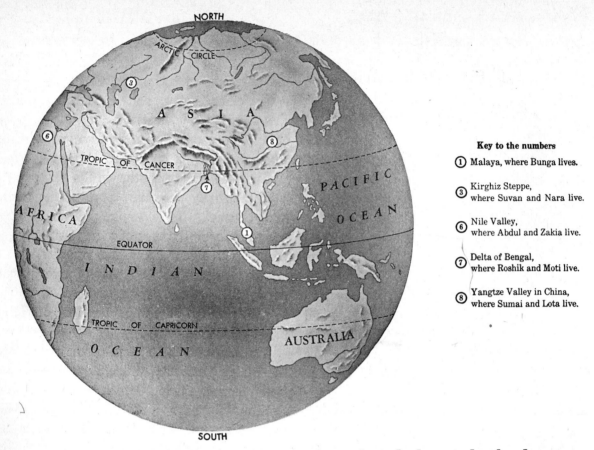

NORTH

ARCTIC CIRCLE

A S I A

TROPIC OF CANCER

AFRICA

PACIFIC OCEAN

EQUATOR

I N D I A N

TROPIC OF CAPRICORN

O C E A N

AUSTRALIA

SOUTH

Key to the numbers

① Malaya, where Bunga lives.

③ Kirghiz Steppe, where Suvan and Nara live.

⑥ Nile Valley, where Abdul and Zakia live.

⑦ Delta of Bengal, where Roshik and Moti live.

⑧ Yangtze Valley in China, where Sumai and Lota live.

This picture of the globe and the two on page 69 show where the boys and girls whom you are meeting in this book live.

Some Differences in Weather and Why

The Equator

You have found that the Negritos, the Eskimos, and the Kazaks live in very different ways because they live in such different kinds of lands. Have you wondered why their homelands are so unlike? Malaya, you know, is always very warm. Baffin Island is always cool or cold. The Kirghiz Steppe has cold winters and hot summers, with the milder seasons of spring and autumn in between.

One reason for these great differences is that Malaya, Baffin Island, and the Kirghiz Steppe

are at different distances from the *equator*. If you do not know what the equator is, now is the time to find out.

Look at your schoolroom globe and you will see that the *equator* is a line that makes a circle round the very middle of it. It is exactly halfway between the *north pole* (the point farthest north on the earth) and the *south pole* (the point farthest south on the earth).

The equator is not a real line on the earth. No one has ever seen it, and no one ever will, for it is not like a line drawn down the middle of an automobile highway. It is just a line

68

Key to the numbers

① Malaya, where Bunga lives.

② Baffin Island, where Netsook and Klaya live.

③ Kirghiz Steppe, where Suvan and Nara live.

④ Congo Basin, where Simba lives.

⑤ The Altiplano, where Pedro lives.

⑥ Nile Valley, where Abdul and Zakia live.

⑦ Delta of Bengal, where Roshik and Moti live.

⑨ Norway, where Erik and Inger live.

⑩ Mexico, where Manuel lives.

⑪ The Pampa, where Roberto lives.

⑫ Eastern Brazil, where Fernando lives.

drawn on globes and maps to help us in comparing the locations of real places on the earth. It is the same with all the other lines that make circles round the globe. They are not real lines on the earth.

If the equator were drawn on the earth itself, it would divide the earth into two equal parts, or halves. We call the halves of the earth *hemispheres*. The earth, as you know, is shaped like a ball. A *sphere* is anything that is round like a ball, and *hemi* means "half." The earth, then, is a sphere, and half the earth is a half-sphere, or a *hemisphere*. The half of the earth north of the equator is called the *Northern Hemisphere*. The half south of the equator is called the *Southern Hemisphere*.

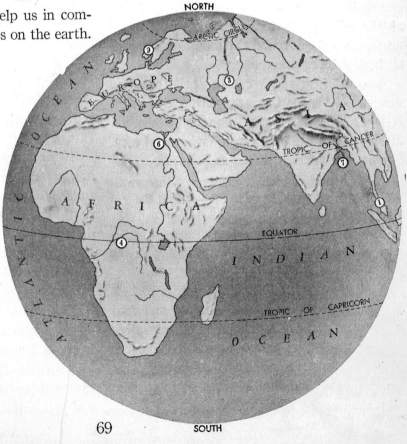

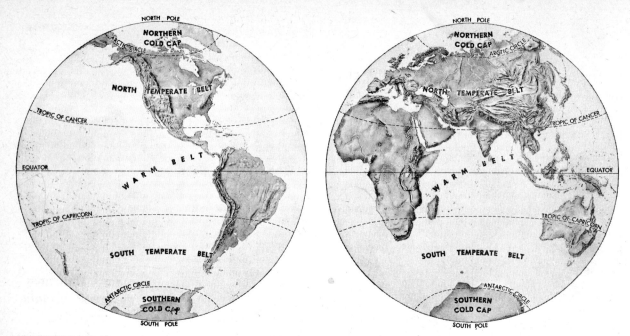

Two maps showing the warm belt, the temperate belts, and the cold caps of the earth.

The Warm Belt of the Earth

You can see from the globe (or the picture of the globe on page 68) that Malaya, where Bunga lives, is near the equator. Malaya and all the other lands that are always very warm are in a broad belt round the middle of the earth on both sides of the equator.

You will hear people call this belt the *torrid zone*, which means the *warm belt* of the earth. It is the belt of greatest year-round heat. A little thinking will help you to understand why.

First ask yourself these questions:

1. What part of each day is usually the warmest? Isn't it the middle of the day, when the sun is highest in the sky?

2. What part of the year is the warmest in our part of the world? Isn't the sun higher in the sky in summer than in winter?

You know yourself that the sun is highest in the sky in the middle of the day, and that it gives us more heat then than at any other time of day. You know, too, that the sun is higher in the sky in summer than at any other time of year, and that it gives us more heat then than at any other season.

In the warm belt of the earth the sun climbs high into the sky every day in the year. At certain seasons the sun at noon is directly overhead; that is, straight up from the heads of the people. For this reason we call the warm belt of the earth the belt of overhead sun.

Now you can understand why this belt is the belt of greatest year-round heat. It is because it is the part of the earth where the sun is most nearly overhead throughout the year. Bunga lives in this belt of overhead sun.

If you want to know how wide the warm belt is, find on the globe the two lines marked *tropic of Cancer* and *tropic of Capricorn*. One is north of the equator, and the other is the same distance south of the equator. You will see that they both make circles round the globe. The warm belt of the earth is between these two lines.

The width of the warm belt, then, is the distance between the tropic of Cancer and the tropic of Capricorn. Since the equator is halfway between these two lines, the warm belt of the earth is half in the Northern Hemisphere and half in the Southern Hemisphere.

70

The Cold Caps

Another thing you can see from the globe (or the upper picture of the globe on page 69) is that Baffin Island, where Netsook lives, is very far from the equator. It is in the Northern Hemisphere, and it is much nearer to the north pole than it is to the equator.

Look more closely and you will see that most of Baffin Island is north of the line marked *arctic circle*. The part of the earth north of this circle is called the *north frigid zone*, which means the northern cold belt. A better name for it is the *northern cold cap*. You can see for yourself that it is cap-shaped, not belt-shaped like the warm belt.

In the northern cold cap the sun is never high in the sky, not even at noon in the summertime. For this reason we say that the lands of the northern cold cap are lands of low sun. This is why they are such cold lands, — very cold in winter, and cool even in summer. The Arctic Ocean, which is in the northern cold cap, is covered with ice the year round. The north pole is in the midst of this frozen ocean.

Penguins are the little "ladies and gentlemen" of Antarctica. They stand and walk upright. They can swim, but they cannot fly.

Far to the south of the equator, in the Southern Hemisphere, is another line which is the twin of the arctic circle. It is the same distance from the south pole as the arctic circle is from the north pole. It is called the *antarctic circle*.

Find the antarctic circle on the globe. The part of the earth south of this circle is the *south frigid zone*, or the *southern cold cap*.

The two cold caps are the parts of the earth farthest from the equator, and the parts that have the lowest sun. This is why they have the greatest year-round cold.

Within the southern cold cap is one of the seven continents. Its name is Antarctica. Antarctica is the loneliest land in the world. Very few people ever go there, and no one lives there all the time. Can you guess why? It is because Antarctica is buried under a thick cap of ice and snow that never melts awa

Not a tree, not a flowering
a bit of grass grows in Ant
no animals on the conti
that live there all t
is no way t
Antarcti
contine

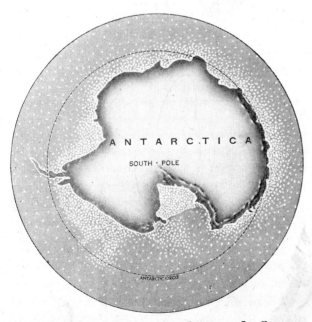

A small map of Antarctica, showing the floating icebergs in the ocean round about it.

The Temperate Belts

You have learned that Malaya is a warm land because it is a land of overhead sun near the equator. You have found that Baffin Island is a cold land because it is a land of low sun in the Far North. Now let us see what the globe (or the lower picture of the globe on page 69) can tell us about the Kirghiz Steppe, where Suvan lives.

You can see that the Kirghiz Steppe is in the Northern Hemisphere, about halfway between the equator and the north pole. It is not in the warm belt, and it is not in the northern cold cap. It is in a belt between the tropic of Cancer and the arctic circle. This is called the *north temperate belt*.

In the north temperate belt the sun is high in summer and low in winter. This is one reason why summer is hot and winter is cold in the Kirghiz Steppe. In spring and fall the sun is higher than in winter, but lower than in summer. That explains why spring and fall are "in-between" seasons, cooler than summer, but warmer than winter.

You can see from the globe that there is another temperate belt, or zone, in the Southern Hemisphere. It is between the tropic of Capricorn and the antarctic circle. This is the *south temperate belt* of the earth.

In the south temperate belt the sun behaves as it does in the north temperate belt, bringing the changes in weather which we call the four seasons: spring, summer, autumn, and winter. You mustn't think, though, that because all the lands in these belts have four seasons they all have the same kind of weather. There are ___ ences among them. In the Kirghiz ___ about one kind of temperate- ___ er on in this book you will ___ nds.

Some Questions to Answer

Use your schoolroom globe or the pictures of the globe on pages 68 and 69, in answering these questions.

1. Where do Bunga, Netsook, and Suvan live — in the Northern Hemisphere or the Southern Hemisphere?

2. In which of these hemispheres do we live?

A List to Arrange

Here are the names of the five "zones" of the earth which you have been learning about. The list needs rearranging so that the names will be in the same order as the "zones" themselves *from north to south* on the earth. See if you can arrange them in the correct north-south order.

North temperate belt
Northern cold cap
South temperate belt
Southern cold cap
Warm belt

What Are the Children Saying?

Imagine that you and your best friend are with the boys and girls whom you have met thus far in this book. You are telling one another about the places where you live. See if you can give the missing words in what is being said about each homeland.

1. *Bunga:* I live in the ____ belt. My homeland is ___ the year round.

2. *Netsook and K'aya:* We live in the northern ____ cap. Our homeland is always ____ or ____.

3. *Suvan and Nara:* We live in the north _____ belt. Our homeland is a land of four _____.

4. *Yourselves:* We live in the _____ temperate belt. Our homeland is not always ___ like Bunga's. It is not always ____ or ____ like Netsook's and Klaya's. It is more like Suvan's and Nara's homeland because it is a land of ____ seasons.

Simba—a Boy of the Congo

A little paddle-wheel steamboat is making its way up the Congo River.

A GREAT FOREST IN AFRICA √

A Land of Many Rivers

Far, far away in Africa the Congo River flows through a great forest. The Congo is a broad, muddy river, deep in some places and shallow in others. The forest is a jungle like the Malayan forest where Bunga lives. Along the river banks the leaves of the crowded trees make thick walls of green.

For hundreds and hundreds of miles the Congo River winds through the forest on its way to the ocean. Many other rivers join it along the way. They are called *tributaries* because they give, or contribute, their waters to the Congo.

Can you picture the work that the Congo River and its tributaries do? They drain off water from a huge stretch of land in the middle of Africa. The land that is drained by a river and its tributaries is called a *river basin*. This one is the Congo Basin.

If you could look down on the Congo Basin from an airplane, the rivers would remind you of brownish ribbons twisting this way and that through the green of the forest. They are brownish because they are so muddy. Along their banks are some good-sized towns, but they are many miles apart. There are smaller towns too, and many little villages, but between each one and its nearest neighbor is a stretch of the thick forest.

On a Congo Steamboat

Picture to yourself a little steamboat making its way upstream on the Congo River. At the stern, or rear end of the boat, a big paddle wheel stirs up the muddy water as it pushes the boat along.

On the middle deck of the boat are some white people who are passengers. They are wearing their thinnest clothes, for the day is hot and sticky. There was a thundershower a while

73

In the shallow water by the shore a family of elephants is taking a shower bath.

ago, but it did not cool the air. Now the sun is out again, and the air feels close and steamy.

"Look!" says one of the passengers. He is pointing to a spot on the river bank. There, in shallow water, stand three elephants taking a shower bath. They are sucking up water with their trunks and squirting it over their backs.

All day the passengers on the middle deck of the boat have been amusing themselves watching for wild animals. They have seen dozens

---

Simba is one of the passengers on the boat.

of ugly crocodiles sunning themselves in the shallows and on sandbanks. They have caught sight of big, lazy hippopotamuses half hidden by tall grass in swampy places along the shore. They have watched bands of monkeys swinging from limb to limb among the trees.

On the lower deck of the boat there is a crowd of Negro passengers. They are natives of the Congo Basin, not people from outside as the white passengers are. The great Congo forest is their homeland.

The natives have on very little clothing, and their dark skin shines as if it were polished. They are talking and playing games to pass the time away. Not one of them pays any attention to the animals that the passengers on the deck above find so interesting. The natives are so used to seeing the wild animals of the forest that they think no more of them than the white passengers do of automobiles on the streets at home.

One of the Negro passengers is a ten-year-old boy named Simba. He is with his father, and they are on their way home from a trading station down the river. Simba is the boy whose home in the Congo forest you are going to see.

74

Simba Gets Home for Supper

It is late in the afternoon now, and the sun has dropped behind the tall trees. Sunset is still an hour off, but as the shadows fall on the river, the damp air begins to feel cooler. It isn't really very cool, but it is more comfortable than it was when the sun was beating down.

Now the little steamboat is turning toward a place on the river bank where there are a couple of tiny huts and some big stacks of firewood. This is one of many wood stations along the Congo River. The boat has used up nearly all its firewood, and so the captain will stop here for an hour or two to take on more. Wood, not coal or oil, is burned to make steam in the Congo River boats.

Supplying the steamboats with fuel provides many of the natives of the Congo Basin with work. They cut the wood in the forest, stack it at the wood stations along the rivers, and sell it as the boats come along.

Simba and his father will get off at this wood station. Their village is a few miles farther on, and they will paddle the rest of the way in a canoe. Simba's uncle is here in his canoe to meet them. He paddles alongside the steamboat. Simba and his father get into the canoe with the things they have brought from the trading station.

Simba's father and uncle drive the canoe forward with strong, even strokes of their paddles. It is the kind of canoe that is called a dugout. This is because it is made by hollowing out the trunk of a tree. The Congo natives all use dugouts which they make themselves.

After sunset the twilight fades quickly into darkness, but Simba's father and uncle keep on

75

At a place a few miles from Simba's village the boat stops to take on firewood.

paddling at the same speed. They know this part of the river too well to need daylight to find their way. Now, as they round a point of land, Simba sees the lights of home. They are not electric lights. They are flickering flames from wood fires in the village street.

As the canoe touches the river bank, Simba jumps out. He lifts his head and sniffs. His nose is almost as good as a dog's. M-m-mm-mmm — pig meat for supper tonight!

Without waiting for his father, Simba runs up the river bank and into the village street. There is a fire burning outside every hut. Yes, Simba's nose was right: over every fire a kettle of pig-meat stew is cooking. Simba thinks it is fine to be at home again.

Another Warm, Rainy Land

You have learned that Simba lives in the Congo Basin, and that the Congo Basin is in Africa. Africa is one of the seven continents. Find Africa in the lower picture of the globe on page 69. Notice that Simba's home is on the equator. In what belt of the earth is it?

You have found that the Congo forest is a jungle like the Malayan forest where Bunga lives. On page 1 you read this about the forest in Malaya:

The forest is the kind which you will find only in the parts of the world that are hot the year round and very rainy.

From this you will know that the weather in the Congo Basin is like the weather in Malaya. It is very warm and rainy at all times of year.

The Congo forest is like the Malayan forest in many ways. The trees are crowded and hung with vines. The tops of the tallest trees make a leafy roof that shuts out much of the sunlight. In many places the plants and creeping vines on the ground are so thick that paths must be cut with knives or hatchets.

The thick forests of this kind in the warm belt are called *tropical rain forests*. You can easily understand why. They are called tropical forests because the warm belt is between the two lines called tropics: the tropic of Cancer and the tropic of Capricorn. They are called tropical rain forests because they grow only in the parts of the warm belt that are very rainy. Simba and Bunga both live in tropical rain forests.

76

Simba's father and uncle drive the dugout forward with strong, even strokes of their paddles.

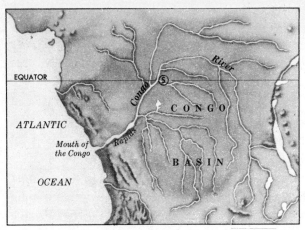

A map of the Congo Basin; that is, the part of Africa which is drained by the Congo River and its tributaries. The letter S shows where Simba and his family live.

Some Things to Think Out

1. You met Simba on a steamboat going upstream on the Congo River. Was the boat going toward the mouth of the Congo, or toward its source?

2. If you were going upstream on a tributary of the Congo River, should you expect to reach the Congo itself? Why, or why not?

3. In our country we have a great river named the Mississippi which has many tributaries. What should you call the land that is drained by the Mississippi River and its tributaries?

4. Why do you think it is that the boats on the Congo River burn wood instead of coal or oil to make steam?

5. Our country is north of the tropic of Cancer. Would it be right to say that we have tropical forests? Why, or why not?

6. Which boy would feel most at home in the Congo Basin — Bunga, Netsook, or Suvan? Why?

Just Suppose

Suppose that you have sent Netsook a picture of Simba. Netsook is looking at the picture. He feels sorry for Simba. This is what he says:

"Why, Simba has hardly any clothes! What a poor hunter his father must be! He will surely freeze to death if his father doesn't get him some clothes before winter."

Why does Netsook think this about Simba and his father? What doesn't he know about Simba that you know?

SIMBA'S VILLAGE

A First Glimpse

If you were going to visit Simba, you would cross the broad Atlantic Ocean in a steamship. Find the Atlantic Ocean on your schoolroom globe, or on the pictures of the globe on pages 8 and 9. This will show you why you would cross this great body of water to reach the continent of Africa from our own continent of North America.

Your ship would take you into the mouth of the Congo River and land you at a town which is a small *seaport*. Seaports are shipping centers. Ships come to them with passengers and goods and take other passengers and goods away.

At this Congo seaport you would take a train inland for about 250 miles. The train passes along a part of the Congo which boats cannot use because there are big rocks in the river. The water races over the rocks and round them, forming dangerous *rapids*. Upstream, at the end of the rapids, you would take one of the Congo steamboats and go on up the river.

Make believe that you have taken this long trip into Africa and that you are now in Simba's village. No matter what time of year it is, the weather is sure to be hot. You need only your thinnest clothes, and before your visit is over you will be wishing you were wearing as little as Simba does.

Simba's village is different from any village you have ever seen at home. It has just one street with a row of tiny houses on each side. After a rain the street is muddy, but when the hot sun comes out it soon dries, and then it is dusty. The houses are close together, and they are so small that we should call them huts.

At one end of Simba's village is the broad, muddy river. At the other end and on both sides is the great forest. A footpath winds through the forest to the next village. It is a narrow, shady path, and if it were not used often, it would soon be filled in with bushes and vines.

At the water's edge are the dugout canoes that are used for getting about on the river. Simba's people travel more on the water than on the land, because paddling is quicker and easier than walking along the narrow, winding paths in the forest.

The first thing you will notice in the village is that everyone is outdoors. The children are playing in the street. The grown-ups are sitting outside their huts. Some of them are just sitting and talking. Others are busy at some kind of work. Everything that goes on in the little village goes on in the street.

There is no danger of anyone being run down by an automobile, for the village street is not part of any motor highway. There are motor roads connecting the towns in the Congo Basin, but they do not run through the small native villages. The only time Simba ever sees an automobile is when he goes with his father to the trading station down the river.

Simba's House

Take a good look at Simba's house, and you will know how all the huts in the village are built. Simba's father built the hut of wood that he cut in the forest. The walls are made of thin strips of wood fastened between posts set in the ground. The walls are partly plastered on the outside with mud.

The part of the hut that counts most is the sloping roof. The roof is thatched, or covered, with a thick layer of palm leaves tied on with vines. If you think leaves a strange sort of roofing, ask Simba about them. He will tell you that palm leaves make a very good roof because they are smooth and slippery, and the rain runs off them quickly. Protection from rain is about all the shelter the Congo natives need.

Simba's house in the little Congo village.

There is nothing to see or do inside Simba's house. There is no furniture, and as there are no windows, the hut is dark. Really, the huts in the village are hardly more than bedrooms for the families. The people sleep indoors on beds of leaves, but in the daytime they stay outside. They eat outdoors, and even when it rains they usually sit under the eaves instead of going inside.

Everyday Sights in the Village

Suppose you walk along the street and see what the people are doing this morning. Nothing unusual is going on, but you will learn some interesting things about the everyday life of Simba's people.

Here are some women working with clay. They are making what we call pottery. They

In the village street the women and girls are weaving baskets and making pottery.

have been down to the river bank to get the kind of clay they need, and they have softened it with water. Now they are molding the clay with their hands. They are shaping it into bowls and jars. When they have finished, they will set the bowls and jars in the sun to dry and harden.

One of the men is weaving a fish trap.

The pottery jars and bowls are used for storing food and carrying water. They break so easily that the women often have to make new ones. Sometimes Simba knocks over a jar or a bowl and breaks it, but his mother doesn't scold him very hard. With plenty of clay close at hand she can easily make a new one.

This morning Simba's mother is not among the pottery-makers. She is weaving a basket of the straw-like ribs of palm leaves. It is a large basket, and she will wear it strapped on her back. Simba's older sister, Panya, is weaving a smaller basket of the ribs of banana leaves. Small baskets are used like pottery bowls for storing food.

The women are not the only weavers in the village. A bit farther down the street a man is weaving a fish net, and another man is weaving a cone-shaped fish trap. The men are as clever at weaving as the women.

80

Simba's father is with some men who are making spears for hunting. They have cut long, straight pieces of wood in the forest, and they are rubbing them with stones to make them smooth. Simba's father has finished this work and is fastening an iron point to his spear. The point was hammered out by a blacksmith in a neighboring village. Simba's father paid for it with monkeys' teeth, which the blacksmith wanted for a necklace.

Perhaps you will think the most interesting work is what is going on down by the river. Simba's uncle and some other men are making a dugout from a big log. A log, you know, is a long piece of a tree trunk.

Hollowing out the log takes a long time, because the wood is very hard. The only tool the men have for this work is a kind of hatchet. They must keep chipping away at the wood and burning it a little until the whole log is hollowed out except at each end. The ends are pointed so that the dugout will slip through the water easily. Wooden paddles must be made, too.

It is noon now, and the sun is beating down from straight overhead. It is so hot that Simba and the other boys are going swimming. Here they come, racing down the river bank.

Splash! The first boy has dived into the water. Splash! Splash! Splash! In go the others. They are all good swimmers, and they love being in the water.

There is one thing, though, that the boys must watch for. There may be crocodiles about. If the boys see one, no matter how far away, they will swim for the shore and get out of the water as fast as they can. A grown-up crocodile is about twelve feet long. Give him a chance, and he will make a meal of a boy in no time. Even though it is so hot, perhaps you would rather not go swimming with Simba.

Swimming and paddling are among the things that Simba likes best to do. He likes games too, and you will often find him playing with his friends in the village street. In some of the games the boys dance and keep time by clapping their hands.

81

On the river bank Simba's uncle and some other men are making a dugout from a big log.

How Simba's village looks from a plane flying low over the Congo River.

Some Questions to Answer

Your morning in the Congo village has shown you that Simba's people make for themselves most of the things they use. Here are some questions which will help you to prove that you have been thinking about what you have seen.

1. Why do Simba's people need houses?

2. Where do they get the materials for building their houses?

3. Why don't they need windows or chimneys in their houses?

4. What use have they for fires?

5. How do they get firewood?

6. What reasons have you to think that Simba's people get some of their food by hunting and fishing?

7. Where do the men get the materials for making the things they need for hunting and fishing?

8. Where do the women get the materials for making the things they need for housekeeping?

9. Why do Simba's people build boats?

10. Where do they get the materials for making dugouts and paddles?

Two Maps for You to Read

Map 1, on page 83, is a sketch map of the neighborhood where Simba lives. See if you can point out these things in it:

The forest   Simba's village
    A tributary to the Congo River
    Some paths through the forest

Map-reading is fun because it helps you to picture to yourself lands you have never seen. Map 2 helps you to picture more of the part of the Congo forest where Simba lives.

In this map *symbols* are used. Symbols are signs that stand for things. For example, on automobile road maps lines that stand for roads connect dots and circles that stand for cities and towns. With the lines and the dots and circles as symbols, the maps show you how to drive from one place to another.

Whatever explains the meaning of the symbols in a map is called a *key* to the map. In order to read what the map can tell you, you need this explanation of the symbols just as you need a key to open a locked door.

With the help of the key, see if you can read Map 2. Point out (1) the Congo River; (2) two tributaries to the Congo; (3) the native villages; (4) the forest; (5) a path connecting Simba's village with another village; (6) a bridge.

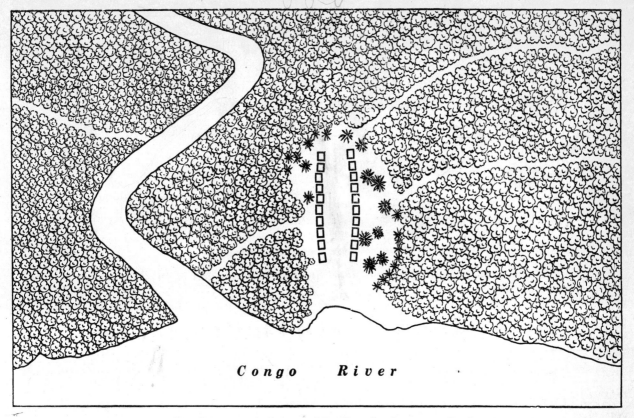

1. *A sketch map of the neighborhood where Simba lives.*

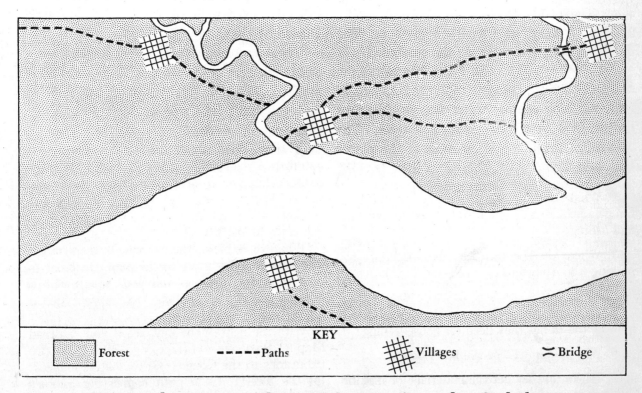

KEY

Forest ----- Paths ▦ Villages ⋈ Bridge

2. *A map showing more of the part of the Congo forest where Simba lives.*

Panya and her mother are at work in their little garden in the forest.

HOW SIMBA'S PEOPLE GET FOOD

Gardening in the Forest

From what you have seen you may have thought that Simba's people live mostly on food that the fathers get by hunting and fishing. They do eat some meat and fish, but much more of their food comes from their gardens. The mothers, not the fathers, do the gardening.

This is one way in which the Negroes of the Congo Basin are different from the Negritos of Malaya. You will remember that the Negritos gather food from wild plants and trees. The natives of the Congo grow most of the plants that give them food. They do a little farming in the forest. Their farms are so small that we should call them gardens.

Another day has come, and it is early in the morning. Panya and her mother are starting off to work in their garden before the sun gets too hot. So are the other girls and their mothers. They have baskets strapped on their backs, but they are not carrying any garden tools.

If you would like to see the gardens, Panya will be glad to take you along. You haven't far to walk, for the gardens are scattered along the edge of the forest, just beyond the village.

If you were alone, you might pass by the gardens and not notice that they were there. How different they look from our gardens at home! They are just patches of ground where only the smaller trees have been cut down. The crops are growing in sunny spots that are not shaded by the tall trees.

There are banana plants as big as small trees, scattered here and there. There are other smaller plants, but nothing is set out in rows, and you can't help wondering if some of the plants aren't weeds.

You are right about the weeds. They grow so thick and fast in this warm, rainy land that if they weren't pulled out, a few every day, they would soon choke out the food plants. But the food plants grow fast too, and as the weather is always warm, they can be grown the year round.

Panya has started weeding now. She is pulling up the weeds with her hands and is tossing them aside. Her mother has taken a stick and is digging at the roots of some plants with wide-spreading leaves. These are manioc plants, and their roots supply the flour for the bread that Simba and Panya eat.

If you wander through the little gardens, you will find that all the girls and their mothers are either weeding or gathering the crops. Some are digging manioc roots as Panya's mother is. Others are picking beans or digging yams. Still others are picking ripe bananas from the big bunches growing on the trees. Later they will go back to the village with their back-baskets filled with food.

No matter what time of year you visit Simba and Panya, you will find their mother working part of every day in her garden. She doesn't need a big garden, because she can grow food plants the year round. When, for example, she has gathered one crop of beans or manioc, she can plant another as soon as she wishes.

Simba's mother grows most of the food for her family, and yet her only tools are a home-made hoe and a digging-stick. She would be surprised to see how many tools your mother uses just for a flower garden.

Simba's mother digs up the ground with her hoe, puts in the seeds, and covers them with earth with her hands. She digs manioc and yams with her digging-stick, and gathers the other crops by hand. She doesn't work at gardening very long in any one day, but she has to keep at it all through the year. If she didn't, Simba would go hungry.

Climbing an oil palm.

Going home with baskets filled with food.

Food and Money from a Tree

Now that we have seen the gardens, let's go and see what Simba and his father are doing this morning. They, too, are just outside the village on the edge of the forest. Simba's father is climbing a tree. It is the kind of tree that is called an oil palm. Oil palms grow wild in the Congo forest, and there are many of them near Simba's village.

Near the top of each tree grows a big bunch of fruit. It looks somewhat like a bunch of grapes, only very much larger. With a sharp knife Simba's father cuts off the bunch of fruit, and it drops to the ground. When he has cut the bunches from several trees, Simba will help him to carry them home.

Each fruit is about the size of a date and has a thin skin. Inside, round the hard stone, or kernel, is the pulp — the soft part of the fruit. The pulp is very oily.

Now Simba's father is throwing the bunches of fruit into a big trough made of a hollow log. Simba steps into the trough and begins to stamp on the fruit. His father steps in and stamps, too. This is the way they squeeze the oil from the pulp. What do you suppose the oil is good for?

85

Simba's mother and a friend are spreading out palm nuts to dry in the sun.

Simba likes palm oil as much as you like butter. His people do not have any butter because they do not keep any cows. Palm oil takes the place of butter in their meals and of fat for their cooking.

The hard kernels are called palm nuts. They, too, have oil in them, but Simba's people have no way of crushing them to get the oil out. Simba's grandfather can remember the days when the nuts were thrown away. To do that nowadays would be like throwing away money.

The natives dry the nuts in the sun and take them to the trading stations. The traders are white men from other parts of the world. They

want palm nuts because they can send them to countries like ours and get a good price for them. Great machines crush the nuts and squeeze out the oil, and the oil is used in making soap and many other useful things.

In exchange for the palm nuts, the Congo natives get things that they need but cannot make for themselves: knives, hatchets, guns, and the bright-colored cotton cloth that the native women like for making skirts. You can see, then, that palm nuts are as good as money to Simba's people.

How lucky it is that there are plenty of oil palms in the Congo forest! You will like to remember that they supply the natives with both food and money.

Hunting and Fishing

Do you remember how excited Simba was the night he came home from the trading town and found that he was going to have stewed pig meat for supper? He was excited because he doesn't often have meat to eat, and when he does, it is a great treat.

You might suppose that if Simba's people eat pig meat they keep pigs, but this is not so. They eat the meat of wild pigs that roam in the forest. The wild pigs are dangerous beasts, much larger than the harmless pigs that are raised on farms. The native men hunt them

86

A wild pig has been killed, and the hunters are carrying it home to the village.

Standing in their dugout, the men let a fish net down into the waters of the river.

with guns and spears, but the animals are hard to track down. You can see, then, why pig meat is a much greater treat to Simba than pork or bacon is to you.

Now and then the men kill monkeys and smaller animals, but they do not often hunt the big animals such as the elephants and the hippopotamuses. Once in a while, though, an elephant comes into the gardens at night and damages the crops. When this happens, the men get to work at once and try to catch it.

First they dig a big, deep hole in the ground where they think the elephant will walk if he comes back. Then they cover the hole with branches so that it doesn't show. If the elephant steps on the cover, he crashes through, and no matter how hard he tries, he cannot get out of the hole. When he has been trapped in this way, the men can kill him with their spears.

Perhaps you can imagine what happens when an elephant is killed. The whole village has a feast of meat that lasts for days. If the elephant has not lost his tusks in a battle with other elephants, the natives have another reason to be glad. Elephant tusks supply the hard white material called ivory, and traders in the towns pay a good price for them.

Simba never eats beef or lamb because his people do not keep cattle or sheep. Cattle and sheep do not stand the hot, rainy weather well,

and there are no good pastures in the Congo forest. Grass such as cattle and sheep need is very, very scarce.

You can understand now why Simba eats much less meat than you do. He eats more fish than meat because there are plenty of fish in the rivers.

The pictures show two native ways of fishing. The men in the first picture are letting down a net into the water. They hope that when they pull up the net it will have caught a good many fish. The second picture shows one of the traps that the natives set for fish. The trap is made so that a fish that swims into it hasn't much chance of getting out.

Simba's father and uncle have had poor luck today—only two fish from their big trap.

Panya is pounding dried manioc roots to make flour, and her mother is making dough.

Simba's Bread and Butter

If you stay for supper with Simba, you will have manioc bread to eat. Panya is at work pounding some dried manioc roots to make flour. Simba has never heard of wheat flour or bread such as we eat, but he can tell you all about manioc flour and manioc bread.

Simba's mother mixes some of the flour with water to make dough. Then she wraps the dough in damp banana leaves and lays it in the fire built outside the hut. When the dough is about half baked, she will take it out of the fire and pour palm oil over it.

You may think the manioc bread rather soggy, and perhaps you will not care for the palm oil, but they are Simba's bread and butter. He eats more manioc bread and palm oil than anything else.

Simba's mother has cooked some beans too, and perhaps you will like those better. Or, if you wish, you may make your supper of bananas, as Simba and Panya sometimes do. Whatever you eat, you will eat it with your fingers, and you will sit on the ground. Simba's people never set a table or use any knives, forks, or spoons.

Simba's Menu

On the blackboard make a list of the things that Simba eats. Then give the right endings for these sentences:

1. Simba's food is more like Bunga's than like Netsook's or Suvan's because ___

2. Simba's people do not have to lead wandering lives to get food from plants because ___

3. Simba eats meat now and then because ___

4. He often eats fish because ___

5. He doesn't eat beef or lamb because ___

6. His people do not keep cattle or sheep because ___

7. He doesn't drink milk because ___

8. He eats vegetables because ___

A Palm-Tree Test

You have found that the oil palms and other kinds of palm trees in the Congo forest are useful to Simba's people in many ways. Tell how the palms help to supply these needs:

1. Food.

2. Houses.

3. Housekeeping things.

4. Nets and traps for fishing.

5. Something to use as money in trading.

A Game of Pantomime

A pantomime is a play without any words. The actors tell the story by motions alone. Here is a way to make a game of a pantomime.

First draw numbers. Pupil number 1 starts by acting out something that you might see in spending a day with Simba. The class guesses what it is. Then pupil number 2 acts out something else from a day with Simba, and the class guesses what it is. Keep on in this way until everyone has had his turn.

Ask your teacher to decide who are the three best pantomime actors in the class. They will be the winners of the game.

Simba's manioc bread is buttered with palm oil.

WORK AND PLAY IN THE GREAT FOREST

Where Seasons Do Not Count

A few days in Simba's village will give you a good idea of how his people live and of the work they do. It makes no difference what month it is; the Congo natives live and work in the same way every month in the year. They never need warm clothing. They never need any better shelter than their huts give them from rain. They do not have to store up food at any one time of year for use later on. They can hunt, fish, and grow crops the year round.

Think how different it is with the Eskimos and the Kazaks. In the Far North and in the Kirghiz Steppe people cannot live in the same way all through the year. They cannot do the same things in winter as in summer.

You will never hear the Congo natives talking of the four seasons as the Eskimos, the Kazaks, and we ourselves do. There is no reason why they should, for in the Congo forest spring, summer, autumn, and winter bring almost no changes in temperature. Temperature means the amount of heat, and the Congo forest is always warm.

But you will hear the natives talking of the rainy seasons and the dry seasons. You might suppose, then, that there are times of year when the Congo forest has little or no rain, but this is not true. When Simba talks of the dry seasons, all he means are the times of year when there is less rain than in the rainy seasons. There is not a single month with so little rain that we should call it dry.

So, you see, the seasons in the Congo forest do not count for much. The weather is always warm and rainy. There are no seasonal changes in weather great enough to make any difference in the needs of the people or in the way they live and work.

Villages That Move

You have found that the Congo natives get their own food, build their own houses and boats, and make most of the things that they need in their work. Getting food is the most important. If they had to, the natives could go without clothes and even houses, but they cannot go without food. Their gardens mean more to them than anything else.

89

From left to right: a bunch of bananas, some manioc roots, and a cluster of oil-palm fruit.

Very likely you know that we have a special name for the earthy stuff in which plants and trees grow. We call it *soil*. If you know anything about farming or gardening, you know that crops need good soil in order to grow well. They take food and water from the soil through their roots. If there is not much plant food in the soil, the crops are small and poor.

You will remember that the Congo natives grow crops in their gardens the year round. This uses up the plant food in the soil faster than in lands where crops are grown only in the warmer parts of the year. After a while so much of the plant food is gone that there is no use trying to grow any more crops.

When this happens, the natives leave the old gardens to the weeds and make new ones in another place. So, little by little, the gardens move away from the village. As the years go by, the time may come when all the gardening land within easy reach of the village has been used.

What do you suppose the natives do when there is no good gardening land left as near the village as they want it? They do what is easiest. They move to another place in the forest and build a new village there. Often the new village is only a mile or two from the old one. Moving is easy. The natives haven't much to carry, and it doesn't take them long to build new huts.

It doesn't take long to start new gardens, either. The men clear a little land just outside the village. All they do is to cut down the smaller trees and clear away the wild plants that cover the ground. Then the women plant the crops. Soon the new gardens are supplying food, and the daily life in the new village is just the same as in the old one.

Weather, Health, and Work

Now that you know how Simba's people live and work, doesn't it seem to you as if they have an easier time than the Eskimos and the Kazaks? They do not have to work so hard because their needs are not so great. Think of all the clothes that the Eskimos and the Kazaks need. Think of the different houses they must have for summer and winter. Think how hard the Eskimos work at hunting, and how much care the Kazaks must give to their flocks and herds.

But the weather that makes life easy for the Congo natives in some ways makes it hard for them in others. The year-round heat and dampness in all tropical forests are unhealthful — so unhealthful that white people cannot live in these lands many years at a time and keep well. Then, too, the hot, damp weather means that the tropical forests are full of insects, such as ants, flies, and mosquitoes, that sting and bite. The bites of some of these insects give people fevers and diseases.

For these reasons the natives of tropical forests are not so healthy as the people of cooler and drier lands. They stand the weather better than white people do, but it keeps them from having what we call "pep."

If you could see a movie showing just how the people of Simba's village spend their days, you might say to yourself, "How slowly they work, and how much time they take off! What lazy people they are!"

They do seem lazy to us, but it isn't really fair to blame them for it. Because of the weather, they don't feel like working very hard, and for the same reason they don't have to.

An Invitation to a Dance

The Congo natives must do some work every day, but they have much more free time than the Eskimos or the Kazaks do. For this reason they have more time for play. One of their favorite pastimes is story-telling. Another is dancing.

If you stay long with Simba, an afternoon will surely come when you will hear the beat of drums from somewhere in the forest. This is the way in which the natives send messages to one another. They know from the way the drums are beaten what the message is.

A swaying bridge of vines crosses the stream.

White people call the drums the "Congo radio." Years ago they often meant war. Nowadays the Congo natives are peaceful, and the drums often mean an invitation to a dance.

The drums are beating now, and everyone in Simba's village is listening. The message is from a neighboring village, and from the smile on Simba's face, it must be a pleasant one. Over and over the drums are saying, "We have killed an elephant. Come this evening and feast and dance."

Soon fathers, mothers, and children gather at the end of the village street. The babies are in slings of cloth on their mothers' backs. Only a few old people who cannot walk the two or three miles through the forest will stay at home.

Everyone falls into line, for they must walk single file along the narrow path shaded by the tall trees. They come to a stream with a bridge across it. The bridge is made of strong vines, and it looks a little like a long, narrow hammock. It swings and sways as Simba's people walk over it. The drumming is still going on, growing louder as our friends get near their neighbors' village. Simba is getting more and more excited. He is thinking of the elephant meat and of the fun after the dancing begins.

Wood fires are blazing in the village. The elephant meat has been partly cooked and is

The "Congo radio" is a big piece of log hollowed out and open at one end.

ready to eat. The drumming stops, and the feasting begins. The women and girls eat in groups apart from the men and boys.

Darkness falls, and more wood is thrown on the fires. As the flames leap up, drumming for dancing begins. Like the "radio" drums, the dance drums are hollow pieces of logs, but they are smaller, and they are beaten on the ends, which are tightly covered with skin. Some of the men start dancing. Others join in. Soon the women are dancing, too, and so are all the children who are not too small.

You will never see a stranger dance. No one takes a partner. No one pays any attention to anyone else. They all prance and whirl and clap their hands in time to the drums. The drums beat faster and faster until the dancers' feet move so fast that you cannot see them clearly. When at last the drumming stops, the dancers drop breathless wherever they happen to be.

This is only the beginning. Soon another dance begins, and then another and another. In the flickering light of the fires, with the black forest round about, the dancing goes on all night long. The children soon drop out. One by one they curl up on the ground and go to sleep. Simba tries hard to keep awake, but he is tired now, and the beat of the drums makes him very sleepy.

After sunrise in the morning, our friends from Simba's village say good-by and start homeward through the forest. They are all tired, but they have had a wonderful time. Already they are looking forward to the next dance in their neighborhood. Perhaps they will give it themselves.

When Simba Goes to Town

When you first met Simba, he was coming home from a trading town with his father. This was Simba's first trip in a steamboat, and he thought it was great fun. Usually he and his father paddle to the town in their dugout.

You know now what Simba's father takes to the trading town on these trips: palm nuts from the fruit of the oil palms. In exchange he gets things that he needs but cannot make himself.

Simba likes going to town even better than going to feasts and dances. The traders have so many strange things on their shelves that he never tires of looking at them. On this last trip he saw a pocket flashlight, and oh, how he wanted it! He has decided that when he is grown up and can do his own trading, a flashlight is the first thing he will buy.

Then, too, there are the automobiles that Simba sees on the streets in the town. The first time he saw one he was frightened, but now he isn't the least bit afraid of them. He hopes that some day he will have a chance to ride in one.

Simba knows that in the town there is a building where native children like himself go to learn things from books. This puzzles him. He doesn't see how a boy can learn anything from lines of little black marks on paper. Simba, you see, cannot read or write. Neither can any of the other children in his village, and perhaps none of them will ever go to school.

You mustn't think, though, that because Simba and his friends do not go to school they are not learning anything worth while. The boys are learning from their fathers how to hunt and fish; how to build huts with roofs that won't leak; and how to build dugouts which will be as swift as any on the river. The girls are learning from their mothers how to cook and how to make baskets and pottery. Most important of all, they are learning how to be good gardeners.

In all the little villages scattered far and wide in the Congo Basin children like Simba and Panya are learning what they need most to know: how to make a living in the great forest. You will like to remember this as you start for home, where all children go to school.

Some Questions about Seasons

1. In the language that Simba speaks there is no word for winter. Can you explain why?

2. When Suvan speaks of a dry season in the Kirghiz Steppe, he means a season of drought. Does Simba mean the same thing when he talks of the dry seasons in the Congo Basin? Why, or why not?

3. When the weather is hot we say that the temperature is high. When the weather is cold we say that the temperature is low. What should you say about the temperature in all seasons in the Congo forest?

4. Why don't the seasons count in the Congo forest?

5. Do the seasons count where you live? How would your life be different if every month were like July? if every month were like January?

Can You Correct These Sentences?

The fact given in each of these sentences is right, but the reason for it is wrong. How should you change each sentence to make it wholly correct?

1. The Congo natives have gardens because they like to grow flowers.

2. Crops can be grown the year round in the Congo Basin because the soil never wears out.

3. Simba's people sometimes move their villages because they get tired of living in the same place.

4. Moving is easy because Simba's people have pack animals to carry their belongings.

Making Comparisons

Comparing people and things means seeing how they are alike or unlike. Here are some helps for you in making comparisons among the four groups of people you have visited: the Negritos of Malaya, the Eskimos of Baffin Island, the Kazaks of the Kirghiz Steppe, and the natives of the Congo Basin.

1. Two of these groups live in parts of the world that are rather unhealthful. Which two groups are they? Why are their homelands less healthful than the homelands of the other two groups?

2. The people of one of the groups have no way of getting about except on their own legs. Which group is it? Why don't they need other means of transportation?

3. What means of transportation have the other three groups? Are any of them like the means of transportation that you use?

4. All four of the groups carry on trading. Can you give a reason for this that is true for all of them?

5. They all trade without using money. What does each group use instead of money, and why?

Something to Do

Write a few sentences telling what Simba and Panya are learning which will help them to make their living when they grow up.

Volunteer Teamwork

Make a model of Simba's village on the bank of the Congo River.

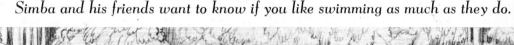

Simba and his friends want to know if you like swimming as much as they do.

Pedro of the Andes

Here is Pedro's father with some of the llamas that he uses as pack animals.

A COOL LAND IN THE WARM BELT

People Who Keep Llamas

The animals that you see in the picture are called llamas. Perhaps you have never before heard of them. A llama has a long neck like a camel, but it is a smaller animal. It has a thick coat of wool like a sheep. In our country we never see llamas except in the zoos.

In this story you will meet a boy who knows all about llamas. His name is Pedro, and his people are Indians. They live among some of the highest mountains in the world. The mountains are called the Andes, and they are in the continent of South America.

Pedro's people keep llamas, and they also keep sheep and alpacas. Alpacas look somewhat like llamas, but they haven't such long ears. Their wool is soft and very thick.

The picture shows that Pedro's people use llamas as pack animals. For their size the llamas are strong, and they can walk long distances with packs on their backs. They can climb up and down steep mountain trails easily because they have sharp hoofs that keep them from slipping.

Pedro will tell you that you must never overload a llama. You may tie a pack weighing about a hundred pounds on its back, but the pack must not be heavier than the animal is willing to carry. If it is, the llama will lie down and will not budge until the pack is made lighter.

Pedro's people are fond of their llamas, and they treat them well. The llamas deserve good treatment, for they are willing workers and they are useful in more ways than one. The wool helps to supply Pedro's people with clothing, and the dried manure is a valuable fuel because wood is scarce. When the animals die, their skins make good leather.

Pedro's House

Pedro doesn't live in a village. His house stands by itself in a big, open stretch of level land. From the doorway Pedro can see other houses, but they too stand by themselves with open land round about them. In the distance he can see a long line, or range, of mountains.

The picture shows that Pedro's house is about the same size and shape as Simba's house in the Congo forest. But Pedro's house is not built of wood as Simba's house is. It is built of stone and of bricks made of mud and dried in the sun. Wood is scarce in Pedro's land because there are not many trees. The roof of the house is thatched with coarse grass.

If you peep into the house, you will see a stove and some low platforms along the walls. The platforms are made of earth packed down hard. They are covered with skins and woolen blankets. Pedro's family use the platforms for beds and seats just as Netsook's family use the snow benches in their igloo.

Outside the house are the corrals. They are open spaces with stone walls round them. You will easily guess that the corrals are pens for the animals. In the daytime the sheep and the alpacas graze in the open, often some distance from the house. So, too, do the llamas when they are not carrying goods for Pedro's father. At night all the animals are shut up in the corrals.

From what you have learned so far, do you think Pedro's land is warm? Think what you have found there: (1) sheep and other animals with thick coats of wool; (2) people who wear woolen clothes; (3) skins and woolen blankets for bedding.

A Surprise

If you answered "no" to the question, you were right. Pedro's land is not warm. It is a very cool land. Knowing this, you may be surprised to find that Pedro lives in the warm belt of the earth. Look at the upper picture of the globe on page 69 and you will see that Pedro's homeland is between the equator and the tropic of Capricorn.

If you ask Pedro where he lives, he will say, "In the altiplano." *Altiplano* is Pedro's word for "high plain." It means a stretch of level land which is very high. Our word for land of this kind is *plateau*. The altiplano, or plateau, where Pedro lives is higher than most of the mountains in our country. Yet, high as it is, the ranges of the Andes Mountains which surround it are ever so much higher.

Pedro's house is built of stone and mud bricks because wood is scarce in the altiplano.

When you visited Netsook, you learned that Baffin Island is cold because it is a land of low sun far from the equator. Pedro's altiplano is cool because it is so high.

You know that when we say that a tree is 100 feet high, we mean that its top is 100 feet above the ground. We measure its height from the ground. We measure the height of land from the ocean, or, as we say, from *sea level*. Pedro's altiplano is nearly two and a half miles above sea level. It is well named, for it really is a very high plain.

All over the world the lands that are very high are cool or cold. This is true even in the warm belt, which is the belt of high overhead sun. In that belt it is the lower lands that are warm or hot the year round. Pedro's altiplano is not nearly so cold as Baffin Island, but it is cool enough for him to need woolen clothes the year round.

The picture shows Pedro wearing a poncho. The poncho is a narrow woolen blanket with a slit in the middle so that he can get his head through it. All the Indian boys in the altiplano wear ponchos, and so do their fathers. Pedro thinks his poncho is very good-looking because it has bright-colored stripes.

Under his poncho Pedro wears a woolen jacket. His trousers are woolen, too, and his hat is made of felt. Often he wears a close-fitting woolen cap under his hat. The cap has flaps on each side which he can turn down over his ears if he wants to.

The Indian girls and their mothers wear long woolen skirts. They often wear three or four skirts of different colors, one over the other. Over their jackets they wear bright-colored woolen shawls. They all wear the same kind of hats, very much like the hats that the men and boys wear.

Pedro would be surprised if you were to tell him that summer is much warmer than winter. In the altiplano the temperature changes so little from month to month that summer and winter haven't much meaning. The days are chilly most of the year, and the nights are always cold. Even in the warmest part of the year the only time when the sunshine is really warm is in the middle of the day.

The nights are so cold that Pedro needs a warm bed. Every night he sleeps on a llama skin with the thick wool left on it, and he covers himself with woolen blankets.

Off for the Altiplano

The picture of the globe on page 8 shows that South America is connected with our own continent of North America by a narrow strip of land. A narrow strip of land connecting two larger bodies of land is called an *isthmus*. This one is called the Isthmus of Panama.

The globe shows also that the altiplano is in the western part of South America. If you are going there, you may take a ship from some seaport in our country. Or, if you wish, you may take an airplane.

If you go by ship from a seaport on the eastern coast of our country, you will have a chance to see the Isthmus of Panama. Your ship will pass through the isthmus from the Atlantic Ocean to the Pacific Ocean. Perhaps you know why this is possible. It is because a waterway for ships has been cut through the

Here is Pedro wearing his striped poncho.

This is the railroad station where you will find Pedro's father and his llamas.

isthmus. This waterway is called the Panama Canal. If it were not for the canal, your ship would have to sail all the way round the southern tip of South America.

When you reach the seaport on the west coast of South America where you are to land, the easiest part of your journey is over. From here a train will carry you up and up from the coast to the high Andes.

Of course the railroad cannot climb straight up the steep mountainsides. It twists and winds, and, even with the engine pulling its best, the train moves slowly. Every now and then the track crosses a deep river valley on a bridge so high that you wonder how it was ever built.

The highest mountain peaks that you see from the train are white with ice and snow. They are so high and cold that never, even in summer, are they bare. They always wear their beautiful caps of snow and ice.

Higher and higher you go. If you are like most people from lower lands, you may find it a little hard to breathe. If you ask why, you will be told that you are now more than two miles above the sea, and that at such heights the air is thin. Until you get used to the thin air, you may feel rather uncomfortable.

At last the train runs through a pass, or gap, in the mountains and comes out on a level plain. This is the altiplano — the high plateau where thousands of Indians like Pedro's family live. It stretches away for miles and miles, but it is hemmed in by mountains.

At the station where you leave the train you will see Pedro's father and a number of other Indians with their llamas. The llamas have bags of ore strapped on their backs. The ore is crushed rock with bits of tin and silver in it. It has been dug from a deep mine several miles away on a mountainside.

There are many mines in this part of South America, for the rocks deep in the ground are rich in tin and silver. Many of the Indians work part of the time as miners, digging the ore in the mines. Others, like Pedro's father, are paid to carry the ore to the railroads on the backs of their llamas. In this way the llamas earn a little money for their Indian masters.

The railroads carry the ore to the coast, and from there ships carry it to our country or to countries in Europe. You can think of many things that are made of tin or silver. When you see some of these things, perhaps you will remember Pedro's father and his llamas.

Can You Give These Names?

See if you can give the name of

1. The continent where Pedro lives.

2. The strip of land which connects that continent with North America.

3. The waterway for ships through this strip of land.

4. The high mountains of South America.

5. The high plain, or plateau, where Pedro lives.

Some Things to Explain

1. You know that Simba and Pedro both live in what we call the warm belt of the earth. Why, then, is Pedro's land so cool? How can you be sure that the Congo Basin must be one of the lower lands in the warm belt?

2. You learned on page 95 why Pedro's house is not built of wood as Simba's house is. What reason have you to think that the altiplano is not a very rainy land?

3. Pedro's people keep flocks of sheep and other animals, but they haven't any tents. Do you think they are nomads like the Kazaks? Give a reason for your answer.

4. What reason have you to think that there must be more or better grass in the altiplano than in the Kirghiz Steppe?

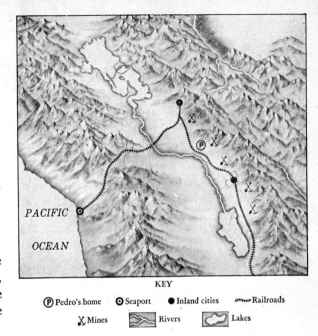

PACIFIC OCEAN

KEY

Ⓟ Pedro's home   ◎ Seaport   ● Inland cities   〰 Railroads

X Mines   〰 Rivers   ⬭ Lakes

A map of part of the altiplano.

A Map to Read

Here is a map of part of the altiplano and its bordering mountains. It shows how you could reach Pedro's home from the west coast of South America. Under the map is the key. With the help of the key, point out these things in the map:

1. The place in the altiplano where Pedro lives.

2. Some ranges of the Andes Mountains.

3. A town which is a seaport.

4. The railroad that runs from the seaport to the altiplano.

5. Two inland cities, far from the coast.

6. Some mines.

7. Two lakes in the altiplano.

8. A river that flows from the larger lake to the smaller one.

99

The llamas earn money for their masters by carrying ore from the mines to the railroads.

Pedro's mother and oldest sister are spinning wool from the sheep and the llamas.

AT HOME WITH PEDRO AND HIS FAMILY

Pedro's Mother at Work

Let us pretend that Pedro's father has taken us home with him. Pedro's mother is sitting outside the little house spinning wool. She draws out the fine, wavy hairs, or fibers, of the wool and, with the help of a wooden stick called a spindle, she twists the fibers into yarn.

Pedro's oldest sister is spinning, too. The younger children are playing with balls of colored yarn. Pedro's mother colors the yarn herself. She mixes dyes of bright red, yellow, green, and blue, and dips the yarn in them. Pedro's people are fond of bright colors.

You can easily guess what Pedro's mother does with the yarn. She uses it for weaving, for she is the cloth-maker for her family. She weaves all the blankets that keep them warm at night, and much of the material for their clothes. She even weaves the cloth for the bags in which the llamas carry goods on their backs.

The next picture shows how Pedro's mother does her weaving. She uses a wooden frame called a loom. First she strings the loom with threads of yarn all running in one direction. Then she weaves in threads running the other way. In stringing the loom she uses yarn of one color and then another. This is the way she makes the stripes in the cloth.

The wool that Pedro's mother uses comes from the sheep and the llamas. Once a year Pedro's father clips the wool from the animals with sharp shears. Then Pedro's mother washes it, brushes it, and stores it away ready for spinning whenever she needs it.

If Pedro's mother has more wool than she needs, his father sells some of it in the nearest town. He doesn't often have much wool from the sheep and the llamas to sell, but he usually sells all the alpaca wool. This is because the alpaca wool is the best of all, and it brings the highest price.

100

How Pedro Helps His Father and Mother

Pedro is out on the plateau today, a mile or so from the house, and he has his dog with him. He is looking after his father's sheep and alpacas. The animals are nibbling the grass, and Pedro is watching to see that none of them wander away. A chilly wind is blowing, but Pedro's poncho keeps him warm.

There is plenty of grass on the plateau for the animals to eat. This tells you that the altiplano has more rain than the steppe where Suvan lives. Pedro's people do not have to wander about in search of grass as Suvan's people do. They can live in the same place all the time because there is grass enough near their homes to feed the animals the year round.

Much of the grass is short, but there is one kind that grows in bunches and is rather tall. Pedro calls this kind of grass *ichu*. He will tell you that ichu is useful in two ways. It makes good pastures for the animals and good thatch for the roofs of houses.

Although there is plenty of grass in the altiplano, trees are scarce. They grow only in the small, deep-sided valleys which streams have cut in the plateau. The valleys are few and far between, and the trees that grow in them are small.

Three of the alpacas in Pedro's flock.

It is easy to understand why the altiplano is a hard place for trees to grow. The plateau is always windy, and always cold at night. Even after a warm day, the night often brings a frost. Too much wind and cold are the chief reasons that the altiplano is almost treeless.

Luckily there is no season too cold for the grass to keep on growing, or for the flocks to graze out of doors. At night the animals keep warm by crowding together in the corrals.

You will be surprised to see what Pedro is doing as he watches his father's sheep and alpacas. He has a spindle like his mother's, and he is spinning wool. In the altiplano the Indian boys, as well as the girls, learn to spin when they are small. By looking after the animals the boys help their fathers, and by spinning wool they help their mothers.

You might think that when the boys grow up, they would give up spinning, but they don't. Everyone spins — men, women, boys, and girls. You will often see them spinning as they walk. The men and the children are a great help to the women in this way.

Almost every day you will find Pedro out in the pastures with his father's flocks. Looking after the animals isn't very hard work, but it doesn't leave Pedro much time for play. When his little brother is older, the two boys will take turns in caring for the animals.

Weaving striped cloth for a poncho.

101

The End of the Day

Pedro hasn't any watch, but he can tell by the sun about what time it is. The sun is highest in the sky at noon. Then, as it moves toward the west, it sinks lower and lower in the sky. Before it drops behind the western mountains, Pedro starts for home. He must get back with the flocks before dark.

Pedro gathers the sheep and alpacas together and starts them toward his house. He talks to them and waves a stick to keep them trotting along. If one of them darts off in the wrong direction, Pedro sends his dog to drive the animal back.

When Pedro reaches home, he drives the sheep and the alpacas into the corrals for the night. His father has already put the llamas in their corral.

Pedro's mother is getting supper. She is washing the seeds of a plant called quinoa. She will cook the seeds in boiling water and a little sheep's milk to make a porridge. Quinoa porridge tastes somewhat like the cooked oatmeal that we often have for breakfast.

With his porridge Pedro will have some bread that is hard and crisp. The bread too is made of quinoa. Pedro's mother makes her own flour by pounding quinoa seeds to a powder. When she bakes bread, she bakes enough to last a number of weeks.

Tomorrow night perhaps Pedro will have chuño for supper. Chuño is the Indian name for dried potato. Pedro's mother cooks the chuño in boiling water. Sometimes she cooks meat with it.

Pedro likes meat, but he doesn't have so much as you might expect. In this way Pedro's family is somewhat like Suvan's family. Their animals are too useful in other ways for many to be killed for meat. Pedro's father would never think of killing a llama or an alpaca for food, and it is only now and then that he kills even a sheep.

Sometimes Pedro has stewed chicken to eat, for his mother keeps some hens. The foods that he eats most often are quinoa bread and porridge, chuño, and soups. When his mother cooks a little meat or a few vegetables in a soup or a stew, Pedro thinks he has a fine meal.

Soon after supper Pedro's family go to bed. The animals are quiet in the corrals now, and the night air has grown very cold. How glad Pedro is that he has a warm bed! He slips in between a llama skin and some woolen blankets on one of the platforms in his house. He snuggles down and closes his eyes.

Pedro will sleep soundly until daylight. When the sun rises from behind the eastern mountains his mother will wake him and give him his breakfast. Then he will take the flocks out to the pastures again.

Pedro and his dog drive the sheep and the alpacas home for the night.

Pedro's mother is washing quinoa seeds for a porridge for supper.

A Missing-Word Test

Two words are missing in each of the sentences. All the missing words are given in the list. Choose the right words for each sentence.

List of Missing Words

animals	grass	sheep
cloth	ichu	spinning
father	llamas	yarn
	pastures	

1. Pedro's mother uses woolen ____ to weave blankets and _____.

2. She has help from Pedro and his _____ in _____ the wool into yarn.

3. The wool comes from the _____ and the _____ that Pedro's father keeps.

4. Pedro looks after the _____ when they are grazing in the _____.

5. The animals eat ____ and other kinds of _____ that grow in the altiplano.

Something to Do

Draw a picture of a llama. Under it write down the different ways in which llamas are useful to Pedro's people.

Can You Answer These Questions?

There is a "weather answer" for each of these questions. Can you give it?

1. Why is there more and better grass in the altiplano than in the Kirghiz Steppe?

2. Why are there no forests in the altiplano?

3. Why does Pedro need woolen clothes?

4. Why does he need a warm bed every night in the year?

5. Why haven't the words "summer" and "winter" much meaning in the altiplano?

Some Food Lists

1. Make a list of the foods that Pedro eats which come from animals. Have you any reason to think that Pedro's father does any hunting? Why, or why not?

2. Make a list of the foods that Pedro eats which come from plants. Do you think that Pedro's father does any farming? Give a reason for your answer.

3. Since Pedro's father keeps sheep and other animals, you might expect the family to eat more meat than they do. Explain just why it is that they do not eat a great deal of meat.

Pedro's father is plowing his land to make it ready for planting his crops.

FARMING IN THE COOL PLATEAU

Planting Time

Now that you know about Pedro's food, you will guess that his people do a little farming. The only crops they can grow in the cool, windy plateau are kinds that are not easily harmed by the frosty nights. They raise a few vegetables, but by far the most important of their crops are quinoa and potatoes.

The picture shows how Pedro's father plows his land to make it ready for planting. He doesn't use a plow that was made in a factory as farmers in our country do. He turns over the soil with a homemade plow which is just a strong piece of wood with an iron point. The plow is heavy, and Pedro's father uses a pair of oxen to pull it.

Pedro's father is only part owner of the oxen. He and three of his neighbors bought the animals together, and they take turns using them in their farm work. Sharing the oxen is a good plan, because none of the men does enough farming to need a pair all his own.

After Pedro's father has plowed his land, Pedro's mother and the children help him with the planting. They sow the quinoa seeds in

Pedro's father and mother will put each seed potato into the ground by hand.

one field and plant the seed potatoes in another. They do the planting by hand, and use rakes to cover the seeds with earth.

Quinoa is a kind of grain, and it is raised for the new seeds that form on the stalks. The seeds in the ground sprout quickly and send up green shoots, but after that the stalks grow slowly. About six months must pass before the new seeds are ripe and the crop is ready to be harvested.

The potatoes grow more quickly, and while the plants are growing, the field must be weeded. Pedro's mother and the girls do most of this work, but they do not have to weed so often as Simba's mother and sister do. Weeds, as well as crops, grow much more slowly in the cool, windy altiplano than in the warm, rainy Congo forest.

Harvest Time

The quinoa plants grow to be from two to four feet high, and each stalk carries a new "ear" of small white seeds. When the seeds are ripe, the harvesting begins. Harvesting, you will remember, means the gathering of crops.

Pedro's father cuts the quinoa stalks by hand with his sickle.

His way of threshing is to beat the seeds off the stalks with a stick.

Harvesting grain means the cutting of the stalks in the fields.

The picture shows how Pedro's father harvests his quinoa. He cuts the grain with a sharp-bladed tool called a sickle. Perhaps you have seen people in our country using sickles to cut small patches of grass.

After Pedro's father has cut the quinoa, he stacks the stalks in rows in the fields. He leaves them there to dry for a while. Then he carries the bundles of stalks home and starts his threshing.

Threshing grain means getting the seeds off the stalks. In our country we have big machines that do this work very quickly. Pedro's father threshes his quinoa by hand, and it takes him a long time. He spreads the stalks on a bare piece of hard ground and beats them with a heavy stick to knock the seeds off.

The potatoes that Pedro's father grows are smaller than ours and yellowish in color. When they are ready for harvesting, Pedro's mother helps in digging them from the ground. You will be surprised to see what Pedro's family and their neighbors do with their potatoes.

Tramping on the potatoes every few days helps them to dry in the sun and the wind.

They do not put them in sacks or barrels and carry them away from the fields as soon as they are dug. They leave them lying in long rows on the ground in the fields.

The potatoes freeze in the cold at night, and thaw and dry in the sun and wind in the daytime. Every few days the people go out and tramp on them. This squeezes some of the water out of the potatoes and helps the drying along. After a long time the potatoes are so dry that they will keep for years without spoiling. You will remember that the chuño that Pedro eats so often is dried potato.

Farming and Weather

You have learned that in the altiplano there is not much difference in temperature through the year. Do you suppose, then, that Pedro's people plant their crops of quinoa and potatoes at any time of year when they happen to feel like it?

No, they don't, and the reason is easy to understand. To begin with, the weather is a little warmer at the time of year when the sun is highest than it is at other times. More important than this, the months of highest sun are the months when the altiplano gets most of its rain. During the rest of the year the weather is pretty dry.

As you would expect, Pedro's people do their farming when the weather is best for crops. They grow their yearly supply of food during the months which are the warmest and rainiest.

Although Pedro's people have other things to eat now and then, they depend more on quinoa and potatoes than on anything else. If something happens so that either crop is small, they may have to get along with less food than they need.

Pedro will tell you that now and then there is a bad year with less rain than usual, and then the potatoes do not grow so well as they should. Or there may be a year when there is too much cloudy weather at the time when the quinoa is ripening. Plenty of sunshine is needed for the quinoa seeds to ripen well.

The good years, of course, are the years when neither of these things happens. Then the crops are as large as Pedro's people hope for. A good harvest means enough food for the year to come, for both the quinoa seeds and the dried potatoes can be stored away and used as they are needed. Luckily for Pedro's people, there are more good years than bad.

Work for Everyone

Our Indian friends in the altiplano do not have an easy life. The women spend long hours spinning, weaving, and making clothes. They prepare all the food for the daily meals, and they make the pottery jars, bowls, and dishes that they use. At certain times of year they help with the farm work.

The men, too, have much work to do. They must plow the land, plant and harvest the crops, and thresh the grain. They must look after the flocks the year round, and do the shearing. Shearing is the clipping of the wool from the animals. When the men are not busy with the flocks or the crops, they must earn what money they can.

The boys and girls begin to help their fathers and mothers when they are a good deal younger than you are. They grow up learning how to do all the things their parents do. Pedro started helping to look after the flocks when he was seven years old. He is eleven now, and in a few years he will be helping his father with the plowing, harvesting, and threshing.

When Pedro grows up, perhaps he will work in his spare time as a miner. Or, when he has some llamas of his own, he may use them as his father does, to carry ore from the mine to the railroad.

It is lucky for Pedro's people that there are mines in the plateau and the mountains where the men can get work when they want to earn money. They need a little money each year to buy things that they cannot get or make themselves.

There are times, though, when the mines are closed and no workers are wanted. If this happens, Pedro's people have to get along without buying much of anything. But even so, if the crops are good, Pedro's people do not think that they are badly off. Food from their crops, wool from their animals, and houses to shelter them are what they need most. In the

Pedro's mother makes her own pottery.

best years, when crops are good and there is spare-time work for the men in the mines, Pedro's people think they are getting on very well indeed.

Some Farming Questions

1. What are the two most important crops that Pedro's people raise?

2. Why do these crops mean so much to them?

3. Why can't they grow the kinds of crops which are easily harmed by frost?

4. During what part of the year do Pedro's people grow their crops, and why?

5. What sometimes happens to make the quinoa crops poor?

6. What sometimes happens to make the potato crops poor?

Something to Think Out

In countries like ours many of the farmers who raise grain use machines for plowing, planting, harvesting, and threshing. Machines cost a great deal, but they save the farmers much time. Why do you think it is that the Indian farmers in the altiplano do not use machines in raising quinoa?

107

Saturday morning, and the whole family is going to market in the nearest town.

MARKET DAYS AND FIESTAS

When Saturday Comes

Pedro is looking forward to Saturday of this week. Saturday is market day in the town nearest his home. It is the day of the week when all the Indians of the neighborhood go to town to do their buying and selling. Pedro's family go to market nearly every Saturday.

There are many towns scattered here and there in the altiplano, and each one has its weekly market day. It may be Monday or Tuesday or any other day, but it is always the same day in each week.

Now Saturday has come, and Pedro's family are ready to start. Pedro's father has led one of the llamas out of the corral and is tying two bags of wool on its back. He has dressed up the llama for market day by tying some bright-colored woolen tassels on its ears.

Pedro's mother has put on her best skirt over two or three others, and her brightest-colored shawl. On her arm she carries a basket. In the basket are two chickens. If she can sell the chickens, she will have money to buy some dyes that she wants for coloring yarn.

Off they go, with Pedro's father driving the llama. The town is several miles away, but they will all walk except the baby sister. She rides on her mother's back.

When Pedro and his family reach the town, they go to the market square. This is a good-sized open space with streets leading into it from all sides. The square is already crowded with Indian families who have come in from the country and with people who live in the town. Many of the men from the country have brought wool that they want to sell, as Pedro's father has.

The Day's Business

Pedro's father will take his wool to one of the merchants in the town. If the merchant doesn't want to pay him as much money for the wool as he thinks it is worth, Pedro's father will try another. He will sell the wool for the best price he can get. With the money he will buy things that he needs or wants. What he needs most today is a new sickle.

Pedro's mother and the other Indian women from the country sit on the edge of the sidewalk round the square. They spread out the things they wish to sell, so that the people who pass by may see them. Some of them have vegetables to sell. Others, like Pedro's mother, have chickens. Sometimes they exchange things with one another, but the townspeople are their best customers.

Market day is play day for Pedro and the other Indian children. They do not race about as we do, but they have fun together in the market square. There is a fountain in the middle of it, and the children like to splash the water with their hands. As long as the children do not bother the grown-ups or run away and get lost, they may do much as they please.

In the afternoon the Indian families start for home with the things they have bought. Pedro's family are going home happy today. The wool has been sold, and the llama is stepping along with only the empty bags on its back. Pedro's mother has her dyes, and his father has the new sickle. The children are

Sitting on the edge of the sidewalk, the Indian mothers wait for customers.

tired, but they have had such a good time that they do not mind the long walk home.

Fiesta Fun

If you ask Pedro when he has the most fun, he will say, "At the fiestas." These are special celebrations in the town. Pedro's family never stay away from a fiesta if they can help it. The Indian families from the country start for the town early in the morning and stay all day.

The market square is bright with flowers and flags, and all the townspeople are there as well as the Indians from the country. There are parades and dances to watch. The dancers are men, and they wear all kinds of fancy costumes.

109

Pedro and his family are coming home from market tired but happy.

Good-by to Pedro as he stands in the square watching the dancers.

Some of them wear hats trimmed with big feathers of different colors, and many wear masks over their faces. Some of the masks are like animal faces, and others are just funny faces. There is a band of drummers and flute-players to make music for the dancing, and it plays all day long.

Some of the young men of the town have bags of bright-colored bits of paper called confetti. They toss handfuls of the confetti into the air, and it falls on the crowd like a shower of colored snowflakes. The young men have rolls of bright-colored paper tape too. When they throw these rolls into the crowd, the tape unwinds and tangles itself round the people.

Pedro and his friends do not take any part in the celebration, but they have a wonderful time looking on. They love to hear the music and watch the dancing, and they think the showers of confetti and of paper tape are great fun.

We shall say good-by to Pedro and the other Indian children as they stand in the market place watching all that is going on. They are having some real fun now, but we shall not forget that they are children who spend more time at work than at play.

Can You Explain?

1. You have found that when Pedro's family need to buy things, they buy them with money. How are they different in this way from the other groups of people you have visited?

2. How can Pedro's father earn money?

3. How else can the family get money?

Like and Unlike

1. Which of these lands is most like the altiplano?

The Congo Basin   Malaya
The Kirghiz Steppe   Baffin Island

2. Each of these words will remind you of some likeness between the altiplano and the Kirghiz Steppe. Explain what each likeness is.

Grass   Trees   Animals   Clothes

3. Each of these words will remind you of some difference between the altiplano and the Kirghiz Steppe. Explain what each difference is.

Rain   Farming   Crops   Tents

4. The different groups of people whom you have visited get the things they need in different ways. Which of these sentences explains why their ways of getting things are not alike?

a. They speak different languages.
b. They like to do different kinds of work.
c. They live in different kinds of lands.

110

Abdul and Zakia in Egypt

Abdul and Zakia are helping their father and mother to pick cotton.

THE LAND OF THE NILE

Children Who Pick Cotton

Do you live in one of the warmer parts of the United States where farmers raise cotton? If you do, you have often seen people picking cotton in the cotton fields. But if you have always lived in some colder part of our country, you have never seen a cotton field. Cotton is a plant which needs much warmth. It grows slowly, and it needs nearly seven months of warm weather without any frost.

The children in the picture are at work in a cotton field. They are picking the fluffy white fiber from the plants. You can see from the way the children are dressed that they are not Americans. The boy in the middle is named Abdul. At his right, partly hidden among the cotton plants, is his sister. Her name is Zakia.

The cotton field belongs to Abdul's father. Early last spring he plowed the field and planted cotton seeds. It is autumn now, and the plants have grown up. The new seed pods have opened, and you can see the white fiber in which the seeds are hidden. It is the fiber that makes the cotton plant so useful.

Abdul's father grows other crops besides cotton. He grows wheat, corn, and another kind of grain called barley. He also grows vegetables. The weather is so warm that he raises crops the year round. He doesn't have to stop in the wintertime as farmers in colder lands do.

But here is a surprise for you. *The land where Abdul lives is always very dry.* Sometimes a whole year goes by with hardly any rain. How do you suppose Abdul's father can be a farmer in such a very dry land?

111

Flying over Abdul's Land

The name of the very dry land where Abdul and Zakia live is Egypt. Look at the picture of the globe on page 9, and you will see that Egypt is part of Africa. What boy whom you have visited lives in a very rainy part of Africa?

Let us pretend that we are flying over Egypt in an airplane. How different it looks from the Congo Basin! At first all we see below us is yellowish-brown sand and bare rock. There are no trees, and there is so little grass that we cannot see it from our plane.

You will know at once that this bare, brown land is a great desert. It is called the Sahara Desert, and it stretches all the way across northern Africa. It is one of the driest lands in all the world.

Perhaps, as you look down, you will see a cluster of tiny black dots in the desert. They are the black tents of a band of nomads. Abdul would tell you that the nomads are called Bedouins, and that they live a wandering life with their camels, sheep, and goats.

Now we can see a change in the land below our plane. A long, narrow strip of green runs through the desert. It is a strip of green fields with a river flowing through it. The name of the river is the Nile, and the green strip is its valley. Along the banks of the river are many little villages with palm trees round about them.

A street in the village in the Nile Valley where Abdul and Zakia live.

Green places with trees in a desert are called *oases*. Wherever you find an oasis, you may be sure there is water. The water may come from a stream, or it may come from springs or wells. Because there is water, trees will grow and crops can be raised.

An oasis may be just big enough for one village or town, or it may be larger, but not many oases are very large. It all depends on how much water there is for the people and the crops. The Nile Valley is the largest oasis in the world, and it has many towns and villages. Millions of people live there, and most of them are farmers. In one of the villages in this great oasis we shall find Abdul and Zakia.

"Father Nile"

Look again at the picture of the globe on page 9, and you will see that the Nile is a very long river. Its source, where it begins, is in the rainy part of Africa. From there the Nile flows northward through the great desert to the sea.

The map on page 114 gives you a better idea of the Nile Valley. You can see that the valley is like a ribbon, and that it broadens out at its northern end. There it is shaped like a fan with a broken edge.

The fan-shaped part of the valley is called the *delta*. Notice that at the beginning of its delta the Nile splits into a number of different streams. Each one flows by itself to the sea. So, you see, the Nile has a number of different mouths.

It is the Nile itself that makes the great oasis. It brings water to the dry part of Africa from the rainy part. Because it waters the thirsty land along its banks, the people of the valley and the delta can have farms and gardens.

Great ditches have been dug to carry water from the Nile to the farm lands beyond its banks. They are called canals. Smaller canals

112

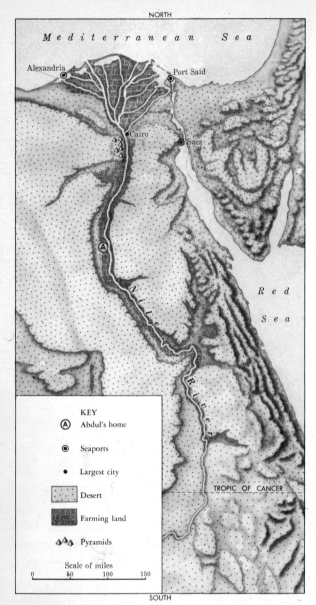

KEY

ⒶAbdul's home

◉ Seaports

• Largest city

Desert

Farming land

▲▲▲ Pyramids

Scale of miles

0   50   100   150

A map showing the valley and the delta of the Nile River in Egypt.

"Father Nile" never does stop flowing. For thousands of years it has been bringing to Egypt the precious water that makes the crops grow and gives the people food.

Reading the Map

Here are some interesting things that you can find out about the Nile and its valley by reading the map.

1. Does the Nile flow from north to south, or from south to north?

2. Does it flow from a warmer part of Africa to a cooler part? (Notice that it flows northward from the tropic of Cancer.)

3. Into what sea do the mouths of the Nile empty?

4. How can you tell from the map that the valley and the delta of the Nile are used for farming?

5. How can you tell that the land beyond the valley is desert?

6. Four Egyptian cities are named on the map. Which three of them are seaports?

7. What city is at the head of the Nile delta, where the river splits into a number of different streams? How can you tell that this is the largest city in Egypt?

8. On the map is a *scale of miles*. With a strip of paper measure the space between Cairo and the village where Abdul lives. Then use the scale to find out how many miles that space stands for. If you were going to travel in an airplane from Cairo to Abdul's village, how far should you have to fly?

What Am I?

See if you can give the right word for each blank space.

1. I am the bare brown land in Egypt. I am a _ _ _ _ _ _.

2. I am the ribbon of green that runs through the bare brown land in Egypt. I am an _ _ _ _ _.

3. I am the water that makes the ribbon of green that runs through the bare brown land in Egypt. I am a _ _ _ _ _. The Egyptians are my people, and they call me " _ _ _ _ _ _   _ _ _ _."

branch off from the main ones. From the canals the water runs into ditches in the fields where the crops are planted.

The Egyptians call the river "Father Nile" because it takes such good care of them. If it should stop flowing, the green oasis would soon be as bare and brown as the desert. The crops would die of thirst, and the people would soon starve.

114

The people of the village do their buying and selling outdoors in the market place.

IN ABDUL'S VILLAGE

A Morning in the Market Place

Abdul and Zakia live in a good-sized village on the west bank of the Nile. The houses are small, and the streets are narrow, crooked lanes. The only broad roadway is the one along the river bank between the outer row of houses and the river.

There are many tall palm trees in the village. They are a great help because of the shade they give. Shade is very much needed in a land where the sky is nearly always clear and the hot sun beats down all day long.

Near the center of the village is the market place. This is an open piece of ground with buildings round about it. The building with the dome that is shaped like a beehive is the village mosque, or church. Every morning people who have things to sell and people who wish to buy gather in the market place to do their business.

As you look around the market place, you will see that the people are dressed in cotton clothes. The men wear long gowns of blue or white cloth, and small, close-fitting caps. Over their caps some of the men wear small turbans, which are strips of cloth wound round their heads. The women wear black dresses with long skirts, and black shawls or veils over their heads.

This is the kind of clothing that the Egyptian villagers wear at all times of year. In the Nile Valley the weather is never cool enough for the people to need heavy clothes.

Many of the people in the market place have things from their farms to sell. Some have sacks of wheat or corn. Others have onions and tomatoes. Still others have baskets of beans or peas. Wandering about among the people are the little donkeys which have brought the grain and vegetables to market in baskets or bundles on their backs.

Then there are the regular merchants and the peddlers. The merchants sell such things as cotton cloth, copper pots and dishes, coffee, sugar, and salt. The peddlers walk about selling cigarettes, cheap candy, and watery lemonade.

Abdul and his father are in the market place this morning to buy a pair of new saddle baskets for their donkey. Abdul has a copper coin which is worth about a fourth of one of our copper cents, and he is trying to decide what kind of candy to buy with it.

Abdul's father is talking with a merchant about the saddle baskets. The merchant has named the price and Abdul's father says it is too much. He tells the merchant what he is willing to pay for the baskets, but the merchant shakes his head. It may be an hour or more before the two men agree on a price. When they do, it will be less money than the merchant first named, and more than Abdul's father first said he would pay; but they will both feel that they have done well.

If you spend the morning in the market place, you will find that all the business is done in this way. No one but a stranger would think of paying the first price that is asked for anything. The buyers and the sellers all like to argue over prices, and they wouldn't enjoy doing business in any other way.

What price for a pair of saddle baskets?

Abdul's little house is built of mud bricks.

Abdul's House

Abdul and Zakia live in the little house that you see in the picture. Most of the houses in the village are very much like it. The walls are made of mud bricks, and the roof is flat. Sloping roofs are not needed in a land where there is so little rain.

Abdul's father made the bricks himself. He took mud from a place on the river bank and mixed it with bits of straw. Then he cut it in blocks and set the blocks in the sun to dry and harden. Perhaps you know why he mixed straw with the mud. If he hadn't, the bricks would have crumbled to pieces as soon as they dried. Abdul will tell you that in making mud bricks you must use straw to hold the mud together.

After Abdul's father had made his bricks, he built the walls of his house. He left an opening for the door, and two small square holes for windows. If you think the house is rather dark, you are right. More windows would make it lighter, but they would also let in more heat. In Abdul's land houses are built to keep the people as cool as possible in the hot weather.

116

The house has two rooms. In the tiny kitchen Abdul's mother has a baking-oven made of sun-dried mud. For firewood she uses dry cotton stalks and cornstalks. In the other room there is a platform of earth packed down hard, and a low table. Abdul's family sleep on grass mats on the platform and eat their meals sitting on grass mats on the floor. The floor is nothing but the ground itself.

For the roof of the house Abdul's father used the trunks of palm trees. He laid the trunks side by side and covered them with layers of palm leaves. Then he plastered the leaves with mud. Abdul's family use the roof as their storeroom. They keep their sacks of grain there, and their vegetables, and their bundles of cotton stalks and cornstalks.

Abdul's house would never do in a rainy land like the Congo forest, where Simba lives. The rain would not run off the roof. Worse than that, the rain would soon soften the bricks. Before long the walls would fall and the roof would cave in.

Even in a land as dry as Egypt, mud bricks do not wear very well, and the houses have to be repaired often. Houses of stone or of brick such as we use would be better, but only the well-to-do Egyptians can afford them. The farming people use mud bricks because mud and straw are the building materials which they can get most easily and most cheaply.

Zakia is grinding corn to make corn meal.

At Home with Zakia

This morning, while Abdul is off with his father, Zakia is at home helping her mother. She is grinding corn between two stones to make corn meal. She often grinds wheat seeds in the same way to make flour.

Zakia's mother is making a fire in the baking-oven. When Abdul and his father come home from the market place at noon, they will find a meal of corn bread, beans, and onions ready for them.

Bread and vegetables are the foods that Abdul's family eat most. They grow their own vegetables and raise their own wheat and corn.

117

How the dates are gathered from the trees.

Zakia helps her mother to wash the clothes.

They eat almost no meat because the only farm animals they keep are a donkey and a pair of bullocks. Bullocks are small oxen, and the Egyptian farmers use them for plowing and threshing. There is a mud-brick shed for the bullocks and the donkey built against one wall of Abdul's house.

For desserts Abdul and Zakia eat dates and other fruits. Dates, as you perhaps know, grow on trees called date palms. Like all other palm trees, date palms need plenty of warmth to grow well. They grow best in desert oases, where their roots can reach water and their feathery tops are in the hot sun. There are many date palms in the great Nile oasis.

If you ask Abdul and Zakia what their favorite drink is, they will say, "Coffee." Their father buys the coffee, and their mother boils it very carefully in a copper pot. She makes it sirupy by boiling sugar with it.

This afternoon Zakia and her mother are going down to the river to wash clothes. Many of the other women and girls will be there washing, too. They will beat the wet clothes on stones to get the dirt out. Then they will take them home in baskets balanced on their heads, and lay them on the rooftops to dry.

Every day Zakia and her mother go a number of times to the river to get water. They bring it home in big jars, and these too they balance on their heads. There are no round shoulders among the Egyptian women and girls. Try balancing a heavy book on your head and see if it doesn't make you stand up straight.

Zakia likes to go to the river for water or to help with the washing, because she loves to watch the boats. Dozens of little boats sail by every day, carrying goods from place to place in the great oasis. Now and then Zakia sees one of the fine passenger steamers which carry visitors from far-away lands up and down the river.

Zakia often wonders where the people on the steamers have come from, and why they want to see the land of the Nile. But she likes

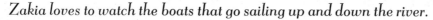

Zakia loves to watch the boats that go sailing up and down the river.

the little Egyptian boats best. Their sails make
her think of the wings of big birds.

Choose and Finish

In each sentence one of the three parts in
parentheses (like this) is right, and the other two
are wrong. Choose the part that makes the sentence correct, and then finish the sentence in your
own words.

1. Abdul and Zakia eat mostly (fruits and nuts)
(bread and vegetables) (meat and fish) because _ _ _

2. They eat almost no (meat) (dates) (sugar)
because _ _ _

3. Abdul and Zakia wear clothes made of
(woolen cloth) (cotton cloth) (furs) because _ _ _

4. Their house is built of (sod) (stone) (mud
bricks) because _ _ _

5. The roof is (sloping) (rounded) (flat) because _ _ _

A Palm-Tree Test

1. Suppose you knew nothing about the Nile
Valley except that palm trees grow there. What
would this tell you about the weather?

2. How do the palm trees help to supply
Abdul's people with building materials?

3. Why are the villagers glad of the shade that
the palm trees give?

4. From what kind of palm trees that grow in
Egypt do the people get fruit?

5. Why do palm trees of this kind grow well
in desert oases?

Some Make-Believe

1. If you are a boy, make believe that you are
Abdul, and tell about a morning in the market
place with your father.

2. If you are a girl, make believe that you are
Zakia, and tell how you help your mother.

YEAR-ROUND FARMING

How the Weather Helps

Winter is the time when Zakia sees the most
passenger boats on the river. This is because
summer is so hot in the Nile Valley that people
from cooler lands do not like it. They come
mostly in the winter, when the weather is more
comfortable.

The Nile Valley is a lowland, and if the
Egyptian part of it were in the warm belt of
the earth, the winters would be as hot as the
summers. But, as you can see from the map
on page 114, most of Egypt is just outside the
warm belt, north of the tropic of Cancer. It is
in the part of the north temperate belt where
the sun is high in summer and lower, but not
very low, in winter. For this reason the winters
are cooler than the summers, but they are not
cold.

The winter weather is what we call mild —
not too hot and not too cold. The nights are
chilly, but there is never any frost. The days
are pleasantly warm with blue sky and bright
sunshine. Because the winters are mild and the
winter days bright and sunny, the Egyptian
farmers can grow crops the year round.

Outside each village are the fields where the
people grow their crops. Nearly every village
family has some farm land, but most of the
farms are very small.

In all, there are thousands of square miles
of farming land with fine, rich soil in the long
oasis of the Nile. Why, then, do you suppose
the farms are so small? It is because so many
millions of people live in the oasis that each
family can have only a little of the farming land.

If crops could be grown only in the summertime, each family would need a larger farm, and
not so many people could live in the Nile
Valley. But because the winters are mild, each
farmer can get at least two crops from the same
piece of land every year.

Autumn plowing makes the land ready for the planting of winter crops.

You will find that Abdul's people talk of their summer crops and their winter crops. The summer crops are planted in the spring and harvested in the autumn. The winter crops are planted in the autumn and harvested in the spring. There is something growing in most of the fields at all times of year.

The Winter Crops

Let us imagine that we have reached Abdul's village in the late autumn. Abdul's father and

The seeds of grain are sown by hand.

the other men are at work in the fields. Their summer crops have been harvested, and now they are plowing the fields for the winter crops.

The picture shows that Abdul's father uses a heavy wooden plow much like the one that Pedro's father uses in the altiplano. His two bullocks walk back and forth in the field, pulling the plow. The plow turns over the soil and makes it ready for the seeds.

In a day or two Abdul will help his father to sow wheat in this field. Next week they will sow barley in another field. They will scatter the seeds by hand.

Soon the wheat field and the barley field will be green with the young blades of the plants. The stalks will grow fast during the winter, and early in the spring the grain will be ready to be harvested.

In the meantime, Abdul's father will plant a good many rows of beans, peas, onions, and other vegetables. He will also plant a small patch of clover for the donkey and the bullocks. All the land in the little farm will be at work for the family during the winter months.

120

When the new seeds of wheat and barley are ripe, Abdul and his father cut the stalks of grain with sickles. They tie the stalks in bundles and leave them in the fields to dry.

Do you remember how Pedro's father threshes his quinoa? Abdul's father threshes his grain in a different way. He spreads the stalks on the ground as Pedro's father does, but he doesn't beat them with a stick. Abdul will tell you that his father uses a *norag* for threshing. It looks somewhat like a big sled, for it has wooden runners. But it also has a number of small iron wheels with sharp edges. Abdul's father hitches his bullocks to the norag, and they drag it round and round over the stalks of grain. The sharp iron wheels break up the stalks and knock off the seeds.

After the threshing, Abdul's father puts the seeds in sacks. Abdul drives the donkey into the field, and his father puts a sack of grain in each saddle basket. The donkey makes one trip after another between the field and the house, carrying the grain home. Abdul walks behind him with a stick in his hand. If the

At harvest time the grain is cut with sickles.

donkey gets lazy and slows down too much, Abdul gives him a little poke with the stick.

Abdul's father sells the barley, but he keeps the wheat for making flour. He raises enough wheat each winter to supply the family with flour for a year. The wheat and the barley are grown for the seeds, but the stalks are not wasted. They make good feed for the donkey and the bullocks.

121

After the grain has dried, it is threshed with a norag drawn by bullocks.

The donkey carries home the sacks of grain.

The Summer Crops

The fields do not have much time to rest in the spring after the winter crops have been harvested. Soon Abdul's father is plowing again, making the land ready for his summer crops. This time he plants cotton and corn. Cotton and corn are summer crops because they need hotter weather than wheat and barley do.

The corn grows faster than the cotton and is ready to be harvested earlier. The seeds grow in bundles called "ears," and each ear has a leaf-like covering called a husk. When the seeds are ripe, Abdul and his father pick the ears from the stalks by hand. Zakia and her mother often help them in this work.

Again there is work for the donkey. Now, instead of wheat or barley, he carries home the ears of corn. Zakia and her mother tear off the husks and dry the ears on the roof of the house.

After that, whenever they want corn for corn meal, they bring down some of the ears and rub the seeds off.

In September the bolls, or seed pods, of the cotton begin to open, and the picking starts. The bolls open a few at a time for a good many weeks. Because of this, the cotton cannot be picked all at once. It must be picked every few days as new bolls open.

During the cotton harvest the women and children work in the fields with the men, picking the fiber from the bolls. The children are clever at this work, and they pick quickly and well. The families do not go home at noon. They eat their lunch in the fields and then lie down to rest before they go to work again.

Abdul's father and the other farmers put their cotton in sacks ready to be sold. A merchant comes to the village to buy it. Later he will send some little boats to take the cotton away. It goes down the river to a place where it is put through machines which remove the seeds from the fiber. Then the fiber is pressed into big bundles called bales and sent to far-away countries.

Most of the money that Abdul's father earns comes from the sale of his cotton. In some years the price is high; in other years it is much lower. If Abdul's father gets a good price for his cotton, he feels very happy. If he gets a poor price, he has very little money to spend.

122

Little boats come to take the cotton away.

The wheel that lifts the jars of water turns because the bullocks turn the wheels at the right.

Abdul's father wants money to buy the clothes that he and his family wear and the foods that they like but do not grow themselves. In poor years they may not have any new clothes, and they may have to get along with less coffee and sugar than they like, but they do not go hungry. Their little farm supplies enough grain and vegetables to feed them through the year.

Watering the Crops

The soil in the Nile Valley is some of the best in the world, but without the river itself not a bit of the land could be used for farming. Where there is no rain there can be no farms unless crops are watered in some other way.

You already know about the canals and the ditches which carry water from the Nile to the fields in the valley. Watering crops in this way is called *irrigation*. Fields in smaller oases are often irrigated from wells or springs.

If there is a river near your home, you know that sometimes the water is high and sometimes it is low. It is the same with the Nile. The water is very high in the Nile in the autumn and very low late in the spring.

In a number of places great dams have been built across the Nile to hold back water when the river is high. When the river is low, gates in the dams can be opened to let out water needed to fill the canals and ditches. In this way water reaches the thirsty land at all times of year.

There are some places, though, where at times the water in the canals is too low to run into the ditches in the fields. Then the farmers have to lift the water into the ditches.

In the picture on this page two bullocks are turning a water wheel round and round. The turning of the wheel lifts jars of water from the canal and empties them into the ditches in the field. The people of Abdul's village have a number of these big water wheels.

In the picture on page 124 Abdul's father is lifting water with a *shaduf*. The shaduf is a long pole that moves like a seesaw. Hanging by a rope from one end of it is a bucket. Abdul's father pulls down on the rope to lower the bucket into the canal and fill it with water

123

Abdul's father is lifting water with a shaduf.

Fastened to the other end of the pole is a big lump of mud. The lump of mud is heavier than the bucketful of water. So, when Abdul's father loosens his hold on the rope, the pole tips and lifts the bucket of water. Then Abdul's father empties the bucket into a ditch in the field.

Years ago, before the dams were built, the Nile overflowed its banks every autumn, when the water was high. The water spread out and flooded the land. After the flood was over, the farmers planted their crops in the damp soil. By the time the winter crops were harvested, the soil was dry again. So, if the farmers wanted to grow summer crops, they had to lift water from the river with water wheels and shadufs.

Now, with the dams and canals, some of the farmers never have to use shadufs or water wheels. But there are others, like the farmers of Abdul's village, who live where the water in the canals is sometimes not high enough to run into the ditches in the fields. This usually happens only for a few weeks in the spring. Then, to give the summer crops a good start,

the farmers must use their shadufs and water wheels.

When you think of Abdul and Zakia, you will like to remember that "Father Nile" is their best friend. Without the water from the river, the deep soil and the warm sunshine would do them no good. There is just one reason why their homeland is a green oasis supplying food for millions of people. It is because "Father Nile" never goes back on them.

Some Questions to Answer

1. Three things that farmers need in order to grow crops are: (1) good soil; (2) enough warmth and sunshine; (3) enough rain. One of these things is missing in the Nile Valley. Which one is it?

2. How can the Egyptians raise crops in such a dry land?

3. What do they mean by "summer crops" and "winter crops"?

4. Why can the farmers in the Nile Valley grow crops the year round?

Can You Explain?

See if you can explain why the summer in the Nile Valley is hot, and why the winter is cooler, but not cold. If you have trouble explaining, read again what is said about the weather on page 119.

A Crop Test

Here is a list of the crops which Abdul's father raises.

| Barley | Corn | Vegetables |
| Clover | Cotton | Wheat |

1. Which of these are winter crops?

2. Which are summer crops, and why?

3. Which crops does Abdul's father raise for food for his family?

4. Which crops help to feed the donkey and the bullocks?

5. Which crops does Abdul's father sell?

6. Which crops supply Abdul's family with fuel?

124

The great stone pyramids in Egypt were built thousands of years ago.

AN OLD, OLD COUNTRY

The Egyptians of Long Ago

Egypt is a very old country, and the people have been farmers for thousands of years. Perhaps you remember the Bible story of Joseph: how he was sold as a slave in Egypt, and how he became rich and famous as one of the chief officers at the court of the king. Joseph lived nearly three thousand years ago, and yet long before he went to Egypt the Nile Valley had become a green oasis of farms and crops.

The Egyptians of long ago worshiped many different gods. One of their greatest gods was "Father Nile." They worshiped him because he brought the precious water that made the crops grow and gave them food.

While you are in Egypt you will see some of the wonderful temples where the people of long ago worshiped their gods. The temples are built of stone, beautifully carved, and when they were new they were painted in bright colors.

The old Egyptians were great builders, and the huge pyramids that they built were even more wonderful than the temples. They stand on the desert edge of the oasis, and they were built as tombs, or burial places, for some of the kings and queens of Egypt. Every block of stone was cut and set in place without the help of a single piece of machinery. When you see the pyramids you will not be surprised to learn that people call them one of the wonders of the world.

Perhaps you will like best the pictures painted on the walls of some of the tombs and temples — pictures of the Egyptians of long ago. At the bottom of page 126 is a copy of some of these pictures. Don't they remind you of some of the sights you have seen during your visit to Abdul's village?

The pictures painted and carved on the walls of the tombs and temples are not new ones. They were done thousands of years ago, and they show how the Egyptians lived and worked at that time. When you see them, you will know that the Egyptian farmers of today live and work much as the old Egyptians did long, long ago.

The Egyptians of Today

Does it seem strange to you that the Egyptian farmers have not changed their ways of working very much in all these years? Are you thinking that they are old-fashioned not to be using farming machinery as our farmers do?

It is true that we think farmers who plow with wooden plows and oxen and who harvest crops by hand are old-fashioned. But machines for farm work cost a great deal of money, and most of the Egyptian farmers are too poor to buy them. Then, too, their farms are so small that many of the machines such as our farmers use are not really needed.

Abdul's father would probably like a good modern steel plow, but it wouldn't pay him to own a harvesting machine or a threshing machine. His fields are so small that he has plenty of time to cut and thresh by hand all the grain that he can grow.

If you catch yourself thinking that the Egyptian farmers are old-fashioned and behind the times, stop and remember this. They are old-fashioned compared with our farmers, but they have much to be proud of. The old Egyptians who were their forefathers were some of the first farmers in all the world.

Long before our own forefathers knew anything about farming, the Egyptians had learned to plow and plant and grow crops. They had learned how to use the Nile to water their crops. They had already turned part of the Nile Valley into a land of farms when most people in the world were still getting their food by hunting, fishing, and collecting wild seeds and fruits.

A Summary

A summary is a short adding-up of what you know about something. In this summary of the Nile Valley you are to give the correct words to fill the blank spaces.

1. The Nile Valley is a long, narrow _ _ _ _ _.

2. It is a warm land with almost no _ _ _ _.

3. In spite of dry weather, the people are able to grow _ _ _ _ _. This is because they can get _ _ _ _ _ for their crops from the Nile.

4. This way of watering crops is called _ _ _ _ _ _ _ _ _ _.

5. The Egyptians grow crops in _ _ _ _ _ _ as well as in summer. This is because the winter weather is never _ _ _ _.

6. The Egyptian farmers do not use _ _ _ _ _ _ _ _ in their work.

7. One reason for this is that the farms are _ _ _ _ _ in size.

8. Another reason is that the farmers haven't _ _ _ _ _ enough to buy machines.

Correcting Wrong Ideas

Here are some things that Simba, Netsook, and Suvan think. What could Abdul tell them that would change their ideas?

1. Simba thinks that all parts of Africa are rainy with thick forests like the Congo Basin.

2. Netsook thinks that when people talk about winter they always mean very cold weather.

3. Suvan thinks that no one who lives in a dry land can get enough food by raising crops.

Volunteer Teamwork

1. Make a model of Abdul's house.

2. Give a play that will tell the story of the farm work that the villagers do.

Roshik and Moti in India

Roshik's mother is outside her kitchen cutting up some fish to cook for lunch.

THE BENGALIS AND THEIR HOMELAND

A Land of Three Seasons

Roshik and his sister Moti are Bengali children. Their skin is brown, and their hair is black and shiny. They live in Bengal, which is part of the country of India. India is in the same continent as the Malay Peninsula and the Kirghiz Steppe. Which continent is it?

India is a large country, and the Bengalis are only one of its many groups of people. This is worth remembering because the different groups of people live in different ways. One of the reasons they live differently is that some parts of India are rainy and some are dry; and some parts are higher and cooler than others. You will not want to make the mistake of thinking that all the people of India live as the Bengalis do.

In the picture you see Roshik and his mother. It is almost noon, and Roshik's mother is cutting up some fish to cook for lunch. What a strange way she has of doing it! She holds the knife between the toes of her right foot.

It is the time of year which Roshik's people call the cold season. The Bengalis never speak of spring, summer, autumn, and winter as we do. They divide the year into three seasons instead of four. They call them the hot season, the rainy season, and the cold season. Does Roshik look as if he were dressed for cold weather?

You will easily guess that the cold season in Bengal is not cold at all. To us it would seem like summer. The Bengalis call it cold because the rest of the year is even warmer.

The hot season in Bengal is well named. It is so hot that if you were there you would not want to run or jump or play any outdoor games. Roshik doesn't mind the heat because he is used to it.

The rainy season is well named, too. How it does rain! For three or four months there is hardly a day without heavy storms that last for hours. Often the thunder rolls and the lightning flashes. The rivers overflow their banks, and the fields are changed into lakes and ponds.

The rainy season is not quite so hot as the hot season because the storms cool the air a little. But the air never feels cool because it is so damp. It feels steamy all the time. If you visit Roshik in the rainy season, you will find that even when the sun is out nothing will dry.

Your clothes will be damp all the time and your shoes will get moldy.

The cold season is the pleasantest time of year because the air is somewhat cooler and much drier. There are many clear, sunny days when hardly a cloud is to be seen in the sky. The water drains off the fields, and little by little the rivers fall until they are within their banks again.

A Great Delta

The map on the next page shows that Bengal is partly in the warm belt of the earth and partly just outside it. When you reach the part where Roshik and Moti live, you will find yourself in a plain that is very low and flat.

The plain spreads out for hundreds of miles, and it is crisscrossed by so many streams that you will soon lose count of them. It is a beautifully green plain, with palms, bamboos, and other trees, and great stretches of fields where crops are growing.

128

Getting about in boats is easy in the delta of Bengal because there are so many streams.

The map on this page shows that two great rivers meet and join in the plain of Bengal. They are the Ganges River and the Brahmaputra River. You can see that they rise, or begin, in some very high mountains on the northern border of India. They flow across the plain of Bengal, but before they reach the sea they split into a number of branches. Like the Nile, the Ganges and the Brahmaputra have a number of different mouths.

Perhaps you have guessed that this green, watery plain of Bengal is a great delta. It is one of the largest deltas in the world. When you think how low and flat it is, and how many streams it has, you will understand why it is flooded in the rainy season. When the streams rise and overflow their banks, the people can go sailing over the fields in boats.

The houses in this flat, rainy delta are on mounds which the people have built; that is, on heaps of earth higher than the fields. If the houses were on land as low as the fields, they would be flooded with water in the rainy season.

Even in the cold season, when there is the least rain, the delta is a watery land. There are many more streams than roads, and the people go about a great deal of the time in boats. In the rainy season, when the fields are flooded, the mounds with the houses on them are turned into islands. Then, for most of the people, boats are the only way of getting about.

Reading the Map

You have learned that there are parts of India which are very different from the delta of Bengal. By reading the map on this page you can find out for yourself what some of these differences are.

1. Point out the Himalaya Mountains. They are on the northern boundary of India, and they are the highest mountains in the world.

2. Are these mountains in the warm belt of the earth, or in the north temperate belt?

3. Point out some tributaries to the Ganges River which rise in the Himalaya Mountains.

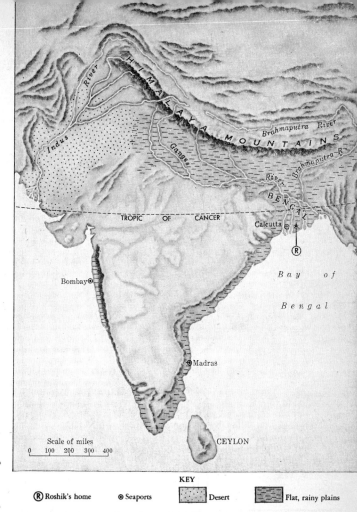

A map of India.

4. What does the map tell you about the land through which the Ganges and its tributaries flow? (Use the key to find out.)

5. What is the name of the bay into which the mouths of the Ganges empty?

6. Find another river farther west which also rises in the Himalaya Mountains. What is its name?

7. Through what kind of land does this river flow on its way to the sea?

8. The three largest cities of India are named on the map. How can you tell that these cities are seaports?

9. Which one of the three cities is in the delta of Bengal?

10. Suppose you were going to travel in an airplane in a straight line from Calcutta to Madras. Use the scale of miles to tell about how far you would fly on that trip

When there are no guests, Roshik's family have their meals in the living-room hut.

SEEING ROSHIK'S HOME

Lunching with Roshik's Family

Let us imagine that we have traveled across the great flat plain of Bengal to Roshik's home. We have chosen the cold season for our visit. Can you explain why?

We have reached Roshik's home just in time for lunch. The boys will have lunch with Roshik and his father. The girls will wait until the boys have finished. Then they will have their lunch with Moti and her mother. In Bengal the boys and girls do not eat their meals together.

We shall have lunch in a hut that Roshik's family use only when they have guests. It is a small, one-room hut with no furniture. Roshik's mother has spread a clean cotton sheet on the floor for us to sit on as we eat our meal.

First Moti and her mother bring us boiled rice and a thick soup of peas and beans. After that we have some vegetables and fish cooked with yellow curry powder. Curry powder is a seasoning, and Roshik and Moti are very fond of it. We do not like it so well as they do, for it burns our tongues like red pepper.

Roshik's family have rice at every meal, and they eat fish and vegetables at least once a day. They grow the rice and the vegetables themselves. They catch the fish, too. Roshik often goes fishing with his father.

The Five Little Huts

After lunch you will have a chance to see more of Roshik's home. It is a five-room home, but each room is a hut by itself. The huts are built round an open yard on a flat-topped mound of earth. The mound makes a safe place for the huts in the rainy season, when the lower land around it is often under water.

One hut is the guest room, where Roshik and Moti have entertained us at lunch. Another is the kitchen, where their mother cooks the meals. There is a mud-brick fireplace in the kitchen, but nothing else except some brass pots and pans for cooking and some large pottery jars. The jars are for storing food and carrying water. On one side of the kitchen hut is a porch, where Moti and her mother do much of their housework.

130

Roshik's father is making some of the bamboo matting used for the walls of the huts.

Two of the huts are bedrooms. Here there are low beds, but no other furniture. The beds must be hard, for they are made of wooden planks, and the mattresses are nothing but mats woven of grass. Hanging from the roof are some shelves. On these Roshik's mother keeps the cotton clothes that her family wear and the sheets that they use for bedding and floor coverings.

The fifth hut is the living room and dining room all in one. Here Roshik's family have their meals when they have no guests, and here they sit when the rain drives them indoors. This little hut has no furniture, but along the walls there are rows of brass plates, jars, and bowls, and some chests for storing food.

The living-room hut has a small front porch, and here you will see the fishing poles and nets that Roshik's father uses, and the paddles for

his boat. The porch is more like an outdoor storeroom than anything else.

There are two other huts, a little apart from the five that the family use. One is a shed for the pair of bullocks that Roshik's father uses in his farm work. The other hut is round, and it is a storehouse for the rice that Roshik's father grows.

How the Huts Are Built

You can see from the pictures how the huts are built. For the frames the Bengalis use slender bamboo trunks, and for the walls they use matting. They have two ways of making the matting. One way is weaving, and for this they use the stems of a tall, tough kind of grass. The other way is by tying strips of split bamboo to bamboo rods used as crosspieces.

Whichever way the matting is made, it is so firm and tight that the walls are rainproof. In the rainy season they become very damp, but they do not let the rain through. Roshik will tell you that the matting makes good walls for another reason too. It lets more air into the huts than other kinds of building material do. Houses that are rainproof and as cool as possible are what Roshik's people need.

As you would expect in such a rainy land, the roofs are steep. Except for the kitchen hut, the roofs are thatched with layers of rice straw. If the thatch of straw is put on well and kept in good repair, it never lets any rain through.

The kitchen roof is made of corrugated iron; that is, sheets of iron bent into wavy grooves and ridges. Perhaps you can guess why. If the kitchen roof were thatched, it would not be safe in the cold season, when the straw dries out. A spark when Roshik's mother was cooking might easily set it afire.

The iron roof, though, is much hotter than the thatched roofs. This is one reason why Roshik's family do not use iron for the roofs of the other huts. Another reason is that they have to buy the iron. The rice straw for thatch comes from their own fields.

The floors of the huts are made of earth beaten down until it is hard and flat. Then they are painted with a thin coating of mud mixed with water. This strange kind of paint dries quickly and gives the floors a smooth, hard surface. Whenever it begins to rub off, Roshik's father puts on another coating.

---

4   *A glimpse of the orchard and the pond.*

The Garden, the Orchard, and the Pond

Back of the huts on one side of the yard is the vegetable garden. Here Roshik's family grow beans, peas, and other vegetables. They plant them every month or two, so that they are never without them. Each morning Moti and her mother gather enough vegetables of one kind or another for the day's meals.

In another place near the huts is an orchard. You will see some banana trees there, but most of the fruits will be strange to you. Perhaps you will like best the sweet, juicy mangoes from the mango trees, or the big golden-yellow papayas from the papaya trees.

As you walk about this little Bengali home, you will find that Roshik's family have a pond. A little stream flows out of the pond to the lower land beyond, but the ground is so full of water that the pond never dries up. As water flows out, more comes in from the ground. This changing of the water keeps the pond fresh and clean.

133

The pond is very useful to Roshik's family. They take their baths in it, and they wash the dishes and the clothes in it. Moti and her mother have a great deal of washing to do because all the family wear white cotton clothes, and because cotton sheets are used for bedding and for floor coverings at meal times.

Roshik's family do not take their drinking water from the pond. They get it from a well which they share with neighboring families. The neighboring homes are much the same as their own. Each one is a group of little huts on a mound above the surrounding fields, and each one has a garden, an orchard, and a pond.

Some Food and Clothing Questions

You have been with Roshik and Moti long enough to know what they eat and what they wear. Can you answer these questions?

1. Where does the rice that they eat come from?

2. Where are the vegetables grown?

3. Who catches the fish that Roshik and Moti eat?

4. What are some of the fruits that they eat, and where do they get them?

5. Why do you suppose Roshik's mother didn't give you a glass of milk with your luncheon?

6. Of what material are Roshik's and Moti's clothes made?

7. Is this a cool or a warm material?

8. Why is it a good clothing material for children of the delta of Bengal?

Helping Friends to Understand

Here are some things that some of your other friends in far-away lands want to know about houses in Roshik's land. Can you answer their questions?

1. *Pedro:* Why do Roshik's people use matting for house walls? The cold wind must blow right through it.

2. *Abdul:* There is always plenty of mud in a delta. Why don't Roshik's people have mud-brick houses?

3. *Suvan:* Why do they put such steep roofs on their houses? I don't see any use in that.

4. *Netsook:* I don't know what the roofs are covered with. What is it? Does it keep the houses warm?

Another Question

If you have friends at home who live on farms, perhaps this is the question that they will want answered: Why are the homes in Roshik's land built on mounds of earth above the fields where crops are grown?

134

Moti and her mother use the pond as a laundry for washing the sheets and clothes.

On plowing days Roshik takes his father's breakfast to him in the fields.

THE HOT SEASON AND THE RAINY SEASON

Plowing and Planting

The hot season in the delta plain begins in March. Day by day the sun climbs higher in the sky. Week by week the weather grows hotter and hotter. There are showers now and then, but the heavy rains do not begin until about the middle of June.

The hot season is the time when Roshik's father plows the fields for his crops. He gets up at sunrise and goes off to the fields with his plow and his bullocks. His plow is much like the one that Abdul's father uses. It is a clumsy tool, not nearly so good as the plows that farmers in our country use, and Roshik's father must go over the fields with it again and again to make the soil ready for planting.

Roshik's father does not plow every day. He chooses the days after there has been some rain. Then, as the plow turns over the soil, the moisture sinks in. For the crops that Roshik's father grows, the soil must be well broken up and very damp before the seeds can safely be planted.

On plowing days Roshik takes his father's breakfast to him in the fields. He goes out about nine o'clock with some boiled rice for his father to eat. By that time his father is hot, tired, and hungry, and he is glad of a little rest. The bullocks need a rest, too.

By noon it is too hot to work any longer. Roshik's father goes home, and he and Roshik bathe in the pond before lunch. The water is rather warm, but it is cooler than the air, and how good it does feel! Roshik bathes in the pond every day in the year to keep clean, but he likes his baths in the hot season best.

After lunch the whole family sleeps or rests for two or three hours. This is the hottest part of the day, too hot for any kind of work. Even the children want to keep quiet, and they often take long naps.

In the late afternoon, when the air is a little cooler again, Roshik's father often goes back to the fields. He plows until sunset. Then he comes home and takes another cooling bath in the pond before supper.

Roshik's father plants two crops in his fields: rice and jute. Jute is a plant which is grown for the long fibers in the stems. Jute fiber is used for making rope, twine, and very coarse kinds of cloth. Have you ever seen the coarse brown cloth called burlap? Burlap is one of the kinds of cloth made from jute.

Roshik's father plants his jute about the middle of the hot season, and his rice toward the end. He grows rice chiefly for food for his family. He grows jute for the same reason that Abdul's father grows cotton. He sells the fiber, and in this way he earns money.

When the Rains "Burst"

In June, usually about the middle of the month, the rainy season begins. The first rains come so suddenly that people say that the rainy season "bursts." Thick black clouds gather quickly, and such heavy rain pours down that it does seem as if the clouds had burst. After they have spilled their rain, the sky clears, but it doesn't stay clear very long. Soon more clouds gather, and down comes more rain.

As soon as the rainy season begins, the fields become very muddy. Then, when the ground can hold no more moisture, the water begins to rise in the fields. You might think it would drown the rice and the jute which have been planted, but it doesn't. They need watery fields, and they grow so fast that they keep their heads above the rising water.

You wouldn't like the weather in the rainy season, especially if you do not like thunder and lightning, but you would enjoy seeing the fields. When the sun comes out, the water sparkles and the green blades of the rice and jute wave gently in the breeze. From the people's homes on the mounds the fields look like a bluish-green sea. And from boats on the swollen creeks and streams the mounds with their trees and huts look like islands.

The Best Fishing Season

After the rainy season begins there is no more farm work to be done until late July or early August, when the jute will be ready to be harvested. Now Roshik's father and the other farmers have plenty of time to go fishing. Roshik loves to go fishing with his father.

In deep water Roshik and his father fish with poles and lines. In shallow water they often wade in and scoop up the fish in baskets shaped like umbrella tops. Often they put traps or a net in a stream in the morning and go out in the evening and collect the fish that have been caught.

Roshik's father makes his fish poles out of bamboo. He weaves his fishing nets of coarse grass that grows along the streams, and makes his traps and baskets of straw and bamboo. He catches fish at all times of year in the waters near his home. But the best fishing is

136

Two Bengali ways of fishing: Roshik with a basket, and his father with a net.

To harvest the jute, the men wade into the water and cut the stems with sharp knives.

in the rainy season, when there is water almost everywhere. You can understand now why Roshik's family have so much fish to eat.

When the jute is ready to be harvested, there will be several weeks when Roshik and the other boys will have to do the fishing without their fathers. The nets are too heavy for Roshik to handle alone, but he is clever at scooping up fish in shallow water, and he knows how to set traps and take the fish out of them. So, although Roshik's father will be busy in the jute fields, the family will still have fish as often as they want it. Roshik is proud to be the fisherman for his family.

Harvesting the Jute

Harvesting the jute is wet work, for it is done before the rainy season ends. Roshik's father and the other men wade into the fields and cut the stems of the plants with sharp knives. Often they work in water above their waists.

After the jute has been cut, the farmers tie the stems in bundles and soak them in the

water for about three weeks. This loosens the fiber so that it can be pulled from the stems easily. After the fiber has been dried in the sun, it is ready to be sold. It takes Roshik's father about six weeks to harvest his jute, remove the fiber from the stems, and dry it.

Perhaps you know that crops which are grown for sale are called "money crops." Jute is a special money crop for Roshik's father just as cotton is for Abdul's father.

Roshik's father takes his jute in his boat to a market town a few miles from his home. There he sells it to a jute merchant. He always hopes to get a good price for it, because this is almost the only way he has of earning money.

What do you suppose becomes of the jute after Roshik's father sells it? It may go to a mill in the great city of Calcutta. In the mill, machines spin it into coarse yarn and weave it into burlap. Or, the jute may be put in a ship at Calcutta, for Calcutta is a seaport. The ship will carry it to some country like our own, where there are many mills that need jute. Nearly all the jute used in the world is grown in the hot, rainy delta in Bengal where Roshik's people live.

The fibers of the jute are pulled from the stems and then dried in the sun.

A Missing-Word Test

Give the right words to fill the blanks in these sentences.

1. The crops that Roshik's father grows in his fields are ____ and ____.

2. He plows the land in the ___ season.

3. He plants the seeds before the _____ season begins.

4. The crops grow fast because after they are planted the weather is so ___ and _____.

5. The jute is ready to be harvested before the _____ season ends.

6. Because of this, the men have to work in the _____ to cut the jute.

About Money Crops

1. What is meant by a money crop?
2. What is Roshik's father's money crop?

3. What is Abdul's father's chief money crop from his farm in the Nile Valley?

4. Do you live on a farm, or in a part of our country where many people are farmers? If you do, name some of the money crops that the farmers in your neighborhood raise.

5. Can you think of reasons why Simba's people in the Congo Basin and Pedro's people in the altiplano do not raise money crops?

About Fishing

Read these sentences and finish each of them in your own words.

1. Roshik's people eat a great deal of fish because ___

2. Some of the ways in which they catch fish are ___

3. Even when their father hasn't time for fishing, Roshik and Moti have fish to eat because ___

WORK AND PLAY IN THE COLD SEASON

The Rice Harvest

Perhaps you know that rice is a very thirsty plant. It needs so much water while it is growing that in many countries the farmers have to find special ways of flooding the rice fields. But in Bengal there is no need for such work. The heavy rains in the rainy season flood the fields and give the plants all the water they need.

The seeds begin to form on the stalks toward the end of the rainy season, but they do not finish ripening until after the rains are over and the cold season brings sunnier weather. The rainy season ends about the middle of October, and the rice is harvested in November. By this time the water has drained off the fields and the ground is fairly dry.

Roshik's father harvests his rice by hand with a knife. The stalks have grown so tall that he cuts off only the tops, where the seeds grow. Each day he carries home bundles of the stalk-tops. When he has gathered all the rice, he begins his threshing.

Roshik's father spreads the stalk-tops on the ground in the yard. Then he and Roshik take turns driving the bullocks round and

Roshik's father cuts off the rice tops.

138

Outside the kitchen hut Moti and her mother are husking rice with their dekki.

round over them. As the bullocks' hoofs crush the stalks, the seeds fall off. The threshing leaves the stalk-tops bare, and Roshik's father stores them away for feed for the bullocks.

Work for Moti and Her Mother

Moti and her mother sweep up the rice seeds and put them in big round baskets. The first thing they must do is to get rid of the dust and the bits of straw that are mixed with the seeds. This work is called winnowing.

Moti is as clever at winnowing as her mother. She puts a few handfuls of rice seeds in a light tray made of matting. Then she tosses the rice in the air, and as it comes down she catches it in the tray again. While the rice is in the air, the bits of dust and straw are blown away by the wind because they are lighter than the seeds. Moti keeps tossing the rice and catching it until it is well cleaned.

The winnowing takes a long time, and for weeks Moti and her mother spend many an hour at work with their trays. When at last the winnowing is finished, the storehouse is well filled with clean rice. There is enough to supply the family for a year, and perhaps more.

Each little rice seed has a covering called a husk. Before Moti's mother cooks the rice, she pounds the seeds to get the husks off. Husking rice is part of her daily work.

The picture shows how the husking is done. Outside the kitchen hut you see the big wooden bowl and the *dekki* that are used to husk the rice. Moti's mother has put rice seeds in the bowl, and now she is working the dekki.

The dekki works like a seesaw. When Moti's mother takes her foot off the short end, the log at the other end drops down and pounds the rice in the bowl. When she presses on the short end, the log comes up again. Moti keeps turning the bowl as her mother works the dekki.

When the husking is finished, Moti will winnow the rice. The wind will blow the husks away, and the rice will then be ready for cooking.

A Crop with Many Uses

As you know, Roshik's father grows rice principally for food for his family. Like all Bengalis, they eat more rice than anything else. Every year Roshik's father plants enough rice to make sure of a year's supply for his family. In some years the rice grows better than in others, and when this happens, he sells what he does not need. So, in some years, the rice is partly a money crop.

Rice is easy to grow in this warm, rainy land. The hardest work for Roshik's father is the plowing. After the crop is planted, the rain and the sunshine do the rest. The rains flood the fields, and the sun ripens the new seeds that form on the stalks. Then all Roshik's father has to do is to gather the harvest. After cutting jute in mud and water, cutting rice in a dry field seems very easy work.

The seeds, of course, are the most important

Moti is as clever at winnowing as her mother.

part of the rice harvest, but the straw is useful, too. After Roshik's father has finished threshing, he goes back to the fields and cuts the rice straw that he left standing when he cut off the tops. He brings it all home and stores it away carefully.

You will remember that the roofs of all the huts but one are thatched with rice straw. So, you see, each year's rice harvest supplies Roshik's father with material for mending the roofs and keeping them rainproof. The straw makes good baskets too, and good traps for catching fish.

But only a small part of the rice straw is used in these ways. Most of it is fed to the bullocks. This is a great help, especially in the long months of the rainy season. At that time of year other feed for the animals is scarce because most of the grass is under water. If it were not for the rice straw, the bullocks would go hungry.

Roshik's father's jute crop is important because it earns money for him. But his rice crop is much more important. He can get along with very little money, but he cannot get along without food for his family and without feed for his bullocks.

Holiday Time

All through the hot season and the rainy season Roshik and Moti look forward to the cold season. This, you will remember, is not really a cold season, but just cooler than the other seasons. A better name for it would be the dry season, for it is a period of clear weather with very little rain.

Roshik and Moti know that after the rice has been harvested and put away in the storehouse their father will not be busy until the time for plowing comes round again. They will tell you that nearly every year their father takes the whole family on a trip in a boat for a week or two in the cold season.

The boating trip on the streams of the great delta will be a happy holiday.

Roshik's father hasn't a big enough boat for the trip, and so he hires one. Roshik and his father push it along with poles where the water is shallow and with paddles where the water is deeper. They can go almost anywhere they like with it because there are so many streams in the delta.

Roshik's mother packs up rice and vegetables for the trip, and his father takes his fishing poles and lines. Roshik and his father fish as they go along, and Moti and her mother cook the meals on the boat.

What fun they have! The trip is like one long picnic. At night they stop wherever they happen to be and tie the boat to a tree on the river bank. Moti and her mother sleep under the rounded roof of matting at one end of the boat. Roshik sleeps outside with his father.

Now and then they stop somewhere to call on friends, and while the grown-ups talk, the children play. But most of the time they drift along the streams, fishing and enjoying the air that seems so cool. Roshik and Moti think the boat trip is a wonderful holiday. Don't you think so, too?

Something to Do if You Are a Girl

If you want rice to eat, all your mother has to do is to buy a package of rice at the grocery store and cook it. Perhaps she would be surprised to know what Moti and her mother have to do before they can cook rice. Write your mother a letter about winnowing and the dekki, and draw some pictures to go with it.

Something to Do if You Are a Boy

Write your mother a letter telling her what Roshik's father has to do so that his family can have rice to eat, and how Roshik helps him. Draw some pictures to go with your letter.

Some Rice Questions

1. Why do you suppose it is that rice is Roshik's father's grain crop instead of wheat? There are some "weather reasons" for this.

2. Why doesn't Roshik's father have to find some way of flooding his rice field?

3. What is his principal reason for growing rice?

4. How else does the rice crop help Roshik's family?

141

BENGALI BOYS AND GIRLS

The Boys and Their Fathers

If you should stay long with Roshik and Moti, you would find that Bengali boys and girls do not play together. The boys spend most of their time with their fathers, and when they play, they play with other boys. Even in one family, the boys and girls do not play together very much.

Most of the children who live in towns go to school for part of the year. But the Bengali children who live on farms, as Roshik and Moti do, haven't much chance to go to school. None of the girls go, and only a very few of the boys. Roshik has never been to school.

As soon as the boys are big enough, they begin to help their fathers in the fields. They learn first how to harvest rice, and, when they are older, how to plow and to harvest jute. Their fathers take them fishing when they are very small, and long before they are grown up they are good fishermen.

Part of the work of the boys is to take the bullocks out to feed on the grass that grows along the banks of the streams. The boys often play games while the bullocks are feeding. But they must not forget about the bullocks, because if they do, the animals may get into the fields and eat some of the crops. If this happens, the boys are sure to be punished.

What Roshik and the other boys like best is going to market with their fathers. There are many little market towns scattered over the great delta, and most of the farming families live within easy walking distance of at least one or two.

Roshik's father always goes to market once a week even when he is busiest with his farm work. When he isn't very busy, he usually goes every other day. Nearly always he takes Roshik with him. Sometimes they walk and sometimes they go in their boat.

You might think from this that Roshik's father has a great deal of trading to do, but he hasn't. He never has much money to spend, and except for cotton cloth there is not much that he needs to buy. If you think over how Roshik's family live, you will see that they make or get for themselves most of the things that they need and use.

Roshik's father goes to market mostly to meet his friends and talk with them. Now and then he buys something, but not often. Going to market is just a habit that he and the other farmers have. They like to talk about their crops and exchange news of their families.

Roshik likes going to market because he sees so many other boys there. While their fathers talk, the boys play games and have a fine time. Sometimes their fathers give them small coins to buy candy.

The Girls and Their Mothers

The girls never go to market. They stay at home and help their mothers. Moti has never been away from home except on the boat trips in the cold season. She has never played with any boy except her brother.

Moti cannot remember when she first began to help her mother with the daily work. She is big enough now to help with the cooking and the cleaning and washing. And, as you know, she helps to winnow and husk the rice. She is learning all the things she will need to know when she grows up and has a home and family of her own.

Every day Moti and her mother go to the well where the families of the neighborhood get their drinking water. Her mother carries a large pottery jar, and Moti carries a smaller one. They fill the jars at the well and bring them home balanced on their heads just as Zakia and her mother do in Egypt.

Often there are other girls and their mothers at the well. The mothers like to talk together just as the fathers do at market. This gives the girls a chance to play games and have fun together.

Perhaps you think that Bengali girls have to work so much that they don't have a very good time. They do work harder than the boys because they help in the kinds of work that must be done every day in the year. But they have dolls and other toys that their fathers and mothers make for them, and in spite of all the work they do, they have time for play.

When you think of Roshik and Moti you will like to remember that there are millions of children in the great delta of Bengal who live as they do. Their way of living may seem strange to you, but they are comfortable in their little homes and they have as good a time in their way as you do in yours.

A Summary

Read these sentences and finish each in your own words.

1. The delta of Bengal is a very warm land because _ _ _

2. It is a very watery land because _ _ _

The boys take the bullocks out to feed on the grass that grows along the streams.

The girls and their mothers go each day to the well to get drinking water.

---

3. It is a land that would seem strange to Netsook and Klaya because _ _ _

4. It is a land that would seem strange to Abdul and Zakia because _ _ _

5. It is a good land in which to raise rice and jute because _ _ _

6. It is a land where fishing is good because _ _ _

7. It is a land where cotton is the best clothing material for the people because _ _ _

8. It is a land where houses need steep roofs because _ _ _

A Comparison

1. March is the month when the hot season begins in Bengal. What season in our country begins in that month?

2. The rainy season in Bengal begins about the middle of June. What season in our country begins in that month?

3. The cold season in Bengal lasts from about the middle of October until about the middle of March. What seasons do we have during those months?

4. What would be a better name for the cold season in Bengal? Why?

143

Sumai and Lota in China

Sumai is picking leaves for the silkworms from a mulberry tree.

THE LAND WHERE SILK-MAKING BEGAN

A Little Girl Who Feeds Silkworms

The little Chinese girl in this picture is named Chu Sumai, and she has a brother named Chu Lota. Chu is their family name. In our country they would be called Sumai Chu and Lota Chu, but Chinese names are written the other way round, with the family name first.

Sumai and Lota live with their father and mother, their uncle, and the grandfather and grandmother who are their father's parents. When their uncle marries, he will bring his wife home to live with the family. In China most families stay together in this way.

Sumai is picking leaves from a mulberry tree. Her father has a small grove of mulberry trees, and he takes good care of them. Sumai is picking the leaves to feed the silkworms

which her mother and grandmother are raising. Silkworms give us the fibers which are used for spinning silk thread and weaving silk cloth.

Silkworm eggs are hardly bigger than pin points, and so the baby worms that hatch from them are tiny things. But if the worms have plenty to eat they grow fast. Fresh mulberry leaves are the best food for them, and the worms have such big appetites that they must be fed every few hours.

The silkworms are kept on shelves and trays in Sumai's house and cared for night and day. How they do eat! For about six weeks Sumai and her mother and grandmother keep picking mulberry leaves and spreading them on the trays to feed the worms.

When the worms have grown to be about three and a half inches long they stop eating

144

and begin to wind themselves up in cocoons. Perhaps you have seen other kinds of cocoons. They are the little cases that caterpillars, which later turn into moths or butterflies, wind round themselves. The silkworm is really a kind of caterpillar.

The silkworm makes its cocoon of a thread-like fiber that comes out of its head — a fiber almost as fine as a thread in a cobweb. The worm wraps itself round and round with the fiber until it is hidden away in the cocoon.

What do you suppose Sumai's family do with the cocoons? They sell them to a buyer for a factory. In the factory the cocoons are unwound and the fibers are twisted to make what we call raw silk. Much raw silk is needed in countries like our own, where many kinds of silk goods are made.

China, like Egypt, is a very old country, and the Chinese have been raising silkworms for thousands of years. They were the first people in the world to use the fine fibers from silkworm cocoons to spin silk thread and weave silk cloth.

Sumai can tell you a story of the beginning of silk-making. It is about a little Chinese princess of long, long ago. Her father was the ruler of China, and her mother was called the Lady of Si-Ling. One day the little princess happened to see some strange worms spinning their cocoons in her father's garden. She told her mother about them.

A silkworm about full grown.

When the Lady of Si-Ling saw the cocoons and unwound one of them, she knew that the little princess had made a wonderful discovery. She had found a fiber which would make lovelier cloth than anyone had ever seen. And so the Lady of Si-Ling was the first person ever to spin thread of silkworm fiber and to weave silk cloth.

This is the kind of story which we call a legend, because it is so old that we do not know whether it is true or not. But we do know that silk-making began in China, and that the Lady of Si-Ling had something to do with it.

Sumai hopes the story is true. She likes to think that it was a little girl who first discovered silkworms making their cocoons.

145

The leaves for the silkworms to eat are spread on shelves and trays in the house.

Discovering Things about China

China is a very large country, one of the largest in the world. If you should travel all over it, you would see mountains in some places, plateaus in others, and plains in still others. You would find parts of this great country so dry that they are deserts, and other parts with just enough rain to make them grassy steppes. You would find still other parts where there is plenty of rain and the land is green with crops.

If you are looking for the parts of China where most of the people live, you will go to the plains which have plenty of rain. There you will find millions of Chinese who are farmers. In one of these well-watered plains you will find Sumai and Lota.

Here are some questions which will help you to discover more about China. Answer them by studying the picture of the globe on page 68.

1. In what continent is China?
2. What ocean does China border?
3. In what belt of the earth is the part of China where Sumai and Lota live?

If you have read what the globe can tell you, you know that China is in the eastern part of Asia, and that it borders the Pacific Ocean. You know, too, that the part of China where Sumai and Lota live is in the north temperate belt of the earth.

Six thousand miles away, across the Pacific Ocean from China, is our own United States. China stretches about as far north as our country does, and a little farther south. The part farthest south is just within the warm belt of the earth.

Sumai and Lota do not live in the warmest part of China in the south, nor in the coldest part in the north. Their home is in central China, about halfway between the north and the south. The summers are hot there, but the winters are rather cold. Often there is a thin coating of ice on the rivers and ponds, and sometimes there is snow. But the winters are not nearly so cold as they are in the Kirghiz Steppe, where Suvan and Nara live.

A Good Land for Farming

You know, of course, that there are twelve months in the year. Where Sumai and Lota live there are only three months of really cold weather: December, January, and February. There are frosts in the late autumn and early spring, but they are not often bad enough to harm crops.

We have a special name for the part of the year that is not too cold for the growth of crops. We call it the *growing season*. How many months long is the growing season in the part of China where Sumai and Lota live?

You can easily understand why farmers like a long growing season. It means that they can raise many different kinds of crops: those that grow slowly as well as those that grow more quickly. Often, too, it means that a farmer can use the same piece of land twice during the year. He can get one crop from it and then another before the growing season is over.

The long growing season is one reason why the part of China where Sumai and Lota live is good for farming. You already know of two other reasons. The land is a plain, level enough to make farming easy, and it has plenty of rain to water the crops. A fourth reason is that the soil is fertile. This means that in the soil there are the kinds of plant food that crops need in order to grow well.

Here is a list of the helps to farming in this part of China:

1. A plain with much level land.
2. Plenty of rain.
3. A long growing season.
4. Fertile soils.

These helps to farming are worth remembering, and they are easy to remember if you understand them.

146

Everywhere on the rivers and canals in central China you will see junks and sampans.

Proving That You Understand

Here are some questions for you to talk over in class. By thinking out the answers you can prove that you really understand why the part of China where Sumai and Lota live is good for farming.

1. Why is it easier to raise crops in level plains than in rough, mountainous lands?

2. Why is it helpful to farmers to have plenty of rain?

3. In some lands, such as the Nile Valley, crops are grown without the help of rain. How can this be done?

4. Why is it helpful to farmers to have a long growing season?

5. Why do farmers want fertile soil?

Up the Yangtze River

To visit Sumai and Lota you must first cross the Pacific Ocean in a ship or an airplane. If you go by sea, the crossing will take you about three weeks. If you fly, it will take you only about five days. You may choose whichever way of traveling you think you will like better.

Try to imagine that you have made this long trip across the Pacific Ocean. You are now in Shanghai, a seaport on the coast of China. Shanghai is near the mouth of a great river called the Yangtze. Sumai and Lota live far inland in the valley of the Yangtze River.

From Shanghai you will travel inland about a thousand miles on a steamer that carries passengers up and down the Yangtze. You cannot go by train because the railroad runs inland from Shanghai for only about two hundred miles. You might go by automobile, but the road would be rough much of the way. You will be much more comfortable on the boat.

The Chinese have not built railroads and automobile roads all over their great country as we have. There are a few railroads and paved highways, but not many for such a big country. In central China people travel mostly on the rivers and canals. The canals have been dug to connect the rivers, and together they make miles and miles of waterways for boats.

The Yangtze is a long, winding river with many tributaries. *Yang* in Chinese means "blue," but this isn't a very good name for the river because it is so muddy that it looks yellowish-brown. Sometimes, after heavy rains, the Yangtze overflows its banks and floods the countryside. A bad flood is a terrible thing. It destroys crops and sweeps away homes, and often many people are drowned.

Your trip on the Yangtze will be slow, but there will be many interesting things to see. You will pass so many other boats that you will soon see for yourself how much the Chinese use the waterways of their country.

There are steamers and motorboats on the river, but there are many more junks and sampans. The junks have straw sails, and they carry all kinds of goods.

These Chinese children are not off on a holiday boating trip; the sampan is their home.

The sampans are smaller boats, and they too carry goods from place to place. Often the man who owns the sampan has no other home for his family. As you pass these little floating homes, you will see the children playing on the decks. The little children are tied like dogs on ropes to keep them from falling overboard.

You will see men fishing from sampans and other kinds of boats. Some are using poles and lines; others are using big nets. They may be fishing to get food for their families. Or they may be men who fish for their living and sell what they catch in the towns and villages along the river.

You will not have to travel far up the Yangtze to know that most of the people in its valley are farmers. The farming land begins just outside Shanghai. A flat plain stretches away from both banks of the river as far as you can see. Scattered over it are many small villages. Except where there are roads, foot-paths, or waterways, all the land between the villages is divided into small fields for crops.

It is springtime, and the farmers are plowing. Each one is guiding a wooden plow drawn by a big, strong animal called a water buffalo. The men and the buffaloes are working ankle-deep in mud and water. These are fields where rice will be planted later on.

Farther on, the plain is narrower, and there are hills near the river. The bushes growing in rows on the hillsides are tea plants. Perhaps you know that the Chinese are great tea-drinkers. They all drink tea at every meal. All over central and southern China tea bushes are grown for their leaves. It is the leaves, dried in a special way, that are steeped, or soaked, in boiling water to make tea.

Now your boat is passing through another broad part of the Yangtze Valley. This part is called the Yangtze Plain. The land is mostly level, but you can see low hills here and there. At a town near the inner margin of this plain you will leave the steamer. A motorboat will take you on a canal to the village where Sumai and Lota live.

148

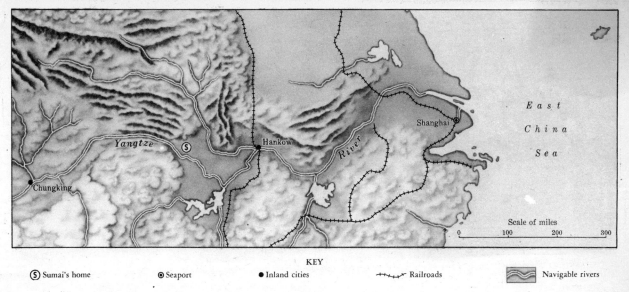

KEY

(S) Sumai's home   ◉ Seaport   ● Inland cities   ⊢⊣⊣⊣ Railroads   〰〰 Navigable rivers

A map of the central part of China, where Sumai and Lota live.

✓ Reading the Map

The map on this page shows the part of China where Sumai and Lota live. It gives you a chance to prove that you are getting to be a good map-reader. Don't forget that the key to the map is there to help you.

1. Find Shanghai on the map. How should you know that Shanghai is a seaport if you hadn't already been told?

2. Trace your route up the Yangtze River from Shanghai to Sumai's home.

3. Notice that the Yangtze River is shown by a double line like this: 〰〰 What does the double line mean?

4. *Navigable* is a new word to you. A navigable river is one which can be used by good-sized boats. Point out some navigable tributaries of the Yangtze.

5. Prove by the map that you cannot travel from Shanghai to Sumai's home in a railroad train.

6. You might make the trip in an airplane. About how many miles should you fly? To find this out you must use the scale of miles to measure the distance in a straight line from Shanghai to Sumai's home.

Something to Do

Draw some pictures to show what you saw on your trip up the Yangtze River.

This is the kind of net used by many Chinese who earn their living by fishing.

149

A VILLAGE OF FARMING FAMILIES

The Village and the Farm Land

As your motorboat chug-chugs along the canal, you pass several small villages. Then you come to a place where the canal joins a stream. Here there is a larger village. This is the one where Sumai and Lota live.

The picture on page 150 shows that the houses are built round the meeting place of the canal and the stream. The three hump-backed bridges make it easy for the people to get from one part of the village to another. All the land round the village is used for farming.

There are about fifty families in the village, each one living in its own house. Nearly all the villagers are farmers. Among the few men who are not farmers are the barber, the shoe-maker, and the shopkeepers.

Why do you suppose the families live crowded together in the village, instead of having their houses on their farms?

It is because farming began long, long ago in China, and for hundreds of years there were robbers and bandits about. In those days people were afraid to live in scattered farmhouses. They felt much safer living together in villages. This habit, begun so long ago, has never been broken.

You will be surprised when you see how small the farms are. The man who has the largest one has only five acres of land, and most of the farms are only about half as large as that.

Have you any idea how much an acre of land is? If you haven't, measure off a distance of 200 feet somewhere out of doors. Imagine a square with sides as long as that, and you will know about how large an acre is. Five acres of land make a tiny farm in our country, but in China they make a good-sized one.

There are no empty spaces beyond the fields that belong to the village where Sumai and Lota live. The farm lands of their village join the farm lands of the neighboring villages. The countryside is one great stretch of crop land divided into tiny fields and dotted with villages. Here and there, within easy reach of every ten or twenty villages, is a larger market town.

It will not take you long to see Sumai's village. Perhaps you will like to go into the little shops and see what is sold there. The shops are near the bridges, where all the people can get to them easily.

One shop is a grocery. The grocer sells salt, sugar, tea, and a few other things that the villagers do not get from their own farms. He doesn't sell canned vegetables, fruits, and meats as our grocers do. Such foods cost too much for the villagers to buy them.

The second shop is the kind we call a dry-goods store. The man who owns it sells the cotton cloth which the villagers use for making clothes. Most of the cloth is either blue or white. The shopkeeper sells thread, needles, and buttons too, and the broad-brimmed straw hats that the farmers often wear in hot weather.

The third shop is the one that Sumai and Lota like best. It is the shop where candy, nuts, and tobacco are sold. These are things the villagers like but do not really need. When they have a little extra money, the men buy tobacco and the women and children buy nuts and candy.

The shoemaker and the barber have their shops side by side. The shoemaker makes cloth slippers and straw sandals. He doesn't make leather shoes because the villagers cannot afford to buy them.

The barber shop is closed this afternoon because nearly all the men are at work in the fields, and the barber hasn't any customers. He is sitting on the bridge near his shop, fishing. The barber likes fishing, and his family will be glad if he catches a few fish for supper.

Sumai and Lota are crossing the hump-backed bridge where the barber is fishing.

Sumai and Lota at Home

Two children are crossing the bridge where the barber is fishing. They are Sumai and Lota, and they have come to meet you and take you home. The picture shows how they are dressed. They wear cotton clothes the year round, but in the winter their mother puts thick linings of cotton batting in their coats and trousers to keep them warm.

You will like these Chinese friends because they are full of fun. They will want you to play games with them, and Lota will let you fly his kite. Kiteflying is a favorite sport with Chinese children.

Sumai and Lota live on the edge of the village, and their home is inside a brick wall. They will let you in through a gate and lead you through a tiny vegetable garden into the courtyard. This is a piece of open ground, and

the house is built round three sides of it. On the fourth side is a long shed.

You can see from the picture that the house is one story high. It is built of brick, and the roof is covered with tiles. The house is divided into small rooms opening into each other. The middle room is the living room, and it has a door opening into the courtyard. The two corner rooms are kitchens, one for each side of the house.

In the left side of the house are the bedrooms for Sumai and Lota and their parents. In the right side are the bedrooms of their grandparents and Uncle Lu. The rooms of the grandparents are the largest. The Chinese are very good to the old people in their families, and always give them the best of what they have.

If you go into any of the sleeping rooms, you will think: "What strange beds! How hard

152

The house is built round three sides of the courtyard, inside a brick wall.

and cold they must be!" The beds are wide brick platforms about two feet above the floor. There are straw mats for mattresses, and cotton quilts for coverlets.

Sumai and Lota do not mind their beds being hard, for they have never slept on anything softer. And the beds are not cold in winter, for they are warmed by heat from the kitchen stoves. The warm air comes through pipes running from the kitchens along the floors of the bedrooms.

The shed is partly a storehouse and partly a tool shed. At one end of it is a big stall for the family water buffalo. In the courtyard a few pigs and chickens are picking up whatever they can find to eat.

The buffalo and the pigs and chickens are the only farm animals that Sumai's father keeps. He does not keep cattle or sheep because he cannot spare any land for pasture or for growing feed for animals. His farm is so small that he must use every bit of the land for growing food for the family.

The pigs and chickens are easy to keep because they manage to live on weeds and garbage. Sumai and Lota never have any beefsteak to eat, or any milk to drink, but they do have eggs and a little pork and chicken.

Nearly every family in the village keeps a few pigs and chickens, and a water buffalo for plowing. The buffaloes can be kept cheaply because they eat the grass that grows along the roadsides and the waterways. This, with rice straw, gives them enough to eat.

Back of Sumai's house are the mulberry trees which supply food for the silkworms. When the worms are being fed, the living room and some of the bedrooms in the house are filled with straw trays on which the mulberry leaves are spread for the worms to eat. During these weeks Lota and his father and uncle have to sleep on the floor in the shed.

When you have seen Sumai's home, you will know what all the village homes are like. They are all much the same except in size. Each house has as many rooms as are needed for the

153

Sumai and Lota spend much of their playtime in the courtyard.

number of people in the family. If the family grows larger, another room or two is added.

Can you guess why the houses are built of brick? It is because wood is scarce. But this is not because there is too little rain for trees. It is because the rainy parts of China are so crowded with people. Long ago most of the forests were cut down, so that the land could be used for raising crops.

A Meal with Sumai and Lota

If Sumai and Lota invite you to have a meal with them, you may expect to have boiled rice to eat. Very likely there will be bits of pork, chicken, or fish mixed with it. There will be a bowl of it for each of you.

Don't look for a fork or spoon, for you will not find one. You must eat your rice with chopsticks, as the Chinese do. Hold the two round, smooth sticks between the fingers of one hand, as Sumai does. See how she picks up a little rice between the ends of the sticks and pops it into her mouth without spilling any.

Eating with chopsticks looks easy, but it isn't. How the sticks do slip! Halfway to your mouth the rice falls back into the bowl. All you can do is to keep on trying, and after a while you will learn the trick.

Perhaps you will have noodles instead of rice to eat. Noodles are thin strips of dough made from wheat flour. They are rather like macaroni, only they are yellowish because in making them eggs are mixed with the flour.

Sumai's mother makes the noodles herself and then boils them. If she has a little meat or fish on hand, she mixes it with the noodles just as she does with the rice. Noodles are even harder to eat with chopsticks than rice is, for they are more slippery.

For a drink you will have hot tea in a little china cup. There will be no lemon or cream to put in it, and no sugar. The Chinese do not sweeten their tea. Are you wishing you could have a glass of milk? There isn't a drop of milk anywhere in the village because no one keeps a cow. If you don't like tea, you will have to drink water.

154

Sumai and Lota drink tea with every meal. They eat more rice than anything else. They have noodles, vegetables, meat, and fish fairly often, but they eat rice every day. Often they make a whole meal of plain boiled rice and tea.

Are you thinking that Sumai and Lota must get tired of eating so much rice? Perhaps they do, but rice is a very good food and it keeps them strong and well.

Eating their rice with chopsticks.

Some Questions about the Yangtze Plain

1. Is the Yangtze Plain near the ocean, or is it far inland in China?

2. How does its surface help to make it a good land for farming?

3. What has happened to the forests that once covered this plain, and why?

4. Why do the farming families live in villages?

5. Why do they build their houses of brick instead of wood?

6. Why are their farms so small?

Can You Explain?

1. Make a list of six kinds of food that Sumai and Lota eat. See if you can explain how their family gets each kind.

2. Suvan thinks it strange that Lota doesn't drink any milk. Give the reason so that Suvan will understand.

3. Nara thinks that Sumai must be cold in the wintertime because she hasn't any woolen clothes. See if you can explain how Sumai's cotton clothes keep her warm in winter.

4. Roshik thinks it strange that anyone should want pipes in a house to carry heat from the kitchen to the bedrooms. Why does he think that? Give the reason which explains why there are such pipes in Lota's house.

Volunteer Teamwork

Give a little play, showing how there is a chance for three shopkeepers, a shoemaker, and a barber to make a living in Sumai's village.

Chinese boys have great fun flying kites.

IN THE RICE FIELDS

Making the Fields Ready

All the way up the Yangtze River you have seen farmers plowing their muddy fields with water buffaloes. That is what the men of Lota's village are doing now. They are making the fields ready for planting rice.

The rice seeds have already been sown in seedbeds in corners of the fields. The green blades have pushed up through the earth and are growing fast. It is past the middle of May, and early in June the little plants will be ready to be set out in the plowed fields.

All the fields round the village are separated from one another by low banks of earth. Here and there between the banked fields are ditches filled with water from the canal and the stream.

Lota says his father's farm land is not all in one piece. It is made up of three different fields scattered among fields belonging to other families. In all three of them Lota's father will plant rice.

Two of the fields are ready for planting, and today Lota's father and uncle are at work in the third. The buffalo is pulling the plow through the mud. Lota's father is walking barefoot behind the plow, guiding it and driving the buffalo.

Uncle Lu is at work with a hoe. He is breaking up the lumps of earth that the plow turns over. Though the field is small, the two men work days and days getting it ready for planting. They must make the soil fine and soft, and they must mix with it the kind of material which we call fertilizer. The fertilizer will make the soil rich in the kinds of food that rice plants need in order to grow well.

Lota wants to tell you more about the water buffalo. This is what he says:

"The buffalo is a fine animal for plowing the rice fields. Pulling a plow in the heavy mud is hard work, but the buffalo is strong. He has broad hoofs, too, and they keep him from sinking into the mud too deeply and getting stuck.

156

Lota's father is plowing a rice field with his water buffalo.

"When the buffalo has finished a day's work in the fields, I drive him along the banks so that he can get some grass to eat. Then I take him to the buffalo pool. The pool is just outside the village. He goes into the pool with the other buffaloes and lies in the water to cool off.

"When he is cool enough he comes out of the water. I drive him home and put him in the shed. I give him some rice straw to eat. I like our water buffalo, and I take good care of him."

Planting Time

Now the fields are ready and the day for setting out the rice plants has come. Our Chinese friends have their breakfast of rice and tea at sunrise. The grandmother is not well enough to work in the fields, but everyone else except Sumai will help with the planting. Sumai is staying at home to help her grandmother with the housework.

Off they go to one of the three rice fields. The field looks like a little pond because it has been flooded with about six inches of water. The banks round the field keep the water from running off.

Look across at the next field, and you will see how the water got in. Over there two men and a boy are pedaling a homemade machine that washes water from a ditch up a trough and

A bath in the pool cools the buffaloes off after a day's work in the fields.

dumps it over the bank into the field. Only yesterday Lota was out helping his father and uncle to finish flooding their field in this way.

When you were visiting Roshik and Moti in Bengal, you learned that rice is a very thirsty plant and grows best in fields that are under water. This is why the Chinese farmers flood their rice fields.

Now today's work is beginning. Lota's mother is in the seedbed at the corner of the field. The seedlings, or little rice plants, are about twelve inches high. Lota's mother gently draws them by handfuls from the mud and ties them in bundles with bits of grass.

157

Lota often helps to pedal the machine that floods the rice fields with water.

Lota carries the bundles of seedlings to his father, his uncle, and his grandfather. The three men plant the seedlings in straight rows in the watery field. Watch Uncle Lu as he works. He takes four or five seedlings from a bundle, plunges them into the water, and presses their roots down into the mud. Then he takes a step forward and plants another little bunch.

With Lota's mother in the seedbed, the three men in the field, and Lota for errand boy, the work goes fast. At noon Lota goes home. Soon he comes back with Sumai, bringing rice and tea that their grandmother has sent for lunch. They all sit down on the bank to eat and rest a while.

After lunch the work starts again, and before sunset the whole field is planted. During the next few days the other two rice fields will be flooded and planted.

The other families in the village are planting their rice fields, too. Soon the farm land is green with the blades of rice. Sumai thinks the rice fields are a lovely sight in summer, and you will think so, too. They are loveliest of all on a sunny day when a breeze ripples the water and the green stalks dip and nod as if they were bowing to one another.

Why do you suppose the Chinese farmers take such care in making ready their rice fields and setting out the plants? It is because rice is their chief food. Their farms are so small that every bit of rice land must grow all the grain it possibly can. If the farmers were careless, the rice crops would be small, and the people wouldn't have enough to eat.

Hot Weather and the Harvest

Summer brings the hot sunshine and the rain that make the rice grow well. Some years there is enough rain to keep plenty of water in the fields. When there is too little rain the farmers spend many a day pedaling the machines that pour water from the ditches into the fields.

Lota helps all he can with the pedaling, but he cannot keep at it as long as his father and uncle can. It is terribly hot work, and his legs get so tired! From time to time the fields must be weeded, and Lota helps in this work too. Weeding isn't so bad; it is rather fun to wade round in the water and feel the soft mud between his toes.

When the rice stalks begin to turn yellow and the new seeds start to ripen, the farmers let the fields dry out. Now all the children can be a

The men plant the rice seedlings in straight rows in the flooded field.

At harvest time the rice is cut with sickles and stacked in the fields to dry.

great help. They fly their kites near the fields. The kites and the shouts of the children scare away the birds that would like to steal the rice seeds from the stalks.

September is harvest time. The men and women cut the rice stalks close to the ground with sickles. They tie the stalks in bundles and stack them in the fields to dry. Later the men carry home the bundles of grain.

Then comes the threshing in the courtyard. No one in the village has a threshing machine, and so the work of getting the seeds off the stalks is done by hand. Lota's father and Uncle Lu beat the stalks on a wooden frame. The seeds fall on a big piece of cloth laid on the ground to catch them.

After the rice has been winnowed it is stored away in the shed. Lota's mother will husk it a little at a time as she needs it. The straw too is saved, and not a bit of it is wasted. Some of it will be fed to the water buffalo, and the rest will be burned as fuel in the kitchen stoves.

"Thank the Harvest"

Because rice is their daily food, the people of the village are happy when the crop has been gathered and they know they have enough to last until another September. When the harvest is over, they have a three-day celebration which they call "Thank the Harvest." Sumai and Lota look forward the whole year to these holidays.

Early the first morning the people of the village go out to the fields. There they give thanks for the soil, the sun, and the water which have made the rice crops grow well. Then they walk back to the village and the fun begins.

The village is decorated with colored paper flags and ribbons, and at night the bridges are strung with colored paper lanterns. Bands of traveling entertainers who go from village to

How Lota's father threshes his rice.

159

What fun it is to watch the entertainers at "Thank the Harvest"!

village during the celebration give shows in the streets. There are funny plays with songs and dances. There are acrobats who do wonderful jumping and tumbling, and jugglers who keep balls and sticks flying in the air without ever dropping one.

Then there are the stilt walkers. They wear funny costumes and masks, and their stilts make them twice as tall as the people in the crowd. They parade through the village playing tricks like clowns. Best of all is the blue-and-yellow dragon. It is made of cloth and wire, and there are four men inside it. The dragon rolls its red eyes, flaps its ears, and wiggles its long tail, and all the time there is music from little bells inside it. Before the dragon leaves the village it dances a jig, and then the men come out of it and bow to the crowd.

The entertainers come to the village hoping that if the people like their shows they will give them money. They do not expect much, for they know that the people haven't much to give, but they always get a little.

What fun "Thank the Harvest" is for all the children! But the grown-ups enjoy it just as much. The Chinese are jolly people, and they like all kinds of shows and fun and make-believe.

Rice Work to Put in Order

Here is a list of the different kinds of work that Sumai's family do so that they can have rice to eat. The list would be better if the kinds of work were put in the right order. See if you can arrange them in that way.

Flooding the fields	Plowing the fields
Harvesting the grain	Threshing the grain
Planting the seedlings	Weeding the fields

Winnowing and husking the rice

Some Rice Questions

1. Is rice a summer crop or a winter crop in the Yangtze Plain? Why?

2. Why does it take so much work to make the rice fields ready for planting?

3. Why isn't the flooding of the fields so easy in the Yangtze Plain as in Bengal?

4. Why are water buffaloes good animals for work in the rice fields?

5. Why do you think it is that the Chinese do not use machines for harvesting and threshing rice?

6. How do Lota's people use the rice straw?

7. Why do they have a special celebration after the rice harvest?

8. Why does the yearly rice crop mean so much to them?

160

AS THE SEASONS COME AND GO

Spring and Summer

You have been learning about the work that the people of Lota's village do in the spring and summer to grow the rice which is their daily food. Meanwhile they are also growing vegetables. In their garden they grow melons and peas, beans, carrots, and other vegetables from early spring until well into the fall.

Perhaps you know that most vegetables grow rather quickly. Peas, for example, are ready to be picked about six weeks after they are planted. Because of this, and because the growing season is long, Sumai's family get three or four crops of vegetables from their garden each year.

Spring and summer are also the seasons when the silkworms are raised, for it is then that there are plenty of fresh mulberry leaves. This work keeps Sumai and her mother and grandmother very busy because the worms need so much care. Do you remember how Sumai helps?

Sumai's mother and grandmother usually raise three sets of silkworms, one after the other. There are hundreds of worms in each set. Sumai's father sells each set of cocoons as soon as they are finished.

Silkworm cocoons are the chief "money crop" for the family. The rice and other field crops and the vegetables are grown almost wholly for food. Are you wondering why Sumai's father doesn't sell a good part of his crops, as many of our farmers do? Remember how very small his farm is. It is just about big enough to feed the family, but too small to grow much extra for sale.

Of course Sumai's family must earn some money, for they need clothes, a few kinds of food that they do not raise, and such things as tools and furnishings for their house. The money to buy these things comes mostly from what Sumai's father is paid for the cocoons.

The few coins that Lota and Sumai give to the entertainers they like at "Thank the Harvest" are from the cocoon money. Sumai likes to think that she has helped to earn this money by picking mulberry leaves for the silkworms. She says it is more fun to spend money when you have earned it yourself.

Autumn and Winter

After "Thank the Harvest" the farmers go to work in the fields again. They plow the land where the rice was grown and plant winter crops. Lota's father is planting wheat and soybeans. There is no flooding of the fields now, for the winter crops are not so thirsty as rice is. The rain will give them the water they need.

Soon the fields are again green with young plants. Meanwhile the weather is growing cooler and the villagers are getting ready for winter. The mothers are lining coats and trousers with cotton batting, so that everyone will be warm when the cold weather comes.

For the children autumn is the time for gathering fuel. They go out with baskets and gather all the twigs, leaves, and dry grass they can find. Wood, you know, is scarce in China, and coal costs more than most of the farming

161

Autumn is the time for gathering fuel.

people can pay. They buy a little charcoal for use in the coldest months, but they make their fires mostly of rice and wheat straw, and of twigs, leaves, and grass which in many countries would go to waste.

In the fields the soybeans are growing so fast that they will be ready to be picked before there is enough frost to spoil them. If you ask Sumai why her father raises soybeans, she will say, "We make soy from some of them, and we dry the rest. Then, whenever we wish, we boil some of the dried beans and have bean curd."

Soy is a brown-colored sauce that the Chinese eat on rice. Bean curd looks somewhat like cottage cheese, but it tastes quite different. You might not like it, but Sumai and Lota think it very good. It is a healthful food, and helps to keep them strong and well.

The wheat grows much more slowly than the soybeans. You might think that the freezing weather in winter would kill it, but wheat can stand a good deal of cold. In the coldest weather the plants stop growing, but they do not die. They rest for a while, often under a light cover of snow. Later, when the weather grows warmer, the wheat begins to grow again.

School Days

In December a teacher comes to the village and for a few months there is school in a room back of the barber shop. Some of the children go in the morning, and others in the afternoon. In the evening the teacher gives lessons to some of the children's parents.

Sumai and Lota think it is wonderful to be able to go to school. They know that many Chinese children have no chance to learn to read and write because as yet there are no schools in their villages. Their own school started only a few years ago, and before that hardly anyone in the village could read or write. Now some of the grown-ups are beginning to learn just as if they were children.

The schoolroom isn't very warm because it has only a tiny stove and the fire is kept going only in the coldest weather. But the children are bundled up in their thickly lined clothes, and they don't mind a chilly room.

The Wheat Harvest

School closes late in March. The weather is much warmer now. The mulberry trees are showing buds, and the wheat is growing fast in the fields. It will be ready to be harvested late in April or very early in May.

Lota's father and Uncle Lu cut the wheat stalks with sickles just as they do the rice. They thresh the wheat differently. They spread the stalks on the ground in the courtyard and drive a stone roller over them to knock off the seeds. The water buffalo pulls the roller.

162

During the winter the children of the village have a chance to go to school.

The water buffalo pulls the stone roller that threshes the wheat.

You will remember that Lota's mother makes noodles of wheat flour. She also uses flour to make dumplings to eat in soup. But first, of course, the wheat seeds must be ground to make the flour. The picture shows how this is done.

If you were in the courtyard watching, you would hear the creak, creak of the stone mill-wheel. The seeds are in the hollow in the big piece of stone. As the buffalo walks round the stone, he pulls the creaking wheel that grinds the seeds into flour.

Some years Lota's father has a little more wheat than he needs, and he sells a few bushels. Sometimes he has a few extra bushels of soy-beans to sell. But in most years he has no more than the family need for their own use.

With their crops of rice, soybeans, wheat, and vegetables, Lota's family get enough to eat from their tiny farm. With the money they get chiefly by raising silkworms and selling the cocoons, they buy the few other things they need. But they get their living only by working hard the whole year round.

Something to Remember about China

As you say good-by to Sumai and Lota, you will like to remember that you have seen some of the smallest farms in the world. Millions of Chinese families live on farms as small as these.

In the cities of China there are a good many well-to-do people, and some very rich people. There are some farmers too who have enough land to be well off. But China is so crowded with people that most of them are poor.

In spite of all their hard work, the people like those of Sumai's village are not able to have many things that they don't really need. But if they get enough food from their tiny farms and enough money to buy the other things they need, they are happy. Because they work hard for what they have, they enjoy it.

The wheat seeds are ground into flour between a flat stone and a stone wheel.

163

Questions about the Crop Year

You have learned that Sumai's family could not get along with such a tiny farm if they could use the land for crops only in the warmest months of the year. These questions will help you to explain why they can use the land the year round.

1. Why do they grow their rice during the warmest part of the year?

2. Why can they grow soybeans that are planted in the fall?

3. Why can they grow wheat that is planted in the fall and harvested in the spring?

4. Why can they get three or four crops of vegetables a year from their little garden?

Three Rivers

Three boys and their sisters whom you have visited live in the valleys of great rivers: Abdul and Zakia, Simba and Panya, and Lota and Sumai. Copy these sentences and fill each blank with the name of one of the rivers.

1. The three rivers are the ————, the ————, and the ————.

2. The ———— and the ———— rivers are in Africa.

3. The ———— River is in Asia.

4. The river that flows through a tropical forest is the ————.

5. The one that flows through a desert is the ————.

6. The one that flows through miles and miles of rice fields is the ————.

7. The one that does the most for the farmers is the ————.

8. The one that sometimes causes terrible floods is the ————.

Farmers All — but Different

In Egypt, Bengal, and the Yangtze Plain you have seen three groups of people who get their living by farming; yet many of their ways of living and working are different. Here is a chance to prove that you understand some of the reasons for the differences. Read these sentences, finishing them in your own words.

1. In Bengal and the Yangtze Plain houses must have sloping roofs because ———

2. In Egypt sloping roofs are not needed because ———

3. In Bengal and Egypt light clothing is enough the year round because ———

4. In the Yangtze Plain light clothing is not always enough because ———

5. In Egypt all the crops must be watered by irrigation because ———

6. In Bengal and the Yangtze Plain the farmers do not need to irrigate their fields because ———

7. In Bengal the farmers do not even have to flood their rice fields because ———

8. In the Yangtze Plain the farmers do have to flood their rice fields because ———

Chinese boys and girls are full of fun, and they like to play all sorts of games.

Erik and Inger in Norway

Erik and his sister Inger are on their way to school.

A LAND OF FIVE F'S

The Last Day of School

It is a bright, sunny morning in June, and Erik and his sister Inger are on their way to school. They are rowing to school in their boat. Inger is pulling one oar, and Erik is pulling the other. They keep good time, and the rowboat fairly skims over the water.

You might think from the picture that Erik and Inger are rowing on a river, but they are not. They are rowing on a *fiord*. A fiord is a long, narrow arm of the sea that winds inland among the mountains. The water is smooth and very deep. It is so smooth that it mirrors the steep, wooded slopes along the shore. Higher up, where there are no trees, snow lies in white patches on the mountains. Above all is the blue sky.

Erik and Inger live on a farm on the shore of the fiord, and the village where they go to school

is only a mile away. They can easily walk there by a path through the woods, but on days like this they like to row.

Now Erik and Inger have reached the village wharf — the landing place for boats. They jump out and tie the boat to the wharf. With their books and lunch boxes, they scamper up the hill to the schoolhouse. The school bell is ringing, and they are just in time. The schoolhouse is small, but it is big enough for the children of the village and the farms round about. The rooms have desks, chairs, and blackboards just as your schoolroom has.

This is the last day of school, and the children find it hard to keep their minds on their lessons. The sunshine is streaming through the open windows, the birds are singing outside, and the children can't help thinking about the summer vacation. It seems a long time until three o'clock, when their teachers dismiss them.

165

Inger

Can't you imagine how free and happy Erik and Inger feel as they race down to the wharf? They take their time rowing home, for there is no need to hurry now.

Erik is looking up at the mountainside high above their farm. His eyes are shining.

"That's where I'll be soon," he says.

"Yes," Inger answers, "and I'll come up often and we'll go berrying." Her eyes are shining, too.

The children pull toward their own little wharf at the water's edge. They tie the boat and run up the path to the house. Their mother is standing in the kitchen door.

"Mother!" they shout. "Mother! School is over and vacation has begun!"

Four of Norway's Five F's

Erik and Inger are Norwegian children. Their country, Norway, is in the northern part of western Europe, and it borders the Atlantic Ocean. Look at the picture of the globe on page 9 and see just where it is.

Norway is a country of mountains and valleys. The coast is broken and rocky, and the mountains rise steeply from the water's edge. The Norwegians say that the coast wears a belt of skerries. They mean that there are thousands of rocky islands strung out along the coast of Norway. Many of these rocky islands, or skerries, are small and bare, with hardly a blade of grass and not a single tree. Others are much larger, with soil enough for trees, grass, and crops, and room enough for villages and towns.

The belt of skerries is often called the "skerry guard." This is a good name for it because the skerries really do guard the coast. The open ocean beyond them is often stormy and rough, with huge waves whipped up by the winds. But the water between the skerries

Erik

and the coast is quiet and smooth because the islands protect it from the winds and waves. The water is deep, too. It is so deep that big ocean ships can wind their way among the skerries and go into the fiords.

Norway is often called "a land of five F's." The fiords are one of these F's. There are dozens of these deep, narrow arms of the sea that reach far inland from the coast. They give Norway many good harbors; that is, places where ships can anchor safely.

The map on page 168 shows how crooked the fiords are. You can see that the longer ones split into branches. Many of the branches are very narrow, and the mountains rise like walls on either side.

Wherever the land along the fiords is not too steep, there are farms, villages, and towns. The farms are small because there is not much land in any one place level enough for raising crops. Erik's farm is on one of these bits of land.

Farms are another of Norway's five F's. They are scattered along the fiords and in the valleys all over the country. They are small, but they are not such tiny farms as you saw in China, for Norway is not a crowded country.

The fiords are so beautiful that thousands of tourists from other countries visit them in the summer. They come in ships that sail along the coast inside the skerry guard and make side trips into the fiords.

Among the things that make the fiords so lovely are the dark evergreen forests on the lower mountain slopes. The trees are mostly spruces, pines, and other kinds that never have bare branches. Here and there birches and maples show a lighter green. The forests are still another of Norway's F's.

The higher parts of the mountains are too cold for trees. Up there grassy pastures take

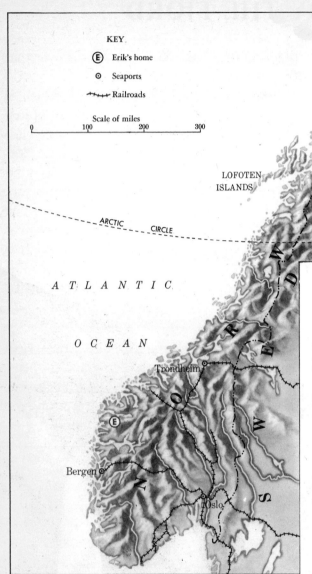

A map of Norway.

the place of forests. Still higher there is nothing but bare rock and snow.

Even lovelier than the forests, many people think, are the waterfalls. These are foaming streams that tumble down the mountainsides into the fiords. They come with a rush and a roar, and many of them plunge over high, rocky cliffs into the deep, dark waters below. The spray that splashes up sparkles in the sunshine, and often you can see a rainbow in it. Add the falls to the fiords, farms, and forests, and you have four of Norway's five F's.

Some Five F Questions

1. Study the pictures on pages 165 and 167. Can you find four of Norway's five F's in them? Point them out.

2. What do you suppose the fifth F is? Here is a help. This F swims in the fiords and in the waters along the coast of Norway. Can you guess what it is?

3. Erik's father divides his time between two kinds of work. These also begin with F. What do you think they are?

Reading the Map

A little reading of the map will tell you more about Norway.

1. Has Norway a long coast line, or a short one?

2. Point out some of the islands of the skerry guard. There are many more than can be shown on this small map.

3. What is the name of one of the groups of islands? How can you tell that this group of islands is in the northern cold cap?

4. Point out some of the fiords. Is Erik's fiord in northern Norway, or in southern Norway?

5. What does the key tell you about the three cities of Norway that are named on the map?

6. Could you reach Erik's fiord from any one of these seaports in a train? Why, or why not?

7. Does the map make you think of any reason why it is hard to build railroads in Norway?

THE FARM BY THE FIORD

A Comfortable House

Let us pretend that Erik and Inger are showing us their farm. You can see from the picture that the buildings are on a piece of gently sloping land bordering the fiord. The rest of the farm land runs part way up the mountainside, where you see the woods. A stream that comes rushing down the mountain supplies the house with water. The water comes through a pipe from the stream.

The house and all the other buildings are built of wood. You can easily understand why when you remember the F that stands for forests in Norway. Nearly all the farmhouses are built of wood, and so are many of the buildings in the villages and towns.

When you go inside the house, you will find it comfortably furnished and clean as a pin. The wood floors are oiled and polished. The walls too are of wood, and they are painted with flower patterns in bright colors. On the living-room floor there are pretty homemade rugs, and on the window sills are pots of flowering plants.

If you should spend a year on the farm, you would know why the Norwegians like bright colors in their houses. The winters are long, and the winter days are short. It snows a good deal, and the sky is more often gray than blue. Brightness indoors helps to make up for the dull weather.

In the kitchen there is a big stove, and in a corner of the living room, a stone fireplace. Wood for the fires is stacked outside the kitchen door and in a woodshed close by. Erik's father cuts all the firewood in the forest himself.

Although the house is heated only by wood fires, it has electric lights and a telephone. This is true of nearly all the farmhouses in Norway, and it is because of one of the five F's. It is the F that stands for falls. There are hundreds of waterfalls, and you have already seen how beautiful they are. Now you will discover that they are useful too.

Falling water has great strength which is called *water power*. With the right kind of machinery, water power can be changed into electricity. Near many of the larger falls the Norwegians have set up machinery of this kind in buildings called power plants. In this way they use the falls to make electricity. You know yourself how electricity can be sent over wires and made to do many useful things. It is because Norway has waterfalls that farms like Erik's can have telephones and electric lights.

Other Buildings on the Farm

Among the other buildings on Erik's farm are a barn for the cows, the horse, and the hens, and two sheds for the goats. The cows are out in the woods this afternoon, and you can hear the tinkle of the bells round their necks.

The farm where Erik and Inger live.

Inger helps in milking the goats.

The goats are grazing a little way up the mountainside. They are nibbling coarse grass and scratchy plants that the cows will not touch. Later this afternoon Inger will help her two older sisters to milk the goats. At milking time she will show you the white goat which is her pet.

Right now Inger wants you to see the outside kitchen, a small building close to the house. This is the family bakery. The meals are cooked in the house, but the baking is done here. As you step inside you smell something that makes you hungry. Inger's sisters are making flatbread.

At a table one of the girls is rolling out dough in thin sheets nearly as big around as a barrel top. The other sister is baking the big round sheets of dough over the red-hot coals of a wood fire. Inger says that flatbread can be made of rye flour, barley meal, or either of these mixed with oatmeal.

When you taste the crispy flatbread, you will wish that your mother made it at home. Inger says that it will keep a long time. Her mother and sisters often make enough of it at one time to last the family for a month or two.

Perhaps you will think that the most interesting building on the farm is the storehouse. Erik and Inger call it the *stabbur*. It stands on

stilts, so that rats cannot get inside and eat the food that is stored there.

The food supplies are rather low now because the family has been using them all winter, but in the fall the bins and shelves will be filled. In the bins you will see what is left of the year's supply of flour, meal, and potatoes. On the shelves are several kinds of cheese, some tubs of butter, and some big stacks of flatbread.

If you climb up into the loft under the roof, you will see a good supply of dried and salted fish. Erik says that these are herring and codfish. He says, too, that in the fall there will be smoked hams and "sides" of bacon hanging in the loft.

The building that Erik wants you to see is the boathouse down on the shore. Inside it is a good-sized boat that can be run into the water over wooden rollers. The sail for the boat is there, too, and the oars. Hanging on the walls are some big nets made of heavy cord, and some strong lines with fishhooks fastened to them.

Do you need now to be told that the fifth F of Norway is fish and that Erik's father is a fisherman as well as a farmer? Wherever you go on the west coast of Norway, you will find farmer-fishermen. By farming and fishing they

Rolling out dough to make flatbread.

get most of the food for their families. The foods they buy are mostly things like coffee and sugar, which they cannot raise on their farms.

Back at the house, Erik's father is just driving his farm cart into the yard. In the cart are some little pigs that he has bought. How they squeal as he pulls them out and turns them into a pen! During the summer the pigs will be fed and fattened, and in the autumn they will be killed. This is how Erik's family get a supply of bacon and ham for the winter.

How the Crop Land Is Used

As you walk round the farm, you will see that all the land that is not too rough and steep is used for crops. Barley is growing in one little field, oats in another, and rye in a third. There is a field of carrots and turnips, and a patch of potatoes.

If you are a city boy or girl who doesn't know much about farming, you may wonder why so much of the land seems to be used just for grass. Erik says that the grass is the beginning of the hay crop. It is wild grass that comes up fresh and green each spring. Later on, when it has grown tall, it will be cut and put in the barn. It makes fine hay for the farm animals to eat.

The crops on Erik's farm are of two kinds: food crops for the family and crops to feed the animals. Feed crops for animals are called *fodder crops*. You might suppose that the turnips and carrots are food crops, but they are not. Like the hay, they are fodder crops for the cows and goats to eat in the winter.

Perhaps you know that farm animals are called *livestock*. On farms like Erik's the raising of fodder crops for livestock is just another way of getting food. The cows and goats are kept because they give milk. The milk and the butter and cheese that are made from it are an important part of the food supply for the family.

Close to the house is a small garden, where Erik's family grow vegetables in the summer. They enjoy eating fresh vegetables in the sum-

Their father brings home some pigs to raise.

mer, for they do not have them in the winter. Fresh winter vegetables in Norway have to come from warmer countries farther south, and they cost more than the farmer-fishermen families can pay for them.

Some More F Questions

1. Which of Norway's five F's supplies material for building houses?

2. What does that F tell you about the weather in Norway?

3. Which of the five F's supplies electricity for lights, telephones, and other uses?

4. Do you think Norway could have that F if it were not a rainy country? Why?

5. Which of the F's explains why ships go far inland among the mountains of Norway?

6. Which two of the F's supply families like Erik's with most of their food?

Some Things to Do

1. Write a letter to your father or mother about the fiords in Norway. Draw a picture of a fiord to go with your letter.

2. Say whether or not you think Norway is a country where it is easy to carry on farming. Explain why you think it is or is not.

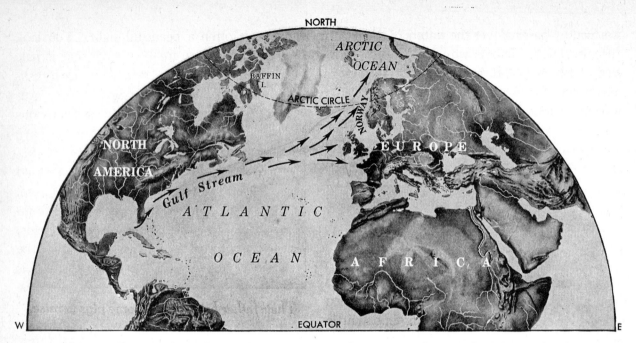

A map showing how the Gulf Stream spreads out into the North Atlantic Drift.

SURPRISING THINGS ABOUT NORWAY

What the Winds Do for Norway

You have found forests and farms on the lower lands in Norway. This is a sure sign of three things: (1) that these parts of Norway are not too cold for trees; (2) that there is plenty of rain; and (3) that there is a growing season long enough for the people to raise crops.

It may surprise you, then, to find that Norway is almost as far from the equator as Baffin Island is. Look at the map on this page, and you will see this for yourself. Do you remember why there are no trees or farms in Baffin Island, where your Eskimo friends live?

Baffin Island, you know, has very long winters with very cold weather. The frozen waters round the island lock it in ice, and for about nine months no ships can reach it. In Norway the winters are cold enough for snow, but not nearly so long or so cold as Baffin Island winters. The waters along the west coast do not freeze over during the winter, and ships can go in and out of the fiords the year round.

There is an interesting reason why Norway, which is so far north, is warmer than Baffin Island. Erik can tell you the reason, for he has just learned it in school.

"Norway," he says, "is warmed by winds from the Atlantic Ocean. The winds are warmed by blowing over the North Atlantic Drift."

The map on this page shows what Erik means. Find the line of arrows marked *Gulf Stream.* You may think of the Gulf Stream as somewhat like a river flowing in the ocean. We call it an *ocean current.* It is a current of warm water that moves northward along the east coast of North America. It swings eastward, spreads out over the colder waters below, and drifts toward Europe.

This is what Erik means by the *North Atlantic Drift.* Trace this drifting of warmer water on the map, and you will see that part of it moves northward along the west coast of Norway.

The winds that Norway has most of the time come from the west; that is, from over the Atlantic Ocean. In crossing the ocean they are warmed by passing over the waters of the North Atlantic Drift. This is why Norway is not so cold as Baffin Island, and why its west coast is never locked in ice. Baffin Island has no such warming winds.

You mustn't think that the winds *feel* warm, for they don't. In winter they feel damp and chilly. But they are much warmer than they would be if they hadn't crossed the ocean and passed over the North Atlantic Drift. If the drift weren't there, Norway would be a much colder country.

The winds do something else for Norway. They bring moisture from the ocean. When they reach the coast and begin to climb the mountains, clouds form and spill much of the moisture. In the winter the moisture falls as snow. The rest of the year it falls as rain.

This is why Norway has plenty of rain for trees and crops. Really, there is too much rain, more than the people need. But it is better for any country to have too much rain than too little. Can you explain why?

Glaciers and Snow Fields

Among the things that visitors to Norway like to see are the glaciers. Earlier in this book you learned about the glaciers of Greenland — those huge tongues of thick, rough ice that creep slowly down to the sea from the great ice cap.

The glaciers of Norway come to an end in the valleys or at the heads of fiords, where the air is warm enough to melt the ice. The end of a glacier is often a beautiful sight. You look into the mouth of a great ice cave that is pale greenish-blue. Out from the cave comes a rushing stream of milky-looking water that races away over a bed of stones. In mountainous countries like Norway many of the rivers have their sources in glaciers.

If you were to fly over Norway, you would soon find out where the glaciers come from. Looking down on the highest parts of the country, you would see miles and miles of snow fields. Beneath the snow there is ice so thick that the snow itself is only a blanket on top of it. It is some of this ice that creeps slowly down the mountains, forming the glaciers.

The snow fields never melt away. Each winter they get a new coating of snow, and this packs down, helping the snow underneath to turn into ice. Each summer the snow melts a little, but not enough to change the snow fields much.

Norway has snow fields and glaciers because it is a mountainous country far from the equator. When you visited Pedro in the Andes Mountains in South America, you learned that even in the warm belt of the earth the high lands are cool or cold. The highest parts of Norway are not so high as Pedro's altiplano, but they are so far north that they are chilly in summer and very cold in winter. Only the lower lands in the valleys and along the fiords are warm enough for farming.

173

The lower end of a glacier in Norway.

A Land of the Midnight Sun

Another thing that tourists go to Norway to see is the midnight sun. This means seeing the sun shining at 12 o'clock at night, when one day is ending and the next is about to begin. People like ourselves, who live where the sun rises and sets every day in the year, find it strange to see the sun shining at midnight.

Do you remember about the "summer day" and the "winter night" in the part of Baffin Island where Netsook lives? During the time of the winter night the sun never rises, and during the time of the summer day it never sets.

All parts of the earth north of the arctic circle and south of the antarctic circle have a period of summer day when there is no sunset, and a period of winter night when there is no sunrise. Thus the part of Norway north of the arctic circle is a "land of the midnight sun."

Erik and Inger do not see the midnight sun because they live south of the arctic circle. In their part of Norway the sun rises and sets every day in the year, but the summer days are very long. The winter days are very short, and even at noon the sun is low in the sky.

Erik and Inger have some cousins living near the northern tip of Norway. Christmas for them comes in the period of the winter night, for there is no sunrise from the middle of November until late in January. But in summer the sun makes up for its absence in winter. It never once sets from the middle of May until late in July. For about ten weeks in each year northern Norway is a land of midnight sun.

Choosing Endings

Each of these sentences has three endings, two wrong and one right. Choose the right ending for each sentence.

1. Ships can go into the Norwegian fiords at all times of year because

   a. Norway has many good harbors.
   b. the fiords never freeze over.
   c. the fiords are very deep.

2. Norway is warmer than you might expect because

   a. it has warming winds from the west.
   b. it is a very low land.
   c. it is a land of high sun.

3. The winds are warmed by

   a. passing over very warm lands.
   b. passing over the North Atlantic Drift.
   c. carrying a great deal of moisture.

4. The west coast of Norway is very rainy because

   a. it has many thundershowers.
   b. it is west of the Atlantic Ocean.
   c. the winds from the west bring much moisture.

5. The moisture falls as snow in winter because

   a. the winter weather is cold.
   b. the land is mountainous.
   c. the winter days are short.

Can You Read These Clocks?

Here are two pairs of clock faces for you to read. One pair shows the length of day and night on the Fourth of July where Erik and Inger live. The other shows the same things for their Christmas Day. Count up the hours of daylight on each of these dates.

Sunrise Time

Sunset Time

Fourth of July.

Sunrise Time

Sunset Time

Christmas Day.

Erik and his older sisters are taking the cows up to the saeter for the summer.

UP AT THE SAETER WITH ERIK

Off to the Mountain Pastures

A week has passed since school closed, and a morning that Erik has been looking forward to for a long time has come. Today he and his two older sisters are going up to the *saeter*. The saeter is their father's pasture land high on the mountainside. Erik and his sisters are taking the cows up there for the summer.

Erik's father is harnessing the horse to the largest of his farm carts. Inger and her mother and sisters are putting bundles, baskets, and bedding in the cart. Erik is racing about, so excited that he isn't much help. The cows are standing by, quietly waiting. The one that gives the most milk is to stay on the farm, but all the rest are going to the saeter.

Now Erik and his sisters are off. The two girls are ahead, leading the horse and cart. One cow is tied to the tail of the cart, and the rest fall into line behind her. Erik comes last. He is carrying a birch switch in his hand.

Inger waves good-by to Erik as he disappears into the woods where a narrow road leads up the mountainside. The road twists and turns among the trees, and it is a slow climb for the horse and the cows. The horse has to stop now and then to rest, and the cows loiter to nibble the grass along the roadside.

Erik's job is to keep the cows moving. When one of them stops to nibble the grass, he uses his switch to start her going again. Erik is so happy that he whistles a merry tune as he climbs the steep, rough road.

After a while the woods begin to thin out, and at last the trees are left behind. Now there are grassy pastures on all sides, and above them bare slopes patched with snow. The air up here is clear and fresh, and a good bit cooler than it was down by the fiord. Now a small hut comes into sight. This is the saeter hut where Erik and his sisters will spend the summer.

The hut is built of logs, and beyond it is a log shed for the cows. Both buildings look as

Milking the cows and making butter and cheese keep the girls busy at the saeter.

if some of the pasture land had climbed onto the roofs. Do you see why? The roofs are covered with sod, and the grass is growing there just as if it were on the ground. In winter the wind blows hard up here, and a thick covering of sod keeps the roofs from blowing away.

It doesn't take Erik and the girls long to unload the cart and move into the hut. They have a picnic lunch of flatbread and cheese, and then Erik drives the cows out to pasture where they can rest and feed. The summer at the saeter has begun. Tomorrow Erik's father will come up to take the horse and cart back to the farm.

Summer Work at the Saeter

There is a good reason, of course, why the cows spend the summer at the saeter. If they stayed on the farm all summer, Erik's father would have to let them eat the grass that grows there, and then what would happen? There would be no hay for them to eat in the winter.

The grass on the saeter comes up fresh and green as soon as the snow melts in the spring. It is good, juicy grass, and good grass means good milk. Each morning the girls milk the cows, and then Erik takes them out to graze in the pastures. Late in the afternoon he brings the cows back, and before supper the girls milk them again.

While Erik is off with the cows his sisters skim the cream from the milk, churn it into butter, and pack the butter in small wooden tubs. They let the skim milk sour and then make cheese from it. They are busy with this work a good part of each day.

Every week or so Erik's father comes up from the farm with the horse and cart. He brings vegetables, bread, and cakes for Erik and the girls, and takes back the butter and cheese that have been made. He stores the cheese in the stabbur on the farm, but he sells the butter. In this way his cows make a little money for him in the summer.

Happy Days

Perhaps you are saying to yourself, "Why does Erik like it up at the saeter? Isn't he lonesome there?"

No, Erik is never lonesome because there are other boys up there. Their fathers too have saeters, and the boys are there with older girls for the same reason that Erik is. The girls make butter and cheese, and the boys look after the cows in the pastures.

Erik will tell you that looking after the cows isn't hard work. Of course you must keep an eye on them and not let them wander away and get lost, but you can do other things at the same time. You and the other boys can play games and go fishing and swimming in the streams.

Each day when Erik takes the cows out to graze, he finds some of his friends to play with. At noon they eat their lunch together. When they separate to take the cows home, they often plan to meet again after supper. The daylight lasts so long that they can play outdoors as late as they are allowed to stay up.

Now and then Inger comes up to the saeter for a day or two. Inger loves to go berrying. In the early summer she and Erik pick wild strawberries. Later on there are blueberries, mountain cranberries, and cloudberries. Cloudberries are mountain raspberries that grow on creeping vines. Often Inger takes a number of baskets of berries home with her.

177

Fishing is one of the things the boys can do while they are keeping an eye on the cows.

Inger comes up to the saeter to pick berries.

Saeter days are happy days for Norwegian children, especially for the boys who spend the whole summer on the mountain pastures. Erik thinks he is lucky to have summer work that gives him so much time for play.

Some Saeter Questions

1. Why are there good pastures high on the Norwegian mountains?

2. Why aren't there any trees up there?

3. Why do the farmers send their cows to the saeters in summer?

4. How does the work at the saeters help the families in getting food and money?

5. Why do the boys like their summers at the saeters?

ON THE FARM WITH INGER

How Inger Helps Her Mother

While Erik is at the saeter, Inger is at home helping with the farm work. She helps her mother to weed the garden, pick vegetables, feed the hens, and milk the goats. Inger is fond of the goats, and she likes to play with them as they graze on the rocky slopes back of the farm.

Inger is carrying some big round cheeses into the storehouse that she calls the stabbur.

From goats' milk mixed with cows' milk Inger's mother makes a brown cheese that the Norwegians like very much. Every week she stores away more cheese in the stabbur for the winter.

When Inger brings mountain cranberries down from the saeter, her mother makes jam of them, and this too goes into the stabbur. When Inger brings cloudberries, her mother puts them in stone jars. Stored in a cool, dark place, the cloudberries keep fresh and taste as sweet in winter as in summer.

Inger is a great help to her mother, but she doesn't spend her whole vacation working. The summer days are so long that she has plenty of time to play with the girls who live on neighboring farms. What good times they do have! They play in the woods, wade in the brooks, pick berries and flowers, and go rowing on the fiord.

Twice a week a boat comes up the fiord from Bergen, a city farther down the coast. It carries passengers, mail, and packages, and it stops at the village where the children go to school. Inger and her friends often go to the village to see the boat come in.

Haying Time

Summer on the farm is a time of getting ready for winter. During the cold weather the ground will be covered with snow. There will be no chance of growing any crops, and the cows and goats will not be able to graze outdoors. Before winter begins there must be plenty of food on hand for the family, and plenty of feed for the livestock.

July is haying time. The grass is tall now and ready to be harvested. The picture shows how Inger's father cuts it. With each swing of his scythe a big half circle of the hay falls to the ground.

Inger's father cuts the hay with a scythe.

Inger and her mother rake up the hay and hang it on the wires to dry.

Why do you suppose Inger's father doesn't use a mowing machine? It is because the farm is so small that it wouldn't pay him to own one. It is better for him to spend more of his time on his farm work than to spend money for farming machines.

Before the hay is put in the barn, it must be dried. This is not so easy in Norway as in some countries, because of the damp weather. The west coast is very damp, and the summer days are often half rain and half sunshine. In weather like this, hay left lying on the ground to dry is likely to spoil in the dampness.

Across the fields Inger's father puts up sticks with wires strung between them. Inger and her mother rake up the hay and hang it on the wires. Here the wind can blow through it, and the wind and sun together will dry it. Inger likes handling the fresh hay because it smells so sweet.

As soon as the hay is dry, Inger and her father and mother get it under cover. They take it off the wires and load it into a little two-wheeled hay cart. The horse hauls the loads of hay to the barn, and Inger's father pitches it into a loft under the roof.

But this is not all that Inger's father does to get hay for his livestock. He goes part way up the mountainside and cuts the grass that grows in small patches there. You will like to see how he gets it down to the farm. A long, strong wire is strung from a tree on the mountainside to a post near the barn. Inger's father ties the hay in bundles. Then all he has to do is to hang a bundle on the wire, and zip! it goes whizzing down to the farmyard.

Inger's father is always glad when his hay crop is safely in the barn. He knows then that the cows and the goats will not go hungry in the winter.

When the hay has dried, it is taken off the wires and carted to the barn.

Inger's Father Goes Herring-Fishing

In August Inger's father and the other farmer-fishermen wait anxiously for word by telephone of the "herring run." When the word comes, it means that the herring are swimming into the waters of the skerry guard from the ocean. These fish live part of their lives far out at sea, but at certain times of year they come in near the coast. They swim in great swarms near the top of the water, and it is easy to catch them in big nets.

The very day that news of the "run" comes, Erik's father and his neighbors go down the fiord in their boats. There are several men to each boat, and they all work together. When they reach the skerry guard, they put out their nets to catch the fish.

If the fishing is good, it takes strong muscles to pull up the nets. But the men are only too glad to tug at a net filled with hundreds of flopping fish. Herring mean both food and money to the fishermen. They sell the fish to the captains of boats belonging to fish merchants in Bergen. The boats are always on hand to take the herring that the fishermen catch.

In some years the fishing is rather poor and the men do not make much money. But they never come back with empty boats. They always bring a supply of herring for each man's family. They need the herring because their farms are too small to supply all the food they must have. They dry the herring and store them away in the stabburs.

In good years the men come home happy. They have money in their pockets as well as herring in their boats. They need money to buy things they want for themselves and their families: things for their houses, winter clothes, and new tools.

More Work in the Fields

By the last of August the days have grown much shorter, but the weather is still rather warm. The grain is ripe, and harvest time has come. There are busy days ahead for our friends on the farm by the fiord.

180

Erik's father and his friends are hauling in a big net filled with herring.

Hanging the grain on posts to dry.

Erik's father cuts the oats, rye, and barley with his scythe. Inger and her mother gather up the stalks, tie them in bundles, and hang the bundles on posts to dry in the fields. When the grain is dry, it is carted to the barn. Later on, Erik's father will thresh the grain with a small machine that turns by hand.

Some of the oats are saved for winter feed for the horse. The rest of the oats and all the barley and rye are ground into flour and meal and stored in the stabbur. Erik's father takes the grain to a mill in the village to be ground.

You will remember that Erik's mother uses oatmeal flour, rye flour, and barley meal to make flatbread. She makes other kinds of bread of these grains, too. If she wants wheat flour, she has to buy it.

Are you wondering why Erik's father doesn't grow wheat or corn on his little farm? The answer is to be found in one word: weather. The summers on the west coast of Norway are not hot enough for either wheat or corn to ripen well, and for wheat there is too much rain. Erik's father raises oats, rye, and barley because the weather is better for these grain crops than for any others.

After the grain harvest comes the digging of the potatoes, carrots, and turnips. Erik's father

digs them all with an iron fork. When at last the potatoes are stored away in the stabbur and the carrots and turnips are in bins in the barn, Erik's father feels that he is ready for winter. He has a good supply of food on hand for the family, and fodder enough for the livestock.

Facts and Questions

The sentences in italics *like this* give facts which you have learned about the farmer-fishermen on the west coast of Norway. The questions are for you to answer.

1. *The farmer-fishermen work hard in summer to get ready for winter.* Why is this? What would happen if they were lazy in the summer?

2. *Their grain crops are oats, rye, and barley.* Why do they raise these kinds of grain? Why don't they raise wheat and corn?

3. *Among their other crops are hay, turnips, and carrots.* Why do they raise them? How do these crops help in supplying the families with food?

4. *The farmer-fishermen take time from their farm work in summer to go fishing.* What do they catch? Why must they take time off to go fishing?

Volunteer Teamwork

Hunt in old magazines for pictures for a schoolroom show which you can call "Norway's Five F's." If you cannot find pictures such as you want, draw them.

Digging the winter's supply of potatoes.

Erik's father cuts his own firewood and hauls it home with his horse and sled.

WORK AND PLAY IN THE WINTERTIME

When the Leaves Begin to Turn

Early in September Erik and his sisters come back from the saeter with the cows. The nights on the mountain pastures are growing very chilly, and soon there will be snow instead of rain up there. Coming down through the woods to the farm, Erik sees that the birch leaves are turning yellow and the maple leaves are turning red. Autumn has come, school opens tomorrow, and winter is on the way.

After all the crops have been harvested, Erik's father works in the woods nearly every day cutting firewood. He stacks the wood and leaves it where it is until after the snow has fallen. During the winter he will use his horse and sled to bring the firewood home as he needs it.

Erik's mother and older sisters are busy now knitting socks, sweaters, caps, and mittens for the whole family. How their needles fly, and what pretty things they make of bright-colored wools! All these wooly things will feel good when the cold winter weather comes.

When the Snow Falls

Now the birches and maples have lost their leaves. The days are short and the nights are frosty. There will be no more outdoor farm work until spring but Erik's family will have plenty to do in the cold weather. His mother and older sisters will be busy with housework and mending. They will milk the cows and goats and make butter and cheese just as they do in summer.

Erik's father will feed and care for the livestock, and he will spend a good deal of time hauling and chopping wood for the fires. He will repair his farming tools and mend his fishing nets.

Soon there is snow enough for Erik and Inger to use their skis. Skis, you know, are long, narrow runners made of wood. You fasten one to each foot and go whizzing down the snowy hills. If you are as good a skier as Erik or Inger, you can get up the hills too. All winter they go to school on their skis.

Do you remember how the country looked when you first saw Erik and Inger rowing to school in June? It looks very different now. The snow lies deep and soft on the ground, and the evergreen trees are frosted with snow and ice. The waters of the fiord look almost black. There is no skating on the fiord because it never freezes over.

During the last months of the year the nights grow longer and longer and the days grow shorter and shorter. The sun rises in the middle of the

Erik and Inger go to school on their skis.

the woods. They cut down a Christmas tree and a little birch tree and drag them both home. The birch is the Christmas tree for the birds. Erik sticks it in the snow near the barn. Then he and Inger trim the tree by tying a great many heads of grain full of seeds on it. They love to see the birds come and pick the seeds off.

On Christmas Eve Inger's mother cooks a special supper, and what a feast it is! Erik and Inger talk of their Christmas *lutefisk* just as we talk of our Christmas turkey. Lutefisk is codfish cooked in a special way, and there are many things to go with it. For dessert there are all kinds of sweet cakes and coffee.

Later in the evening Erik and Inger have their Christmas tree and their presents. Then everyone in the family joins hands, and they all circle round the tree, singing Christmas carols. When the clock strikes twelve, everyone shouts "Glaedelig Jul!" which means "Merry Christmas!" Then Erik and Inger go off to bed.

On Christmas morning Erik's family go to church in the village, and there they meet all their friends and neighbors. Christmas afternoon is the beginning of a whole week of holidays with jolly parties every evening in different people's houses; parties not just for the grownups but for the children too. Erik says the parties are great fun, with music and dancing and good things to eat.

morning and goes to bed in the middle of the afternoon. The noonday sun is never high in the sky, and even when the sky is clear, the sunshine is pale.

Does the wintertime sound unpleasant to you? Inger doesn't think it is. She loves to ski and coast and play in the snow, and to feel her cheeks getting rosy in the clean, cold air. She says the nights aren't always dark; you mustn't forget the moon. Bright moonlight on the snow almost turns night into day, and it makes the countryside look like fairyland.

And then on dark nights you are so cozy in the kitchen at home, with a roaring fire in the stove. Your father is sitting there smoking his pipe and reading a paper. Your mother and sisters are knitting. After you and Erik have finished your homework, your father tells you stories or plays games with you until it is time to slip into your warm feather beds.

Christmas on the Farm

Christmas comes when the days are shortest, but Erik and Inger have a wonderful time. A few days before, Erik and his father go out in

Trimming the Christmas tree for the birds.

Winter Fishing

In the winter the herring again come swimming inshore from the sea, usually late in November or early in December. So, before Christmas, Erik's father makes another herring-fishing trip. But his big fishing trip comes later.

If you were on a mail steamer going up the coast of Norway in January, you would see hundreds of small fishing boats hurrying northward. They are bound for the Lofoten Islands, north of the arctic circle.

The Lofoten Islands are mountains that lift their heads out of the sea. They are bare and rocky, but they are dotted with fishing villages. In January, February, and March the villages are crowded with fishermen, and the harbors are crowded with boats. The reason for this is that in these months there are millions of codfish in the deep waters round the islands.

It is a cold, gray day in January, and the cod-fishing boats from Erik's fiord are racing northward with the others. Erik's father and three neighbors are partners in one of the boats. They own a little hut at one of the fishing villages on the Lofoten Islands, where they eat and sleep during the fishing season.

Each morning hundreds of boats leave the harbors and sail out on the cold, stormy sea. At night they come back with the fish that the men have caught with hooks and lines. The fishermen come ashore tired and often feeling half frozen, but if the fishing has been good, they do not mind.

Winter cod-fishing is hard and dangerous, and sometimes a boat overturns and the men are drowned. But the men keep at it because they need the money that they get for the fish. They sell the cod to merchants who hire men on the islands to salt and dry it.

March comes, and the cod begin to grow scarcer. By twos and threes the fishing boats leave for home. The men carry home the money they have earned and a supply of salted codfish for their families.

Can't you imagine how glad Erik and Inger are when their father is safely home again? The first thing they ask is, "Was the fishing good?" They hope so, for they know their father needs money to take care of them as he wants to.

184

A glimpse of one of the fishing villages in the Lofoten Islands.

If the fishing has been poor, they are sorry their father has worked so hard for so little money, but they don't worry. As long as they have their house, food from the farm to eat, and firewood from the forest, they will not go hungry or cold. If they can't have new clothes, old ones can be made over. Another year perhaps the fishing will be better.

Do you see now why Erik's father and his neighbors divide their time between fishing and farming? Remember these two things: (1) the west-coast farms of Norway are small because the country is so mountainous that there is not much level land; and (2) Norway is so far north that crops can be grown only in the summer.

From these little farms there is no chance of getting much more food than each family needs, and so there is very little extra to sell. In order to earn money, the farmers must do other work, and since they live near the sea, that work is fishing. Fishing, as you have seen, is a way of getting more food, too.

When you think of Erik and Inger on their little farm, remember that their father is one of thousands of farmer-fishermen whose homes are scattered along the mountain-walled fiords of western Norway, and that these men work on the land and on the sea to make a living for their families.

Choose and Finish

In each sentence one of the three parts in parentheses (like this) is right, and the other two are wrong. Choose the part that makes the sentence right, and then finish the sentence in your own words.

1. After the harvest Erik's father works in the (fields) (boathouse) (woods) because _ _ _

Winter cod-fishing is cold, hard work.

2. During the winter he cannot (keep livestock) (grow crops) (earn money) because _ _ _

3. During the winter he goes (hunting) (on a vacation) (fishing) because _ _ _

4. His work at the Lofoten Islands is (hard) (pleasant) (easy) because _ _ _

A Question to Think Out

The question is this: Which is the better land for farming — the west coast of Norway or the Yangtze Plain in China? Here are some helps for you in answering it.

1. In which of these parts of the world is the surface of the land better for farming? Why?

2. Which one of them has enough rain for crops, but not more than is needed?

3. Which one has the longer growing season, and why?

4. Now read the question at the top again. What is your answer to it?

SOME THINGS TO TALK OVER

About Food

In reading about your friends in far-away lands you have learned of a number of different ways in which people get food. Here are some helps for a talk with your classmates about what you have learned.

1. Name one or more groups of people who get part or all of their food in each of these ways:

Hunting   Fishing   Herding
Farming or gardening
Gathering food from wild plants and trees

2. Do your parents buy all your food? If not, how do they get some of it?

3. If people live where they can buy little or no food, what must they do? Give some examples of such people.

4. Give some examples to show that people who get food by farming or gardening raise the kinds of crops that grow best in the lands where they live.

5. Why are farmers and fishermen very important to people who buy all their food?

About Clothes

Here are four topics for you and your classmates to talk over.

1. How the kinds of clothes that we wear are suited to the weather where we live.

2. How we get our clothes.

3. Why some of our friends in far-away lands need clothes quite different from ours.

4. What materials they use for their clothes and why they use them.

About Houses and Fuel

Think over what you have learned in this book about houses and fuel. Give examples to prove each of these facts.

1. People in different parts of the world need different kinds of houses.

2. People who cannot or do not buy building materials use what they can get most easily to give them the kind of shelter they need.

3. People everywhere need fuel.

4. In some parts of the world people need much more fuel than in others.

5. People who cannot or do not buy fuel use whatever kind they can get most easily.

About Transportation

You learned on page 64 what is meant by transportation. See if you can answer these transportation questions:

1. There are two reasons why people everywhere need means, or ways, of transportation. What are they?

2. Among the groups of people whom you have met in this book, which ones use boats as means of transportation, and why?

3. Which groups use animals as means of transportation, and why?

4. What means of transportation are used in our country? You should be able to think of a good many different kinds.

About Continents

In reading about the boys and girls in this book you have learned the names of six of the seven continents of the world. Can you answer these questions about them?

1. In which continent do we live?

2. Which continent is connected with our own by a narrow isthmus?

3. In which continent do the Egyptians and the Congo natives live?

4. Which two continents make up the great body of land called Eurasia?

5. In which of these two continents do the Norwegians live?

6. In which of them do the Kazaks, the Bengalis, the Chinese, and the Negritos of Malaya live?

7. Which continent is a cold, frozen land in the Far South?

8. The seventh continent is Australia. Find it in the picture of the globe on page 5. Which continent is Australia's nearest neighbor?

The Earth and Our Hemisphere

THE WORLD PATTERN OF LAND AND WATER

Two Ways of Dividing the Earth in Halves

The equator, you know, divides the earth into halves which are called the Northern Hemisphere and the Southern Hemisphere. You learned on page 70 that the warm belt of the earth is on both sides of the equator, half in the Northern Hemisphere and half in the Southern Hemisphere. You learned also that each of these hemispheres has its temperate belt and its cold cap. These are important things to remember about the Northern and Southern hemispheres.

Your schoolroom globe shows that south of the arctic circle two great oceans separate North and South America from Eurasia, Africa, and Australia: the Atlantic Ocean east of the Americas, and the Pacific Ocean west of them. A line drawn north and south round the globe through these oceans divides the earth into an Eastern Hemisphere and a Western Hemisphere. The maps on pages 188–189 show the earth divided in halves in this way.

You have learned in your history lessons about the discovery of America by Christopher Columbus. Columbus, you know, was trying to get to the eastern part of Asia by sailing westward across the Atlantic Ocean from Europe. Instead of reaching Asia, which was thousands of miles farther on, he bumped into the Americas.

You have learned, too, how people from Europe began to explore the newly found lands across the Atlantic. Bit by bit they discovered that the new lands were two great continents joined together by the narrow Isthmus of Panama, and that the Pacific Ocean was much broader than the Atlantic Ocean. It was then that map-makers began to draw maps dividing the earth into an Eastern Hemisphere and a Western Hemisphere.

Useful Lines on Globes and Maps

You know that the equator, the tropics of Cancer and Capricorn, and the arctic and antarctic circles are east-and-west lines drawn on globes and maps, not on the earth itself. On the hemisphere maps (pp. 188–189) you will find other east-and-west lines, and on your schoolroom globe you will find still more. *All places on any one of these lines are east and west of one another.*

For example, suppose that Netsook were camping at a place on the arctic circle in Baffin Island. Suppose that at the same time Erik were visiting friends at a place on the arctic circle in Norway. Erik and Netsook would be directly east and west of each other.

Notice that on the hemisphere maps there are also lines running north and south. Look at your schoolroom globe and you will see that all the north-and-south lines meet and cross at the north pole and the south pole. *All places on any one of these lines are north and south of one another.*

A map of the Western Hemisphere.

For example, suppose that Netsook were camping at a place on the north-and-south line that crosses Baffin Island on the map on this page. He would be directly north of the parts of North America and South America through which that line passes. Suppose that you were a South American boy or girl living on that line. Should you be directly north of Netsook, or directly south of him?

You will want to remember that the north-and-south lines and the east-and-west lines drawn on globes and maps are very useful in telling what direction one place on the earth is from another.

A map of the Eastern Hemisphere.

The Earth As It Is—Undivided

Dividing the earth into hemispheres is useful in many ways, but we must never forget that the earth is round, and that the map pasted on a globe is the only true picture of it. When we draw maps of the hemispheres or of any smaller parts of the earth, we are really taking the globe-map to pieces and flattening the pieces out.

The best map for showing how the continents and the oceans are arranged is one which is as much like the globe-map as a flat map can be. The map on page 190 is one of that kind.

189

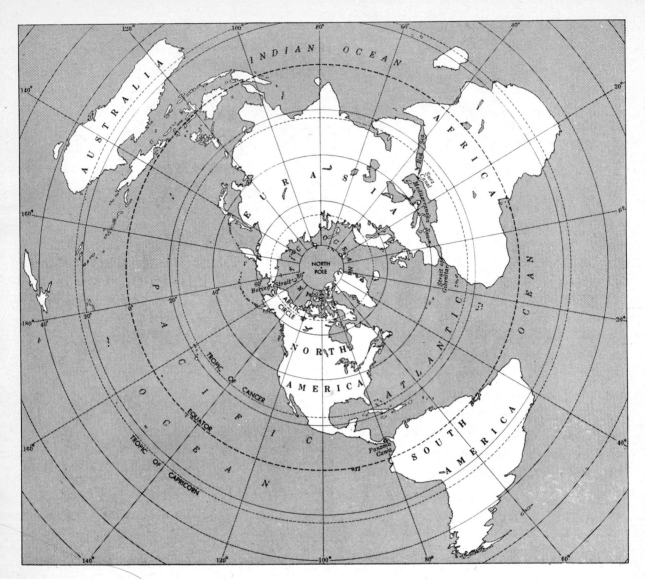

A map of the world showing all the continents except cold, frozen Antarctica.

This map shows a large part of the globe-map flattened out, with its center at the north pole. You may think of it as a "north polar map" because it is rather as if you were looking down on the earth from a point above the north pole. It shows more than one could really see from such a position.

The straight lines that run out from the north pole on the map are like spokes running out from the hub of a wheel. They are all north-to-south lines. You could draw any number of other straight "spoke lines" running out from the polar hub of the map, and they too would all be north-to-south lines.

The circles on the map are east-and-west lines. The one drawn in a heavy dash line is the equator. The ones drawn in lighter dash lines are the arctic circle, the tropic of Cancer, and the tropic of Capricorn. Any circle that you might draw on this map with its center at the north pole would be an east-and-west line.

Notice these things as you study the map:

About the continents: 1. North America and Eurasia are wholly in the Northern Hemisphere;

that is, they are between the equator and the north pole. Together they almost encircle the Arctic Ocean.

2. A large part of Africa and a small part of South America are in the Northern Hemisphere.

3. Australia, the island continent, is wholly in the Southern Hemisphere, but it is not very far south of the equator.

About the oceans: 1. The Pacific Ocean, the Atlantic Ocean, and the Indian Ocean are connected with one another in the Southern Hemisphere.

2. The Arctic Ocean is connected with the Pacific Ocean between North America and Asia, and with the Atlantic Ocean between North America and Europe.

3. The oceans are not separate bodies of water. They form one great world ocean.

In studying the map, did you notice that in one place North America and Asia almost meet? All that separates them is the narrow strip of water connecting the Arctic Ocean with the Pacific Ocean. A narrow strip of water which connects two larger bodies of water is called a *strait*. The one that separates North America from Asia is named Bering Strait.

The Highways of the Oceans

From the map you can learn some important things about travel and transportation between distant parts of the world.

For nearly four hundred and fifty years after Columbus discovered America, the only way of traveling or carrying goods between the lands of the Western Hemisphere and those of the Eastern Hemisphere was in ships. Across the Atlantic Ocean there were direct shipping routes between the Americas and western Europe and Africa. Across the Pacific Ocean there were direct routes between the Americas and eastern Asia and Australia.

But suppose a ship had to go on a voyage from a port in western Europe to a port in eastern Asia. The map shows that for such a voyage the shortest route would be northward across the Arctic Ocean and out through Bering Strait to the Pacific Ocean. Unfortunately, this route could not be used. Ship captains discovered long ago that the entire central part of the Arctic Ocean is blocked by ice the year round.

So, to get from the Atlantic Ocean to the Pacific Ocean, a ship had to start southward instead of northward. It had a choice of two roundabout routes. One was round the southern end of Africa. The other was round the southern end of South America.

The time came when men began to think of ways of shortening these long, roundabout shipping routes. In the year 1869 a canal for ships was dug through the Isthmus of Suez, which joins Africa to southwest Asia. It was named the Suez Canal. You can see from the map that the Suez Canal made the Mediterranean Sea and the Red Sea a short cut from the Atlantic Ocean to the Indian Ocean, and so to the Pacific Ocean.

Later, in 1914, the Panama Canal was finished. This was a waterway for ships through the Isthmus of Panama. It was a short cut between the Atlantic Ocean and the Pacific Ocean through the narrowest part of the Americas.

When the Panama Canal was built, most people thought that at last everything possible had been done to shorten world routes of travel and transportation. By that time airplanes had been invented, but not many people expected they would ever be able to fly long distances over water.

The oceans are the world highways for ships today just as they always have been. Ships are much bigger and faster than they used to be, but they cannot travel on land and they cannot fly. They must stay on the waters of the earth. On many a voyage a ship must take a roundabout route because the straight route to where it is going is barred by land that lies in the way.

The World Highways of the Air

Flying is such a new way of getting about that people do not have to be very old to remember when planes first began to carry passengers and mail. It has given us a world network of highways in the air. It has speeded up travel and transportation tremendously. Think how much faster planes travel than the fastest trains, automobiles, and ships. Think, too, what a free, open highway the air is between any two places on the earth.

Here is just one example of what the use of the air means in saving time in travel and transportation.

Suppose you are in Norway visiting Erik, and you decide to go from there to Egypt to visit Abdul. The map on this page gives you a choice of three ways of making the trip. The trip by sea starts from the Norwegian seaport of Bergen. The other two trips start from Oslo, the capital of Norway. All three end at Alexandria, the great seaport of Egypt.

Answer these questions from the map:

1. Which way of getting from Norway to Egypt is the most roundabout and takes the most time?

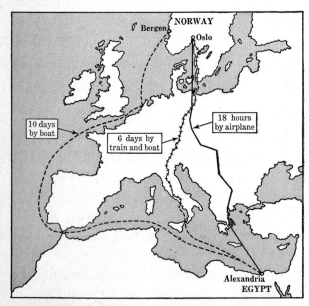

A map showing three ways of traveling from Norway to Egypt.

2. Which one means traveling partly by boat and partly by train?

3. Which one is the shortest and takes the least time?

The route by air from Oslo to Alexandria zigzags a little because the planes stop at a number of cities on the way to land and take on passengers. If you should hire a plane just for your own use on the trip, you could make a nonstop flight in a straight line from Oslo to Alexandria.

The most important thing to remember about flying is that planes can take the direct routes from one place to another, and direct routes are the shortest.

Roads and railroads can follow the shortest routes only where the land is level. Hills and mountains mean that roads and railroads must twist and turn. A ship can take the shortest route between two ports only if there is no land along the direct line between them. A plane can fly a direct course between any two places on the earth because there is nothing in the air to bar its way.

You know, of course, that our country has a network of airways, or flying routes, which connect all our larger cities. Our airways are only a part of the world network of flying routes which connect the different countries and the different continents with one another.

The map on page 193 shows the main airways which connect the continents today. Planes fly regularly over the world airways, carrying passengers and mail, and many airlines also carry freight. On flights over land and over bodies of water which are not too wide, the planes take the shortest routes possible between the cities where they are to make stops.

On flights over the broadest spaces of the oceans, the planes stop at islands. For example, on the long flying route across the Pacific Ocean between North America and Asia there are a number of island stops at which planes land to refuel, or take on more

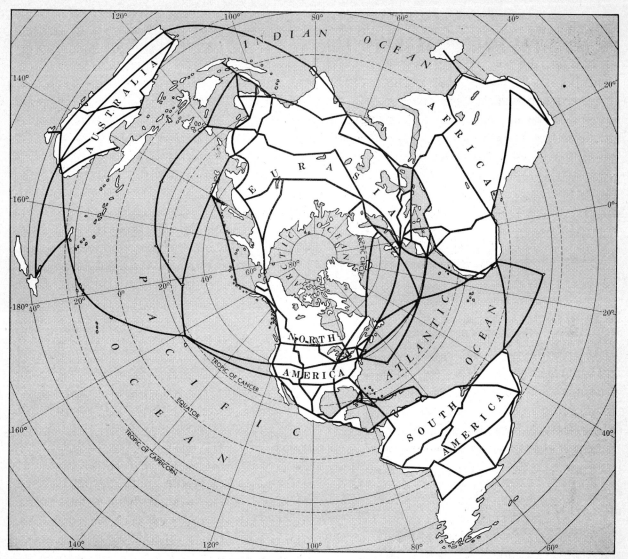

A map showing the main airways of the world.

---

gasoline. At some of these stops they take on passengers as well.

As time goes on, there will be even more travel and transportation by air than there is today. The planes now in use are larger and faster than ever before, and still larger and faster ones are planned. Already there are planes which can carry enough gasoline to make long nonstop flights over land, water, and ice. This means, for one thing, that there may be regular air routes over the frozen waters of the Arctic Ocean and over the great ice cap of

Greenland. You can see from the map how these routes will shorten flying distances between certain parts of North America and certain parts of Eurasia. Shorter flying distances and faster planes will mean a saving of much time in travel and transportation.

By the time you are grown up, and perhaps long before, the airways over the northern cold cap may be in regular use. To understand about them, and about other changes in flying routes, you will want to keep a north polar map of the earth in your mind.

OUR NEIGHBORS TO THE SOUTH

UNITED STATES

ATLANTIC

Gulf of Mexico

MEXICO

TROPIC OF CANCER

Mexico City   Veracruz

WEST INDIES

7

8   9

OCEAN

Caribbean Sea

1
2
CENTRAL
3
4
AMERICA
5
6

Isthmus of Panama

PACIFIC

VENEZUELA

B
GUIANA   S F

COLOMBIA

EQUATOR

ECUADOR

Amazon   River

B R A Z I L

OCEAN

PERU

BOLIVIA

Rio de Janeiro

PARAGUAY

TROPIC OF CAPRICORN

São Paulo

CHILE

ARGENTINA

URUGUAY

Buenos Aires
Pampa   Rio de la Plata

ATLANTIC

PATAGONIA

OCEAN

**Countries of Central America
and the West Indies**

1	Guatemala	5	Costa Rica
2	El Salvador	6	Panama
3	Honduras	7	Cuba
4	Nicaragua	8	Haiti
	9 Dominican Republic		

European Colonies in South America

B British Guiana
S Surinam (Dutch Guiana)
F French Guiana

Spanish America and Portuguese America

After Columbus discovered America, the people of Europe began to call the lands of the Western Hemisphere the New World. The lands of their own hemisphere they called the Old World. At that time no one supposed that there would ever be any way of traveling between the Old World and the New World except in ships.

In those days and for long afterward ocean travel was in small sailing ships. Ocean voyages were slow, even with good winds. The ships were often overcrowded, and on long voyages the supplies of food and water sometimes ran short. Then, too, there was always the chance that a ship might be wrecked in a storm and everybody on board drowned.

In spite of the hardships and dangers, people from Europe began to cross the Atlantic Ocean to make new homes in the New World. As years went by, more and more settlers came to the Americas. You have learned in your history lessons about the people from England and other countries of northwestern Europe who made settlements on the coast of the part of North America which is now the United States. Farther south in the Americas most of the early settlers were from Spain and Portugal, countries which are in the southwestern part of Europe.

The New World settlements of people from different countries of Europe grew into colonies of those countries. In time most of the colonies freed themselves from the rule of the mother countries in Europe. The English colonies which became our own United States took the lead. Others followed, until there was only a scattering of European colonies left in the Americas.

Today the United States is one of twenty-two free and independent countries in the Western Hemisphere. Only one of the other countries is north of us. That country is Canada. Seven are in the southern part of North America, and three are in the West Indies. Ten of the twenty-two countries are in South America.

Most of the countries to the south of us were once colonies of Spain, and their people speak the Spanish language. These countries make up what we call Spanish America. Brazil, the largest of all the countries to the south of us, belonged to Portugal, and there the people speak the Portuguese language. For this reason Brazil is often called Portuguese America.

Wherever the white people from Europe made settlements in the Americas, they found Indians. Little by little they conquered the Indians and took the Americas for their own. You met some of the Indians of today when you were reading about Pedro and his people. There are large numbers of them in certain of the countries of Spanish America.

In Spanish America and in Brazil many of the white men who made the early settlements married Indian women. Their children, who were half Indian and half Spanish or Portuguese, were the beginning of a new kind of people. Today, in many of the countries to the south of us, there are large numbers of these people who are partly white and partly Indian. They are called *mestizos*.

Like our own country, some of our neighbors to the south have many Negroes among their people. Negroes were first brought to certain parts of the Americas to work as slaves for the white people, but there are no slaves anywhere in the two continents now. The Negroes were given their freedom many years ago.

Next year you will be studying about the Americas. You will be learning about our own United States and the countries which are our neighbors in the Western Hemisphere. There is time now for a few glimpses of three of those countries.

Manuel is out for a horseback ride on his father's hacienda.

Manuel Tells about Mexico

The boy in the picture is named Manuel. He is out for a horseback ride before breakfast. If he meets a friend, he will wave his hand and say "Buenos días!" The words are Spanish, and they mean "Good morning."

Manuel is a Mexican boy. His country, Mexico, is our next-door neighbor on the south. It has a Y-shaped framework of mountains that Manuel calls *sierras*. The central part of the country is a rather dry plateau. Parts of the plateau have enough rain for grass to grow, but most of the crops that are raised there must be watered by irrigation. The only lowlands in Mexico are along the coasts.

The map on page 194 shows that the tropic of Cancer crosses Mexico just about in the middle of the country. The northern half, then, is in the warmest part of the north temperate belt of the earth, while the southern half is in the warm belt.

Manuel wants you to know about the weather in Mexico. He says that if the whole country were a low plain, it would all be warm, and the southern half would be hot. A visit to the coastal lowlands would show you that Manuel is right. The lowlands are warm lands.

But, Manuel says, a large part of Mexico is "temperate land." He doesn't mean the half of the country which is in the north temperate belt of the earth. He means all the land in Mexico which is high enough to have mild weather the year round. Part of this land is south of the tropic of Cancer. The plateau of Mexico and the valleys among the mountains make up the "temperate land."

Mexico also has its cold lands. These, as you will easily guess, are the higher parts of the mountains. Some of the highest peaks are capped with snow at all times of year. The one in the picture has a long name that means "The White Woman." The Indians of long ago gave the mountain this name because they thought it looked like a woman lying down with a white robe over her.

Manuel says that the best way to understand the weather in Mexico is to think of it as "up-and-down" weather. In the highest lands the weather is cold, and in the lowest lands it is hot. In the "temperate land" the days are warm and are apt to be hot in the early afternoon. The nights are always cool and often chilly. As you might expect, this is the part of Mexico where the most people live.

196

Manuel's home is in the plateau of Mexico. His father owns a very large piece of land which he calls his *hacienda*. It is used partly for raising cattle and partly for raising crops. The cattle are raised to be sold for meat.

Manuel will lend you a horse and take you for a ride on the hacienda. You will see the cattle grazing in the pastures. You will see fields green with corn and others yellow with ripening wheat. Manuel will point out still other fields of fodder crops. He says that each year's fodder crops are for the cattle that are soon to be sold. The fodder puts the kind of flesh on the animals that makes good beef.

In one place some of Manuel's father's cowboys are driving a herd of cattle along a dusty cart road. The animals are being moved from a pasture where they have eaten most of the grass to a fresh one half a mile away. In another place a couple of men are plowing. A pair of big, strong oxen is pulling each plow, and the sight will remind you of Pedro's father in the altiplano in South America.

Manuel's father is talking of buying a machine plow and a tractor to pull it. They will come, Manuel says, from the United States, because the best farming machinery is made there.

You will not travel far in Mexico without discovering that much less farming machinery is used there than in our country. On the small farms you will not see any machines. Oxen or other animals are the only helpers in the farm work. Even on the big haciendas much work is done with hand tools, but more machines are being used every year.

Here and there on Manuel's hacienda you will see the houses where his father's workmen live. Manuel calls the workmen and their families *peons*, and he says they are Indians and mestizos. He says that Mexico is one of the Spanish-American countries where there are more mestizos and Indians than there are white people.

"The White Woman." The highest point of this beautiful mountain is more than three miles above the level of the sea.

The peon houses on the hacienda are small mud-brick huts with roofs thatched with straw. Each man may use as much land near his house as he needs to raise corn and vegetables for his family to eat, and he is allowed time from his hacienda work for his own farm work. He gets his house and the use of the land as part of his pay. The rest of his pay he gets in money.

Manuel wants you to understand that not all the Indians and mestizos in Mexico are peons. Thousands of them who live in the cities — especially the mestizos — do the same kinds of work that the white people do. Many have businesses of their own. Some are lawyers, doctors, or teachers, and some work for the government. Thousands work in stores, offices, and mills and factories.

Perhaps Manuel will take you home with him for lunch. His house, too, is built of mud-brick, but it is painted a pretty shade of

A Mexican potter painting a design on a jar.

you will find that more of the people make their living by farming than in any other way. On some of the haciendas cattle-raising is important work, as it is on Manuel's hacienda. On others the land is used mostly for raising crops, especially corn and wheat, and in some places cotton. Hacienda farming is "big farming," with hired peons plowing the land and planting and harvesting the crops. Manuel's father would tell you that there used to be more haciendas than there are now. During the last few years a good many of them have been broken up into smaller farms.

In many places there are villages of Indians and mestizos who raise crops on small farms of their own. They live somewhat as Pedro's people do, but their crops are different because of the warmer weather. They grow grain, vegetables, and fruits, and they keep chickens, pigs, and cattle. They raise more corn and beans than anything else, and they cook them in many different ways.

Besides raising most of their food, the people of the farming villages make many of the things they use. Some are skillful potters; they make

pink and it has a tiled roof. It is large and comfortably furnished. As you step inside, out of the hot sun, you will find it delightfully cool, for the thick walls keep out the heat.

The house is built round an open courtyard that Manuel calls the *patio*. The patio is really a garden, gay with flowers and shaded in spots by small trees. Building houses with patios is a habit all over Spanish America. It came with the early settlers from Spain.

If you do much traveling in the Mexican plateau or in the valleys among the sierras,

The plazas, or squares, in Mexican towns and villages are busy places on market days.

By Ewing Galloway, N.Y.

The beautiful cathedral in Mexico City is one of the largest churches in North America.

jars, bowls, and dishes of clay, and paint designs on them in bright colors. Others are clever weavers of baskets and of the big Mexican straw hats that are called sombreros. Still others are skillful weavers of shawls and blankets.

What little money the villagers have, they get by selling these and other things that they make. They sell to one another in their own villages, and to customers in neighboring towns. On market days they load the things they want to sell on donkeys, and off they go to the nearest town, just as Pedro's people do with their llamas.

Every man has a folded blanket thrown over one shoulder. This is his *serape*, and he almost never goes away from home without it. It is hand-woven of wool, and it is always gaily colored. A man's serape, Manuel says, keeps him dry when it rains and warm when the air is chilly. The women wear shawls that cover their heads as well as their shoulders, and for some reason the shawls are almost always blue. If there are babies to be taken along to market, they ride in folds that are rather like big pockets in their mothers' shawls.

There are many other interesting things to see in Mexico besides farms, haciendas, Indian villages, and market towns. Manuel thinks you ought to see some of the mines, because so much of the silver, gold, copper, and other metals that come from them are sold to the United States. Mexico is rich in metal ores, and they make it a great mining country.

Whether or not you see some of the mines, you will surely visit some of the cities. There, Manuel says, you will see how fast Mexico is going ahead with manufacturing, — the making of many different things in mills and factories. Not so long ago the Mexicans bought from the United States and other countries most of the factory-made things they used. Now they are making more and more themselves.

Most of all, Manuel wants you to see Mexico City. This is the beautiful capital of his country, where the president lives and much of the work of the government is carried on. It is in a lovely green valley on the southern margin of the plateau, and the people can see "The White Woman" and another snow-capped peak of the sierras in the distance.

199

Mexico City is one of the largest of all tne cities in Spanish America, and Manuel says it is one of the finest. You will know that he is not boasting when you see its beautiful churches and palaces, its parks, squares, and gardens gay with lovely flowers, and its fine homes, hotels, shops, and government buildings. There is no end to the things you can see and do in Mexico City, and once you have been there, you will want to go back again.

If you wish, you may come home from Mexico in a ship from the seaport of Veracruz. A train from Mexico City carries you down the outer slopes of the Eastern Sierra and across the narrow plain bordering the Gulf of Mexico. As the train zigzags down the steep slopes, the air grows warmer. About halfway down, you begin to run through patches of tropical forest. On the lower slopes and on the plain beyond, crops that need much warmth and moisture are growing. Among these crops are coffee and bananas.

When you reach Veracruz, you are not much farther south than you were in Mexico City, but you are at sea level, nearly a mile and a half lower. You have traveled from the "temperate land" of Mexico to a part of the country which is low, hot, and rainy.

Manuel hopes that you have liked what you have seen of his country, and that you will tell your friends about it. He thinks that next-door neighbors like the Mexicans and the Americans ought to know each other better. Don't you think so, too?

Some Questions about Mexico

1. Why do most crops grown in the Mexican Plateau have to be irrigated?

2. Why is the weather much warmer in Veracruz than in Mexico City?

3. Why is Mexico a great mining country?

4. Where in Mexico do the most people live, and why?

Roberto goes to school in Buenos Aires.

Roberto Tells about Argentina

Roberto is an Argentine boy. He asks you to look at the map on page 194 and notice three things about Argentina. First, it is a large country in the southern part of South America. Second, it is in the Southern Hemisphere. Third, almost all of it is in the south temperate belt of the earth.

In the south temperate belt there are four seasons of the year just as there are in the north temperate belt. But if you visit Roberto in your summer vacation, you will not find him having his summer vacation. It will be wintertime in Argentina, and Roberto will be in school. You will understand why if you study this calendar.

A Calendar of Southern Hemisphere Seasons

	SPRING	
September 22	to	December 22
	SUMMER	
December 22	to	March 21
	AUTUMN	
March 21	to	June 21
	WINTER	
June 21	to	September 22

James Sawders

Straight ahead in this picture of Buenos Aires is the house of the president of Argentina. It is called the Casa Rosada, or the Pink House, because of its color.

The calendar shows that for Roberto Christmas comes in the summertime, not in the wintertime as it does with us. Our winter is his summer, and our summer is his winter. It is the same with the other seasons. Our spring is Roberto's autumn, and our autumn is his spring. The seasons in the Northern and Southern hemispheres are just opposite.

Roberto has two homes in Argentina. One is his father's house in the great city of Buenos Aires, the capital of Argentina. The other is a country house on his father's *estancia*. An Argentine estancia is somewhat like a Mexican hacienda. Roberto spends his summers on the estancia. The rest of the year he goes to school in Buenos Aires.

Three hundred years ago Buenos Aires was nothing but a little Spanish settlement of a few hundred people. Now it is one of the largest cities in the Western Hemisphere; larger than all others except two in the United States. Roberto would like a chance to show you what a fine, up-to-date city it is.

Buenos Aires is on the Rio de la Plata, which is Spanish for River of Silver. The Rio de la Plata is not a true river, and it is not silvery. It is a large wedge-shaped arm of the Atlantic Ocean. Into it pour a number of large rivers which carry so much mud that they make its waters yellowish in color.

Roberto says that the name Rio de la Plata is a reminder of the hopes of the Spanish who first settled on its shores. So is the name Argentina, for it too comes from a word that means silver. The early settlers thought they had come to a land rich in silver mines, but they were mistaken. Argentina's riches are of a different kind.

If you want to know about these riches, go with Roberto to the harbor of Buenos Aires, where the wharves and the ships are. Look at the huge grain elevators — buildings filled with wheat, corn, and other grains. Walk through some of the great warehouses that are packed with wool, cattle hides, and sheepskins. Ask Roberto to point out the buildings of one of the great meat-packing companies. In the packing houses the meat of thousands upon thousands of cattle, sheep, and pigs is made ready to be sold.

Watch the big freighters, or cargo ships, being loaded at the wharves. Huge steel arms called cranes lower bales of wool, bundles of hides and skins, and tons of meat into the holds, or storage spaces, in the ships. Streams of wheat, corn, and other grains pour into the holds through long spouts from the grain elevators.

Ask where the ships are going, and you will learn that Argentina helps to feed and clothe the people of many other countries, especially in Europe. The shipping of food and other products of Argentine farms and ranches to distant lands makes Buenos Aires one of the biggest and busiest seaports of the Western Hemisphere.

If you ask Roberto where the farms and ranches are, he will say, "Mostly in the Pampa." The Pampa is a great plain that stretches far away to the west and south of Buenos Aires. It is one of the flattest plains in the world. The Spaniards who first saw it called it a "sea of grass." The grass grew thick and tall, but there were almost no trees.

The Pampa is the kind of land that we call *prairie*. It has enough rain for a good growth of grass, but not enough for the growth of forests.

Roberto hopes you will be able to fly over some of the Pampa in a plane. From the air it looks like a giant patchwork carpet in shades of yellow, green, and brown. The patches are

Loading a ship with wool at Buenos Aires.

the pastures and the grainfields and other crop lands. The lines that crisscross the patchwork are roads and railroads. The larger clusters of buildings are towns.

The dark-green spots here and there are groves of trees planted for shade and for protection against the winds that sweep over the Pampa. Trees planted on this great plain must be watered until they are old enough to have pushed their roots deep into the ground, where they can get enough moisture to keep growing.

203

The Pampa of Argentina is a giant patchwork of pasture lands and crop lands.

This machine, drawn by a tractor, is planting wheat in a big field in the Pampa.

For a close-up view of the Pampa, you must ride over it in a train or an automobile. Then you will see how big everything is — the pastures, the fields of wheat, corn, and other crops, the herds of cattle, and the flocks of sheep.

You will find that the pastures are fenced with wire, and you will see so many windmills that you will lose count of them. The windmills pump water from beneath the ground for the cattle and sheep to drink. You will find that plowing, planting, and harvesting in the Pampa are done mostly with machines.

In many of the pastures, especially those where cattle are grazing, the animals are not feeding on grass. They are feeding on alfalfa, a plant that has very long roots. The roots go deep down into the ground where there is always moisture, even in dry weather. Years ago the people of the Pampa found they could have much better pastures by plowing up the wild grass and planting alfalfa in its place.

Roberto says that the Pampa used to be mostly a land of great estancias, but that now there are many smaller farms. You will find that "smaller farms" in the Pampa are large, and that estancias are huge.

204

Roberto's estancia is in a part of the Pampa where more cattle than sheep are raised, and where wheat is the principal crop. His house on the estancia is shaded and sheltered by a "windbreak" of trees. It is a large house with a patio, a tennis court, and a swimming pool. The people who work for Roberto's father call it the *casa grande*, which means the "great house." Their own houses are small.

Roberto says that in the summer he spends some of his time with his father's *gauchos*. Gauchos are Argentine cowboys. They live an outdoor life on horseback, and they are wonderful riders.

The gauchos keep the fences repaired so that the cattle cannot stray from the pastures. They watch the windmills to see that the water tanks never go dry. They move the herds of cattle from one pasture to another, so that the animals are always well fed. When the time comes to sell some of the cattle, the gauchos drive them to the nearest railroad station. There the animals are put in cars and sent to Buenos Aires to be killed for beef.

Roberto loves to ride with the gauchos as they go about their work far and wide on the great estancia. He likes to listen to their talk when they are at home doing odd jobs. He sends you this picture and the one on page 200 of Carlos and Luis, the two gauchos he likes the best.

Roberto loves to camp out with the gauchos.

A glimpse of one of the sheep ranches in chilly, windy Patagonia.

The most fun, Roberto says, is when he is allowed to ride so far with Carlos and Luis that they have to camp out overnight and come home the next day. They eat a supper cooked over an open fire, and then Carlos and Luis sing their cowboy songs and tell stories. When bedtime comes, they roll up in blankets on the ground and go to sleep with only the stars above them.

Roberto says that the wheat and other crops on the estancia are raised by tenant farmers. Each tenant farmer rents his house and the land he uses from Roberto's father. More often than not, the farming machines that he uses belong to Roberto's father, too. When the year's crops have been sold, each tenant pays Roberto's father whatever he owes for the rent of the house, the land, and the machines.

Sometimes there are years when the weather is so dry that the crops are poor. Now and then summer hailstorms beat down the grain and spoil much of it. The worst years are when millions of locusts swarm over the Pampa in the hot summer weather. They darken the sky like clouds, and they settle down on the fields to eat the crops. The farmers have ways of fighting these insect enemies, but sometimes they do a great deal of damage.

In spite of droughts, hailstorms, and locusts that come now and then, the Pampa is a wonderful farming and grazing land. Its soils are deep and rich. Its flatness makes it a perfect place for using the big farming machines that save so much time and work. The summer weather is sunny and hot, — the best kind for the ripening of grain.

The winter weather is never very cold, and so the cattle and sheep can graze outdoors in the pastures the year round. There is no need to build barns for them or to raise crops in summer to feed them in winter. Knowing these things about the Pampa, you can easily understand why the Argentinos can send so much meat, grain, and wool, and so many hides and skins to other countries.

Roberto says that when people in other countries think of Argentina, they almost always think of the Pampa. This is not surprising, for the Pampa is the part of the country that most visitors see, and the part where most of the things that are shipped to other countries come from.

Roberto wants you to know that, big as it is, the Pampa makes up only about one fourth of Argentina. All the other parts are different from the Pampa in one way or another.

In the south is the colder part of the country, — the part farthest from the equator. This part is called Patagonia. Roberto says that there is not much farming in Patagonia, because most of it is either too dry or too cold; but you should see the sheep ranches! They are some of the largest in all the world.

Cutting sugar cane in western Argentina.

like giant bouquets of pink and white flowers set in long rows. Later on, the branches bend under the weight of the fruit: peaches, pears, apples, plums, cherries, and apricots. Besides the orchards there are big vineyards where grapes that are used for making wine are grown.

Some of the oases, Roberto says, are Argentina's "sugar bowls." He means that in these oases much sugar cane is raised. Sugar cane grows tall and green like corn. It is grown for the sweet juice in the stalks, and from the juice sugar is made.

Roberto wishes he had time to tell you more about Patagonia and western Argentina, and some of the interesting things about the northern part of the country, but you will have to come again for that. He is glad you have seen something of the Pampa because, after all, the Pampa is the most important part of Argentina.

One thing you would notice if you were to travel all over Argentina is that there are very few Indians and not many mestizos. This is one of the ways in which Argentina is different from most of the Spanish-American countries. Most of the Argentinos are white people.

It will please Roberto if you say good-by in Spanish. "Adiós, Roberto!"

On the west Argentina extends to the crest line of the Andes Mountains. The crest line of a range of mountains is somewhat like the ridge of a roof, only it is not an even ridge. The mountain peaks make it jagged. It is the highest part of the range, and the mountainsides slope down from it on both sides.

From the main range of the Andes other and lower ranges branch off into western Argentina. Between these ranges there are stretches of level land, but it is land with too little rain for crops. Here, Roberto says, are the oases of Argentina, — the lands where crops are grown by bringing water to the fields from rivers that flow down from the mountains.

Each river is like a little "Father Nile" to the land that it waters. From high in the air the rivers look like threads strung with scattered beads of different sizes. The beads are the green oases with their farms, towns, and cities.

Roberto wishes you could see the orchards of fruit trees that cover so much land in some of the oases. In blossom time the trees look

Some Questions about Argentina

1. Why does Christmas come in the summertime in Argentina?

2. Why is the Pampa such a good place for raising cattle and sheep?

3. Why is it such a good place for raising wheat and other grains?

4. What makes Buenos Aires one of the busiest seaports of the Western Hemisphere?

5. Why is the southern part of Argentina the coldest part of the country?

6. Why is it that crops can be raised in the dry lands of western Argentina?

7. Of what building in the United States does the Pink House in Buenos Aires remind you?

Fernando Tells about Brazil

Fernando is a Brazilian boy, and so he speaks Portuguese instead of Spanish. He wants you to know that the full name of his country is *Estados Unidos do Brasil*, or, in English, the United States of Brazil.

The United States of Brazil is the giant country of South America. It is nearly as large as all the Spanish-American countries in South America put together. It is even a little larger than our own United States in North America.

Fernando has learned in school that all of our country is in the north temperate belt of the earth. He wants you to look at the map (p. 194) and see that most of his country is in the warm belt. Only the narrowest part of it is south of the tropic of Capricorn, in the temperate belt of the Southern Hemisphere.

First of all, Fernando wants to tell you a little about the northern part of Brazil. There, not far from the equator, the greatest river in the world winds its way for two thousand miles from west to east. It flows through a great lowland plain covered with tropical forest much like the Congo forest in Africa. It gathers in many tributaries which are themselves large rivers, and it carries their muddy waters to the Atlantic Ocean. Find this great river on the map on page 194. Its name is the Amazon.

Ships go up the Amazon River from a seaport near its mouth. For hours at a time

The books that Fernando reads are printed in the Portuguese language.

passengers see nothing but the broad, muddy river with the leafy wall of forest on the nearer bank. The farther bank is often too far away to be seen clearly. Now and then a dugout canoe, or a launch, or perhaps another ship, passes by. The Amazon and its tributaries are the highways of travel and transportation in the great forest. There are no railroads or motor roads.

No matter what time of year it happens to be, the weather is hot. Around noon dark clouds gather. Then down comes a pouring rain that may last for two or three hours. When the sky clears and the sun comes out again, the air feels sticky and steamy.

207

In northern Brazil there is a great tropical forest with many rivers winding through it.

There are towns along the Amazon and its tributaries, but they are far apart. The forest gives you a lonesome feeling because it seems to have so few people. Most of the people are mestizos and Indians. There are really many thousands of them, but the Amazon forest is so huge that the people seem almost lost in it.

It is easy to understand why there are not very many white people in the Amazon forest. White people find weather that is always so warm and rainy hard to stand. They prefer to live in places where the weather is cooler at least part of the time.

Fernando says that the Amazon forest is Brazil's "Land of Rubber." Trees that have a milky sap from which rubber is made are scattered here and there among many other kinds in the great forest. The sap is called latex. Mestizos and Indians make cuts in the trunks of the trees and hang up little cups to catch the latex as it oozes out.

Gathering latex from a wild rubber tree.

Making one of the balls of crude rubber.

Day after day the rubber-gatherers tramp the jungle paths that lead from tree to tree. They collect the latex in pails and buckets and carry it back to their little camps. They pour the latex, a little at a time, on sticks propped over slow-burning fires. The heat and the smoke harden the latex. After a while there is a big ball of solid rubber to be taken from each stick.

The balls of rubber are called "crude rubber"; that is, rubber ready to be sent to factories for use in making tires and many other things. They are carried away in the ships that come up the Amazon River from the ocean. Fernando thinks you would like to know about Brazilian rubber because the United States is buying all that Brazil can spare.

Perhaps you know that the United States uses more rubber than any other country in the world. Our tire factories alone need millions of pounds of rubber every year. We have always bought our rubber from other parts of the world, because we have almost no land hot and rainy enough for rubber trees.

Before the war most of our rubber came from countries in southeastern Asia where there are great plantations of rubber trees. In 1942 the Japanese captured those countries, and since then we have not been able to get any of their plantation rubber. That is why we are now so short of rubber.

There are millions of wild rubber trees in the great Amazon forest of Brazil, and yet we can get only a very small part of the rubber we need from there. One trouble is that the trees are so widely scattered through thousands of miles of the thick jungle that the gathering of the latex is slow work. Another is that the way of making the balls of crude rubber is also slow.

The greatest trouble is that there are not enough men in the Amazon forest who can be hired to work as rubber-gatherers. Far more workers are needed to gather enough latex and make enough crude rubber to help us out very much. Plans for sending more rubber-gatherers into the forest are now being made. If these plans work out, perhaps we shall be getting more rubber from Brazil before very long.

The map shows that in the east Brazil bulges out into the Atlantic Ocean. Stretching southward from the bulge there is a broad belt of land made up of mountains and hilly uplands. This belt of land is higher than the land in the Amazon forest, and so, even in the north, it is cooler and more comfortable. Winds from the ocean also help to cool this part of Brazil, and to most parts of it they bring plenty of rain.

Near the coast of eastern Brazil there are ranges of mountains that Fernando calls *serras*. In some places the steep, wooded slopes of the mountains rise from the water's edge. In other places there are narrow strips of lowland plains between the outer serras and the sea. Beyond the serras, the hilly uplands stretch away to the west.

Fernando lives in the part of eastern Brazil which has won the nickname of "Coffee Land." He wonders if you know that more coffee is grown in Brazil than in any other country in the world. Very likely your mother uses Brazilian coffee, for the United States is Brazil's best customer for it.

Fernando's home is in the big city of São Paulo, and he is as proud of it as Roberto is of Buenos Aires. He says that if you live in one of the big cities in the United States you will feel quite at home in São Paulo. It has a large central business section with tall buildings. Railroads come into it from all directions. Mills and factories make it a great manufacturing city. Its streets are crowded and busy, for it is a city of more than a million people.

Fernando would like to take you out into the country round São Paulo and show you some of the *fazendas* which make his part of Brazil so famous for its coffee. A Brazilian *fazenda* is a great estate used mostly for raising crops. It may be owned by a single man or by a company. The work is done by *colonos* and hired men. Colonos are tenant farmers and their families.

On the coffee fazendas miles of hillsides are covered with coffee trees set in straight rows.

On the coffee fazendas miles of hillsides are covered with coffee trees set in straight rows. The trees are not tall; they are more like big bushes. In spring they are covered with white blossoms. In May, in the Southern Hemisphere autumn, the trees are loaded with red berries about the size of large cranberries.

From May until August hundreds of colonos on every coffee fazenda are busy stripping the berries from the trees. The women and children join the men in this work. Oxcarts on some fazendas and small railroad cars on others carry the berries away from the groves.

The berries go to some central place on each fazenda. In each berry there are two seeds which we know as coffee "beans." Now the work of getting the seeds out of the berries and drying them begins.

First the berries are dumped into tanks or canals, where they are washed and the poor ones taken out and thrown away. Then the berries are put through machines that remove the pulp from the seeds. Next, the seeds are spread on outdoor platforms to dry in the sun.

The drying may take less than two weeks, or it may take from three to four weeks. It all depends on the weather. Every day or so, workmen rake the seeds to help the drying.

Whenever it looks like rain, the men rake the seeds into heaps and cover them with canvas.

When the drying is finished, the seeds are put through machines that take off their husks. Then, at last, the coffee beans are ready to be put in the big sacks in which they are sent away.

Fernando wants you to know that coffee is only one of many crops that are raised on the rich uplands of eastern Brazil. The list of all the crops is very long. Cotton fields cover big stretches of land, and so do cornfields and rice fields. There are many groves of orange trees, and many orchards of other fruit trees. Besides the crop lands, there are the pastures which are used for raising thousands of beef cattle.

Before Fernando says good-by, he wants to tell you about Rio, the seaport which is the capital of his country. Its full name is Rio de Janeiro, which means "River of January." This seems an odd name for a city, doesn't it?

Fernando says that a Portuguese sea captain sailed into a beautiful mountain-rimmed bay on the eastern coast of Brazil more than four hundred years ago. He thought he was in the mouth of a river. The month happened to be January, and so he called the place Rio de Janeiro. Later, when a settlement was made there, it was called by that name.

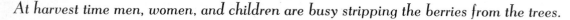

At harvest time men, women, and children are busy stripping the berries from the trees.

By Ewing Galloway, N.Y.

At night, from one of the mountaintops, the lights make Rio look like fairyland.

Rio, Fernando says, is the most beautiful city in the world. Every Brazilian thinks that, and many people who have traveled all over the world feel the same way. It is set in a circle of green, wooded mountains that rise from the blue waters of the bay. The city loops round the bases of the mountains, and in places where it meets the bay there are smooth, sandy beaches. It has beautiful buildings, lovely parks, and miles of boulevards lined with trees and beds of gorgeous flowers. Many visitors think that the loveliest view of Rio is at night from one of the mountaintops.

Fernando hopes you will remember that he has told you of only two parts of Brazil, and only a very little about each of them. It is as if you had told him just a little about two parts of the United States. You would hardly have begun the story of your country. Fernando has hardly begun the story of his.

Some Questions about Brazil

1. Why is Brazil as a whole a warmer country than our own United States?

2. Why are the rivers the highways of travel in the Amazon forest?

3. Why can't we get from that great forest more of the rubber that we need?

4. Most of the Brazilians live in eastern Brazil. What reasons can you give for this?

5. What nickname has part of eastern Brazil won, and why?

6. How did the capital city of Brazil get its name?

Friendly Neighbors

Perhaps you will think of Manuel, Roberto, and Fernando as a committee of three who have tried to give you a little idea of Spanish and Portuguese America. A committee made up of one boy or girl from each of the countries to the south of us would have twenty members. Each one would have a different story to tell, because no two of the countries are alike.

What fun it would be if a committee like that could get together, with two other members, one from the United States and one from Canada! Then it would be an all-American committee, with every one of the free and independent countries of the Western Hemisphere represented. Best of all, it would be a committee representing all the boys and girls of twenty-two countries which are friendly neighbors; boys and girls who want to know one another better. Wouldn't you like to be the United States member?

211

A LIST OF BOOKS FOR OUTSIDE READING

Books marked with an asterisk are especially well suited to be read aloud to the class by the teacher.

Bunga

BRADLEY, MARY HASTINGS. Alice in Jungleland. D. Appleton-Century Company, Inc.

*GATTI, ATTILIO. Saranga, the Pygmy. Charles Scribner's Sons.

GATTI, ATTILIO. Wrath of Moto — a Pygmy Boy. Charles Scribner's Sons.

LOBAGOLA, BATA K. Folk Tales of a Savage. Alfred A. Knopf, Inc.

Netsook and Klaya

"As Told to WILLIAM ALBEE." Kanguk, a Boy of Bering Strait. Little, Brown & Company.

GALL, ALICE C., and CREW, FLEMING H. Top of the World. Oxford University Press.

MACHETANZ, FREDERICK. Panuck, Eskimo Sled Dog. Charles Scribner's Sons.

MACMILLAN, Donald B. Kah-Da; Life of a North Greenland Eskimo Boy. Doubleday, Doran & Company, Inc.

*STEFANSSON, V., and SCHWARTZ, J. A. Northward Ho! The Macmillan Company.

Suvan and Nara

LIDE, ALICE A. Yinka-tu the Yak. The Viking Press, Inc.

*PURDON, ERIC. Valley of the Larks. Farrar & Rinehart, Inc.

SAWYER, EDITH A. Merin and Shari; a Boy and Girl of Mongolia. Thomas Y. Crowell Company.

SOWERS, PHYLLIS A. Our Little Mongolian Cousin. L. C. Page & Company.

Simba

*AKELEY, DELIA J. "J. T. Jr." The Macmillan Company.

*BEST, HERBERT. Garram the Hunter. Doubleday, Doran & Company, Inc.

COMFORT, MILDRED H. Peter and Nancy in Africa. Beckley-Cardy Company. Pages 9–31; 40–48.

ENRIGHT, ELIZABETH. Kintu; A Congo Adventure. Alfred A. Knopf, Inc.

GATTI, ATTILIO. Kamanda, an African Boy. Robert M. McBride & Company.

SINGER, CAROLINE, and BALDRIDGE, CYRUS. Boomba Lives in Africa. Holiday House.

SMITH, EUGENE C. Kongo the Elephant. Alfred A. Knopf, Inc.

Pedro

DESMOND, ALICE; MALKUS, ALIDA; WOOD, EDNAH. Boys of the Andes. D. C. Heath and Company.

*FINGER, CHARLES J. Tales from Silver Lands. Doubleday, Doran & Company, Inc.

GILL, RICHARD C. Paco Goes to the Fair. Junior Literary Guild.

GILL, RICHARD C., and HOKE, HELEN. The Story of the Other America. Houghton Mifflin Company.

HALL, ESTHER G. Mario and the Chuna. Random House, Inc.

MALKUS, ALIDA, The Silver Llama. John C. Winston Company.

Abdul and Zakia

*BAIKIE, JAMES. Wonder Tales of the Ancient World. The Macmillan Company.

COMFORT, MILDRED H. Peter and Nancy in Africa. Beckley-Cardy Company. Pages 263–281.

GERE, FRANCES K. Once Upon a Time in Egypt. Longmans, Green & Co.

HIMES, VERA C. Pepi and the Golden Hawk. Thomas Y. Crowell Company.

HOWARD, ALICE W. Princess Runs Away. The Macmillan Company.

HOWARD, ALICE W. Sokar and the Crocodile. The Macmillan Company.

MEADOWCROFT, ENID L. Gift of the River. Thomas Y. Crowell Company.

Roshik and Moti

BOSE, IRENE M. Totaram; the Story of a Village Boy in India Today. The Macmillan Company.

*MUKERJI, DHAN GOPAL. Hari, the Jungle Lad. E. P. Dutton & Company, Inc.

MUKERJI, DHAN GOPAL. Kari the Elephant. E. P. Dutton & Company, Inc.

RAM MANDAL, SANT. Happy Flute. Frederick A. Stokes Company.

ROOT, CHARLET. The Feast of Lamps. Albert Whitman & Company.

Sumai and Lota

*AYSCOUGH, FLORENCE. Firecracker Land. Houghton Mifflin Company.

CARPENTER, FRANCES. Tales of a Chinese Grandmother. Doubleday, Doran & Company, Inc.

LEE, MELICENT H., and JUNG HO. Chang Chee; the Story of a Chinese Boy. Harper & Brothers.

SOWERS, PHYLLIS. Lin Foo and Lin Ching. Thomas Y. Crowell Company.

WIESE, KURT. The Chinese Ink Stick. Doubleday, Doran & Company, Inc.

WOOD, ESTHER. Silk and Satin Lane. Longmans, Green & Co.

Erik and Inger

ASBJORNSEN, PETER C. East o' the Sun and West o' the Moon. The Macmillan Company.

*CHEVALIER, RAGNHILD. Wandering Monday and Other Days in Old Bergen. The Macmillan Company.

DAVIS, HELEN. The Year Is a Round Thing. Harper & Brothers.

HALL, JENNIE. Viking Tales. Rand McNally & Company.

*HAMSUN, MARIE. A Norwegian Farm. J. B. Lippincott Company.

SCHRAM, CONSTANCE. Olaf, Lofoten Fisherman. Longmans, Green & Co.

SCOTT, GABRIEL. Kari; a Story of Kari Supper from Lindeland, Norway. Doubleday, Doran & Company, Inc.

ZWILGMEYER, DIKKEN. What Happened to Inger Johanne; Inger Johanne's Lively Doings. Lothrop, Lee & Shepard Company.

Mexico

DURFEE, BURR, and McMORRIS, HELEN and JOHN. Mateo and Lolita. Houghton Mifflin Company.

*HOLMES, BURTON, and CASTILLO, CARLOS. Mexico. Wheeler Publishing Company.

LEE, MELICENT H. Marcos, a Mountain Boy of Mexico. John C. Winston Company.

LEE, MELICENT H. Pablo and Petra. Thomas Y. Crowell Company.

PURNELL, IDELLA. Pedro the Potter. Thomas Nelson & Sons.

ROSE, PATRICIA F. In Mexico They Say. Alfred A. Knopf, Inc.

Argentina and Brazil

*BROWN, ROSE J. Two Children of Brazil. J. B. Lippincott Company.

DESMOND, ALICE C. Feathers, the Story of a Rhea. The Macmillan Company.

GILL, RICHARD C., and HOKE, HELEN. The Story of the Other America. Houghton Mifflin Company.

*HUDSON, WILLIAM H. A Little Boy Lost. Alfred A. Knopf, Inc.

POLLOCK, KATHERINE G. The Gaucho's Daughter. D. C. Heath and Company.

*STEEN, ELIZABETH K. Red Jungle Boy. Harcourt, Brace and Company, Inc.

WILLIAMS, HENRY L. Kimbi — Indian of the Jungle. D. C. Heath and Company.

INDEX AND PRONOUNCING WORD LIST

Key

fāte, ăm, câre, ȧsk, ärm, ăccount, sofȧ ōld, ŏdd, ōbey, ôrb, cŏnnect ou *as in* out; natûre
ēve, ĕnd, hēre, ĕvent, makēr, recĕnt ūse, ŭp, fûr, ūnite, circŭs N *as in* boN
īce, ĭll, contĭnents fōōd, fŏŏt; oi *as in* oil th *as in* then

Pronunciation of Personal Names